Raising Sons:
Practical Strategies
for Single Mothers

Raising Sons: Practical Strategies for Single Mothers

by Joann Ellison Rodgers and
Michael F. Cataldo, Ph.D.

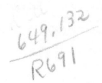

NAL BOOKS

NEW AMERICAN LIBRARY

NEW YORK AND SCARBOROUGH, ONTARIO

Cover photo: Mitchel Osborne/Image Bank

For information address New American Library

Published simultaneously in Canada by The New American Library
of Canada Limited

 NAL BOOKS TRADEMARK REG. U.S. PAT. OFF. AND FOREIGN COUNTRIES
REGISTERED TRADEMARK—MARCA REGISTRADA
HECHO EN HARRISONBURG, VA., U.S.A.

SIGNET, SIGNET CLASSIC, MENTOR, PLUME, MERIDIAN
and NAL BOOKS are published *in the United States* by New
American Library, 1633 Broadway, New York, New York 10019,
in Canada by The New American Library of Canada Limited,
81 Mack Avenue, Scarborough, Ontario M1L 1M8

Library of Congress Cataloging in Publication Data
Rodgers, Joann Ellison.
  Raising sons.

  Bibliography
  Includes index.
  1. Children of single parents—United States.
2. Mothers and sons—United States. 3. Single mothers—
United States. 4. Child rearing—United States.
I. Cataldo, Michael, II. Title.
HQ777.4.R63 1984   649'.132   84-6873
ISBN 0-453-00470-9

Designed by Julian Hamer

First Printing, September, 1984

1 2 3 4 5 6 7 8 9

PRINTED IN THE UNITED STATES OF AMERICA

For my sons, Adam and Jared
—J.E.R.

For my mother, Alice
—M.F.C.

Contents

Preface

This book picks up where the gloom-and-doom reports about sons of divorce and other sources of single-mother parenthood leave off. Where those reports see the family lives of such boys as half empty, *Raising Sons* sees them as half full and waiting to be ably filled to the brim by mothers with the right stuff.

The book owes its attitudes, for the most part, to Joann Rodgers's experiences as a journalist, a feminist, and single mother for seven years of sons now in their late teens. Against a background of ERA, wholesale divorce, changing sex roles, and new social expectations, the concerns and ideas single women have about parenting boys—as contrasted with girls—emerged as a persistent theme in her everyday life and work.

Michael Cataldo, director of behavioral psychology at the Kennedy Institute, associate professor of pediatrics and psychiatry at the Johns Hopkins University School of Medicine, and Joann's longtime friend and colleague, is a leading behaviorist. He searched successfully for data in the ever-expanding literature of behavioral science, in letters from professional colleagues, in his extensive clinical experience, and as he once put it, "in the experience of having a mother." His enthusiastic contributions to the book's approach and message were tempered by a finely honed sense of cautious professionalism his co-author came to welcome as she wrote each chapter and interviewed more than forty mothers and dozens of sons.

The authors have drawn support, where appropriate, from principles and data developed and popularized by Albert Bandura, Donald Baer, Gerald Patterson, Robert Wahler, Edward Christophersen, Haim Ginott, Carl Rogers, Thomas Gordon, and many others. The work of these scientists, some of it cited in the Bibliography, sometimes served as models and guides. Others' contributions are acknowledged in some depth in the Introduction.

But *Raising Sons* departs from previous parenting books in its emphasis on the rapidly changing relationships between men and women as the panorama against which mothers are rearing sons alone; and in its view that such parenting is both healthy and, from society's standpoint, an unprecedented opportunity to redefine and realize successful manhood.

Raising Sons is *not* a report of a scientific study about boys who become men in female-dominated households.

It is about emphasizing the positive in the modern, daily adventure of reaching and teaching manhood in a woman's world. It is about the new social contract that can be formed between mothers and sons just as it is being forged between men and women. It is a personalized exploration of issues and questions many women and their sons are raising among themselves, each other, and to teachers, doctors, psychologists, family, and friends whose lives touch theirs in bad times and good. And it applies what the authors believe are helpful strategies for success in dealing with those issues.

Although the final product is the work of the authors alone, many helped along the way.

Thanks go especially to Caryl Rivers, one of the first to read the completed outline for *Raising Sons*; Arla and Jerry Sussman for their insights and encouragement; Susan Walen, PhD, a clinical psychologist and single mother; and Dorothy and Max Ellison for limitless love, support and tolerance for a mostly absent daughter. Gratitude goes also to Mort Young, Jane Alexander, Scott DeGarmo, Hara Marano, Warren Kornberg, and others who rewrote the Julian calendar to accommodate missed deadlines on stories owed them and offered the treasured gift of time; to Alvonia Boston, a single mother of a grown son who has forgotten more about mothering than most women ever learn; and to Adam and Jared, who know that all mothers do not spend their lives in small rooms behind a keyboard. They not only indulged their mother's tour of duty there, but also, in a gallant display of courtesy to the First Amendment, agreed to publication of many personal stories.

For several years now, Elaine Markson and Geri Thoma have endowed this project with their interest, energy, knowhow, friendship, and support. Words alone can't settle what we owe. At NAL, we thank Maureen Baron, our loyal editor, to whom fell the task of marshaling the manuscript through

the writing and editing process and who from the first supported the authors' concept of the book.

Our greatest debt, of course, is to the many mothers and
sons who shared intimate details of their lives, dreams, successes, and failures. Many of them sought and were given
anonymity to protect their privacy. But they rarely held back.
We hope we have earned their trust.

JOANN ELLISON RODGERS
MICHAEL F. CATALDO

December, 1983

Introduction: When A Boy Is the Man of the House

There is no relationship more intimate than the one between parent and child. In the case of mother and son, that relationship has been widely identified as a particular cause for worry, at least since Oedipus and Jocasta defied the gods. For longer than that, moreover, raising sons has been not only an emotional, social, and cultural role, but a highly political one as well.

Throughout history, mothers of sons—from Abraham's wife Sarah, Mary, and Eleanor of Aquitaine, to Charlemagne's Bertha, Hadrian's Plotina and today's Princess Diana—have received status, security, and power generally denied the mother of daughters.

In more modern times, the real or imagined rewards of bearing sons has persisted, if more subtly. A psychoanalyst once remarked to us that "when women are asked openendedly how many children they have, they will respond with the number if the offspring are girls, but with the number and sex—for example, 'two sons'—if they are boys."

Although most women will publicly insist that health, rather than sex, is the most important consideration in the birth of a baby, their insistence smacks of lipservice. Geneticists in one prominent Massachusetts hospital, for example, reported that a growing number of women have tried to determine the sex of their unborn children before birth in order to abort the unwanted sex. The doctors' concern was not only for the ethical dilemmas posed by such a practice, but for the fear that it would be girls, not boys, who were most often aborted. For a constellation of biological and cultural reasons, many women, even in today's climate of sexual equality, seem to have internalized the idea that being a male is more important

1

than being a female and therefore rearing a male is an undertaking with far more opportunities, threats, and risks.

But if women's perceptions have not changed in eons, much has changed in the last thirty-five years in the American family structure and in the rules under which its members operate. Simply put, record numbers of mothers are raising record numbers of sons alone, and with predictable and justifiable worries about the outcome.

According to the latest census figures, more than 12 million children under the age of eighteen—one in every five—now live in one-parent families. Half of those children are boys and, according to the National Center on Women and Family Law, 92 percent of the single heads of household—representing 11.3 percent of all households in the United States—are mothers. Half of all black children under eighteen live with their mothers alone, again, half of them boys.

The divorce rate has increased the number of single-parent households 100 percent since 1970 and is likely to maintain a steadily high level. As Johns Hopkins University social scientist Andrew Cherlin points out, the next twenty to thirty years will see an entrenchment of current trends in marriage and divorce—"a plateau in family patterns that will last for a while."

Add to this the number of unwed mothers. Since 1970, the number of one-parent families headed by never-married women skyrocketed 367 percent. Although teenagers are having most of these children—270,000 of them a year—the largest rate increases are among women twenty to twenty-four years old, for whom the decision to bear a child out of wedlock was deliberate. According to the Census Bureau in 1981, a growing number of the 1,068,000 never-married mothers are career women who seek children but not husbands.

One of the women we interviewed, a West Coast divorcée in her early thirties with a stable, professional career, recruited a man to father her child with the understanding they would not marry, nor would the father have any obligations to her or the child she eventually bore. "I had one marriage, did not want another, but did want a child," she said. "I am delighted, but I do worry that since it is a boy, he may suffer from lack of fathering. I think it would have been easier in many ways to have had a girl."

At best, most of these 6 million boys in single-mother homes have uneven or uneasy access to their fathers or other close male relatives. In any event, they must live, without full-time fathers, through a number of difficult adjustments. Dependence on their mothers increases, often out of proportion. While they struggle through the usual stages of personal development, they must sort out their parents' behavior, misplaced guilt, and the understandable tendency of many mothers to lock-on emotionally to sons who represent their fantasies and idealizations of strength and security. Often, too, sons may have to deal with mothers who love boys but have come to hate men.

Adding to the angst, social scientists and popular writers are a cadre of contradictions and chaos on the subject of single mothers and sons. Some—like Richard Kulka and Helen Weingarten at the University of Michigan, E. Mavis Hetherington of the University of Virginia, Judith Wallerstein, and Linda Bird Francke—predict lifelong scars for such children; others insist the data are at best fuzzy and that other traumatic life events, before a divorce or in addition to it, are factors in their abnormal psychological profiles. Some of the latest research, however, supports our view: that both mothers and boys growing up with divorced (or widowed or single) mothers have some distinct advantages. Dr. Robert S. Weiss, a sociologist at the University of Massachusetts and Harvard University, has studied more than two hundred single parents from a range of social, economic, and ethnic backgrounds. In the *Journal of Social Issues*, he reports that boys (and girls) of single mothers tend to grow faster, taking and accepting responsibilities. They tend to be more mature, independent, self-disciplined, and unusually self-assured. Mothers of these boys tend to treat them more as equals, what Weiss calls "junior partners"; they feel closer companionship. A Baltimore public relations specialist and divorced mother of two easily described her ten-year-old son as "my best friend." It was a description we were to hear repeated by the majority of mothers and many of the sons we interviewed.

Nowhere is confusion over the role mothers play in the lives of sons more evident than on the subjects of sexuality and homosexuality. The legacy of Freudian analysis, which blamed mothers for sexual aberrations and a whole string of other societal miseries, has been blunted. But not enough.

Mothers are still haunted by the misguided and dangerous belief that there is some surefire formula for raising "masculine" males and, on the flip side, some guaranteed recipe for producing the opposite. They continue to spend anguished time and resources searching for ways to avoid the one and insure the other.

They fret over "conclusions" that are anything but. Recently, for example, while reporting a scientist's conclusions that "sissy" behavior in boys is an accurate tip-off to adult male homosexuality, we discovered that a Johns Hopkins biologist, Dr. James Weinrich, was almost simultaneously concluding that having lots of macho-male chums and being one of the boys served as an equally good crystal ball!

During an interview, Weinrich, a student of psychologist and sex expert Dr. John Money, told one of us: "My guess is that there are many ways to become gay and many childhood signals of homosexual destiny besides sissiness."

He admitted that the failure to pinpoint them is traceable to the fact that unlike sissy activities, other signals, whatever they are, don't involve behavior that sends a mother screaming to the psychiatrist's office, her son in tow.

Indeed, over the years, homosexuality has been attributed to everything from overbearing mothers and passive fathers to one-sex schools, boredom (born of excessive, repetitive heterosexual encounters), genetics, and—of course—divorce.

It should be clear that no one theory has stood the test of time or experience. What "makes" a homosexual is as complex and subtle as the interaction of biochemicals and a myriad of environmental cues and behaviors that engulf a boy from the moment of conception.

"If we have learned anything at all," says Weinrich, "it's that homosexuals are not a single group of people." Another way of putting it is that there is no pattern of behavior or experience to explain the phenomenon for everyone.

Michael D. Storms, a University of Kansas social scientist, theorizes that adult sexual orientation depends on what social stage a boy happens to be in when puberty and sex drive first emerge. According to him, children attach erotic significance to whatever experience is available to them when adolescent hormones begin pumping. Thus boys and girls who mature early, while they are still playing in same-sex groups, learn to love the same sex erotically, whereas those who mature later, when they are involved in mixed groups, become sexually attuned to the opposite sex and develop "straight" sex preferences. His views, based on studies of male and female college students, asked about the intensity and frequency of their sexual fantasies and age at sexual maturity.

Unfortunately, as Weinrich notes, that theory fails to explain a lot of gay behavior. It doesn't work at all for men who as boys were known as sissies and wanted to play with girls, dress up in girls' clothes, and avoid "real" male activities such as football.

What was so startling, in the end, about this confusing picture was Weinrich's remark that "parents of adolescents who are gay are generally taken by complete surprise even today." It is a remark that supports a too-often unheralded truth: There is likely to be no path to or from homosexuality that mothers can predict, follow, or avoid.

The goal of mothering sons, therefore, cannot be posed as a task of avoiding the manufacture of a homosexual, because it is a goal that will inevitably, and blamelessly, elude some of us. To dwell on it may only invite family disaster and build fearful barriers to open communication, tolerance, and caring.

As Weinrich put it, should homosexuality emerge, "it's important to understand that at this stage, there is little you can do to change it. Homosexual boys in straight homes," he adds, "are like deaf children living with hearing adults. The aim must be to help them feel comfortable and grow competent."

That aim is, in a nutshell, the proper goal of all mothers rearing sons. A majority of social scientists, according to a survey of the literature, eschew any cause-and-effect link between single-mother rearing and homosexuality. A recent Kinsey Institute report is one of several reaching that conclusion in recent years. Yet the legacy of mom-made homosexuality remains to thread our best efforts with fear.

Adding to the anxiety is the fact that society tolerates but does not yet truly accept the credibility of single motherhood for male children. Although girls reared by single mothers are, this view holds, probably going to be okay because they have acceptable role models, their male counterparts are ripe for every disaster. By definition, according to this school of thought, there is some underlying "defect" in the single mother, some set of personality and behavioral factors that brought her to the undesirable end of singlehood and which will, ultimately, bring doom to her sons. Depression. School failure. Delinquency. Romantic unhappiness. Homosexuality. Divorce.

How will the boys learn to shoot baskets and check the oil? Or meet aggression? Or man guns? Their mothers will dominate them, fill them with guilt, or even, it is whispered, seduce them. At best, society seems to say, it's suboptimal. Even well-intentioned relatives, teachers, and family friends expect problems, creating self-doubts and, too often, self-fulfilling prophecies.

One need only look around to see evidence of these negative expectations. Newspaper advice columns overflow with psychobabbled advice to "head off" trouble for the "boy without a father." Men are exhorted to become Big Brothers to "fill the vital gap" in the lives of boys from "broken homes." Teachers begin conferences with patronizing sympathy of the what-can-you-expect-with-no-father-in-the-house variety. The rhetoric deliberately ignores the parallel problems of boys reared in two-parent families.

Nancy Rubin, in *The New Suburban Woman*, reports that a recent survey in forty-seven states found that most schools have no programs that take single parenthood into account. Two-thirds of the more than twelve-hundred single parents interviewed for the survey said school personnel automatically assumed their family lives were abnormal, and used the words "broken home" or other damaging stereotyped language when referring to single-parent homes.

Jared and Adam and Joann Rodgers do not consider themselves part of a broken anything, but a whole three-person family. Adam and Jared are also part of other families: their father's, who is remarried and has two stepsons, for example, and several extended families. But if, as is often the case, such boys grow up to be outstanding, comments may reflect surprise or range to some version of "How fortunate he overcame his handicap."

Part of the intellectual bankruptcy of such a position is demonstrated even by well-intentioned scholarship. University of Utah psychologist Michael Lamb, in his book *Contemporary American Families: Children, Work and Housework,* has produced an exhaustive account of studies focused on how children of divorce turn out. "Many," he told a writer for *Working Mother Magazine* (May 1982) "show that children whose parents are divorced or whose fathers are absent are much more likely to manifest signs of psychological maladjustment." But in an amazing (to us) afterthought, Lamb admits that why this happens is unclear.

What he and others must conclude is that the negative outcomes, where they occur, are not so much a consequence of an absent father as of overwhelming physical and emotional demands of the remaining parent, who, in most cases, just *happens* to be female. Whoever remains the primary parent (and that includes single fathers as well as mothers) must absorb and mount defenses against inordinate stresses that have little or nothing to do with gender but a great deal to do with human limitations.

A single mother has often remarked that she needs a wife, not a husband: someone traditionally agreeable to attacking the daily lot of endless chores and nuisances involved in child rearing. It is not the big challenges of raising sons that overwhelm mothers, we suspect, so much as the mundane jobs of cleaning the toothpaste out of the sink and checking the homework.

It would be naive to deny the loneliness that single mothers often experience, the absence of another adult with whom they can compare ideas and share worries. As the Baltimore PR woman told us: "I find myself talking to Ian (her ten-year-old son) as if he were the man of the house. I know it's unfair to him, but sometimes I just need to unburden myself to another human being. I can't always hold it all inside, even if he is just a child."

Sometimes the guilt- and doubt-messages society transmits to single mothers are more indirect, if no less thoughtless. Among the scores of novels for teenagers, many are romances, targeted for girls. A few of these deal with mother-daughter and father-daughter behavior and tensions. What fiction there is for boys, however, is primarily "adventure stories" of the boy-meets-hero variety. A few deal with the themes of sex and male-female tensions, or father-son relationships. We have yet to see one that explored the issues between mothers and sons.

It is surely no accident that the majority of single-parent

series on television have predominantly featured male parent and child pairs genially solving every problem.

Eddie and Dad in the *Courtship of Eddie's Father, Bonanza's* Ben Cartwright and his three sons, as well as the stars of *Different Strokes* and *Silver Spoons*, come to mind. Bruno of *Fame* had a relationship with his late, taxi-driver father any male would envy.

The point is not to suggest that single father and son relationships are portrayed dishonestly, but that honest single mother and son relationships are portrayed only rarely.

In *The Big Valley*, for example, the matriarch in a household of three macho sons was a featured role, but she spent most episodes in quasi-male garb, barking orders and persuading us she was "one of the boys." One of the few recent successful shows to star a single (divorced) mother with visible children is *One Day at a Time*. And Ann Romano has two *daughters*, one of them a prime-time delinquent. In *Alice*, the single mother has a boy, but he is a shadowy character who appears infrequently. In *Nurse*, too, the widowed RN was featured in stories that generally omitted her teenage son. When he was in an episode, a male co-star often had the sage words of advice to solve the inevitable problems the boy can't discuss with mom.

Another program featuring a single mother and child was *Love, Sidney*. The child was female, however, and the mother apparently couldn't handle even that. She turned to good neighbor Sid. He was a creditable father figure, but in a nice twist he also was a former homosexual. The cumulative effects of such programs, like the social values and beliefs they represent, go a long way to perpetuate single mother and son anxieties.

Beyond demographics and pop culture, the social revolution that has witnessed the emergence of the single-female-parent family as a prominent and permanent fixture has also seen unsettling changes in the behavior and expectations of men and women.

Both sexes have been "liberated," willingly or not, from time-honored roles and ideas. The energized, domineering, male-threatening mother is no longer the stuff of fiction but a real person in the boardroom and the master bedroom for millions of boys.

Women now make up 40 percent of the work force and

expect as their due positions of authority and responsibility, whereas men are now expected to diaper and cook and sew and nurture.

By default or design, today's generation of boys will be like no other because so many live with liberated (and confused and ambivalent) mothers and without fathers in their homes full-time. How they are reared will influence generations to come, because, through their behavior, they will pass on their values and beliefs to their children.

The feelings between a mother and son are hard enough to handle with honesty and love. Now, with so many rapid changes crumbling the traditional nature of the mother-son relationship, there is the question of *how* boys should be reared and to what end. Yes, we want males to be male, to take their place comfortably in a two-sex society. But how? What do today's single mothers need to know—and do—to rear normal men of tomorrow? What, indeed, is "normal"?

Without a doubt, successful men of the future will need different skills than their fathers needed, and heightened sensitivity to social change in order to get along. If the sons of single mothers have lots of company, they must still face the trials of growing up without society's blessing and sometimes half-hearted support. To be reared by mothers with their own changing needs, hang-ups, and sexual conflicts adds an historic layer of complication to adolescence. And it's a sure bet that single mothers don't want their sons to be "just like Dad," although they don't want them to be soured on close relationships, either.

Betty Friedan, perhaps the most perceptive chronicler of the woman's movement within the family as well as within society at large, speaks of the "critical mass" of liberated women forming in our social and personal institutions and what that will mean for men as well as women. "Men," she writes, "must change. They must develop the flexibility and sensitivity to their own feelings and the feelings of others—the attunement to life that has been considered up to now feminine."

Tomorrow's men will be living in Friedan's "Second Stage" feminism, in which "female values begin to be shared by the male." It is a shift she believes is "simply a stage in human evolution, necessary for survival."

Yet, again, *what* to do about that has eluded many such

women. Even something as straightforward as wanting to take some of the male chauvinism out of their sons, or prevent its taking root, suggests dire consequences to many mothers.

When two journalists, Lindsy Van Gelder and Carrie Carmichael, asked a group of feminist parents what they did about male chauvinism, they either said nothing or worried aloud that if they tried to put their parenting where their politics were, they risked turning their boys into homosexuals.

In her book, *Growing Up Free*, feminist writer Letty Cottin Pogrebin points out that feminist mothers have far fewer problems translating their philosophies into child-rearing methods for their daughters than for their sons. Although they feel comfortable with daughters who try out for the tackle football team, they chew their nails over sons who don't. It's okay for their daughters to be tough, but not for their sons to be tender.

What is especially disturbing about all this worry is the lack of data to support its necessity. There is, in fact, growing evidence from researchers that although single mothers raising sons is certainly an experience different from conventional, two-parent child rearing, the outcome is far from negative. Moreover, these same studies suggest that the absence of a father in the home at all times is irrelevant to the successful rearing of sons.

Psychologist Robert Brannon, coauthor of *Forty-Nine Percent Majority: The Male Sex Role*, for example, contends that "on the whole, boys raised by single mothers develop less-stereotyped notions about sex roles than children raised in traditional two-parent families where only the father works."

In the context of rearing successful males of the future, the only individuals who would consider that a problem, or cause for alarm, are the terminally naive.

Numerous social studies support Brannon's view that the emergence of a contented, loving, caring man is not necessarily produced in a two-parent home or inevitably aborted in a single-mother home. We believe, and studies confirm, that there is enormous benefit in boys being linked to nontraditional male roles; in boys growing up at ease with feminine life-styles and a firm picture of hearty, competent womanhood.

In a critical look at women between the ages of thirty-five and fifty-five, *Beyond Sugar and Spice* authors Rosalind Barnett, Grace Baruch, and Caryl Rivers have found that women who "have it all," who manage to meld career, marriage, and motherhood, lay claim to the best overall sense of well-being. For single mothers, the sense of personal achievement and competence is equally high, even if their pleasure in life is somewhat reduced. And numerous studies confirm that women no longer care to sacrifice themselves on the guilt-gilded altar of motherhood.

They do, however, need to address certain issues in order to avoid turning out a generation of men denied both traditional male roles and satisfactory substitutes. These issues are important ones for every mother with sons to bring up and, in some special ways, for the single mother.

Even where there is co-parenting, or a supportive and supporting father, the single mother rearing boys in her custody and household deals nose-to-nose and day-to-day with this: If women have the parenting power most of male society claims they have, and if they now are overwhelmingly in a position to exercise that power more or less at will, why not seize the chance to ask some honest and appealing questions? What kind of men do women in the eighties want to raise? How can they do it? How can women fulfill their social trust and rear successful men without betraying their womanhood or alienating their sons?

If boys are being raised under new guidelines—and they are—*Raising Sons* may serve as a new guidebook. It will, we hope, prompt mothers to ask helpful questions about their relationships with their sons. It will outline the issues and choices, and show that awareness of them is half the battle.

The book's essential theme is that single women rearing males is a good thing, not a bad thing; if it is not the most desired family condition, it nonetheless has many positive and desirable aspects. In any event, it is a necessary occurrence for many families in increasing numbers.

To our knowledge, to date, no popular book has focused exclusively on mothers and sons as so many have on mothers and daughters (the women's movement brought them out in clusters) and, very recently, fathers and daughters.

About the book's approach to both the issues it raises and the strategies it proposes: The authors do not have some foolproof formula for single mothers rearing sons. Professional and scientific standards would require careful and exhaustive investigation, which to date has not been conducted, for such an unlikely formula. On the other hand, problems do not always wait for perfect answers, and even in medical treatment and psychotherapy, clinical solutions are attempted by applying well-researched principles even if those solutions have never been specifically tested.

The task, for Michael especially, became one of asking how certain principles could be adapted to the issues facing mothers and sons; could help explain and interpret those principles to mothers raising sons alone so they would not have to cull the scant and decidedly unreliable research on the subject.

Fifteen years' experience with hundreds of families has convinced Michael that many of the problems and challenges confronting single mothers and sons could be solved, avoided, and eased over if mothers had a working knowledge of behavioral principles to add to whatever other resources they called upon in their parenting.

This book about mothers and sons will always emphasize behavior, not motives. Joann tends to operate on the principle that, as her grandfather once put it, "What is, is. Deal with it." In any book about raising sons, she would want to learn and write about what mothers and sons want to *do* and how they might *do* it, and not especially *why*. Unraveling the complicated set of emotional, cultural, neurological, and genetic reasons for any individual set of behaviors is a task happily and admiringly left to psychiatrists, analysts, and others whose orientation is toward mental illness and dysfunction.

If the reader can understand these principles and apply them successfully when and where she wishes to do so, the enterprise would be both worthy and professionally credible. As a result the authors have elected to present a set of behavioral tools with which mothers and sons can design and build a successful contract for growing up. The principles that guide this book we call *behavioral parenting*, and they are as streamlined and few in number as we could make them. They are not, in the parlance of some self-help books, "quick and easy." They will take some thought and a lot of practice to apply well in the lives of mothers and sons.

Raising Sons offers not behavioral Band-Aids but strategies to be tailored to individual styles and needs, together with examples of how to use those strategies to the best advantage.

We have tried to include those topics we found to be important to boys growing up, even if they were not always obvious to the women rearing them. The authors have listened hard to what concerns sons, as well as mothers.

Although the emphasis on single motherhood is central, it serves more as a statement about degree of involvement than exclusivity.

Married mothers and never-married mothers have many of the same concerns and face many of the same issues as single mothers at some stage in the process of rearing boys, for although fathers today take an increasingly active role in parenting, the upbringing of the young male is still essentially the domain of mothers and other female caretakers.

Whatever we say, therefore, has relevance to all mothers and sons. But there is a sense of urgency, born of more focused involvement in the subject, for the single mothers. Clearly, single women face their role as mothers to boys and men with a more intense and starkly defined responsibility. As one newly separated mother of a six-year-old boy told us: "Hurry up and write it [your book], will you? The libraries and bookstores are full of stuff on mothers and daughters, fathers and sons, fathers and children, mothers and children, divorced mothers, remarriages, and every conceivable combination of family relationship except mine!"

Rearing boys in today's environment demands new strategies. It does not, however, call for hand-wringing or maternal guilt. Nor does it warrant the grudging support it now gets from many quarters. After all, many boys in so-called "intact" families have traditionally been reared primarily by mothers because the demands of their work kept fathers away for long periods. Single-mother homes have much in common with traditional two-parent homes because in both, mother is usually the primary parent of younger children. According to Michael Lamb, the fathering movement has not had much practical impact on the amount of time dads spend with their children in a traditional family setting. Boys reared by one or two parents are still influenced by models beyond their parents, including real and fictional adults in school, on television, and in the movies.

If Philip Wylie's "Momism" was perceived as a problem of that living arrangement, there are few data to support the view that it was mom alone who created it. And a huge number of studies now support the view that children reared in an "intact" family full of hostility, distrust, and betrayal are certainly not to be envied above those reared in a calmer, more secure, single-mother household.

For today's women (married or single), raising sons demands a fair mother-son plan, more attention to behavior, and the will to change habits that undermine the plan, together with optimism, an equitable distribution of energy and time, a sense of humor, raw honesty, and genuine affection. Again, we believe behavioral psychology is important because, beyond acne, there are few male concerns that are not matters of compliance, of persuading someone to behave in one way or another. The behaviors that drive sons are the behaviors that drive their mothers. The emphasis here is on what mothers and sons do, not on what they feel or why they do it.

Joann recalls an incident that makes the point. After her son Adam had an accident on the second day of high school soccer practice, the doctor promised him that if he stayed off his broken foot a few weeks, he would heal in time to play a full season with the jayvees. Because that prospect ranked somewhere between getting a car and getting Brooke Shields, he cheerfully learned to maneuver his crutches into the family Toyota and hop between classes with notebooks and *A Tale of Two Cities* under one arm.

That evening at home, however, the first crisis struck.

"Whaddya mean I can't take a bath with my cast," he bellowed. "I'll rot."

Joann's suggestion that he bathe, instead, by dangling his right leg over the tub side precipitated a second crisis. To wit: logistics. Because his parents are divorced, the only person in his household available to ease him and his casted foot in and out of the tub on a regular basis (teenage boys, it seems, need running water hourly) was mother.

"No way!" he intoned, was a *mother* going to see a *son* stripped of jeans, Jockey shorts, and other dignities.

After much eyeball rolling, hand waving, and loud negotiations, Adam and Joann resolved the crises. He kept off his foot and lived to play soccer a full season. He bathed. He did not rot. Nor did he win his bid to rent a male neighbor for bathroom duty or move in with his father for the duration. He simply met the suds in a Speedo swimsuit.

Keeping clean with a broken foot may not appear to be a

world-class problem. But for teenage boys reared by a single woman in a female-run household, the underlying issues are often related to what people *do* about privacy, nudity, emerging sexuality, and masculinity. Male-female relationships and independence are major concerns for all adolescent males. But for boys who are the "men" of the house, the vagaries of growing up carry extra layers of anxiety for them and their mothers.

The popular wisdom today, as we explained earlier, is that boys raised by single mothers are especially vulnerable to all manner of woes.

Admittedly, as a group, boys reared by single women do face increased pressures. Financially they may have trouble because female heads of household earn less overall than men. The annual median income for a family headed by a husband and wife is $23,000, whereas the figure is less than $9,500 for a female head of household with no husband. The boys grow up faster and must often make room in their emotional lives for their parents' lovers or stepparents. They also have added responsibilities at home that fill their days and drain their energies.

But it is our conviction, based on our research and interviews, that relationships between mothers and sons hold as much opportunity for success as any other parent-child relationship; there is nothing intrinsically weak or unnatural or halfway or second-best about them. They may be pressured by obsolete or unrealistic views of traditional family life. The facts, however, do not warrant support of them, if in fact they ever did.

Mothers cannot replace fathers. We don't know many who want to. But as one of the more than forty women intensively interviewed for this book told Joann, "A mother can indeed father, just as a father can mother."

Mothers can, by themselves, be good, loving, effective parents and model persons for their sons. They can do this if their goals are clear, if they know what kind of person they want to raise, and if they have the skills to guide their efforts. Boys raised primarily by women *will* have different views on some things, as well as some different skills, but there is no guarantee that they will be inappropriate or second-rate ones. Indeed, as journalists Van Gelder and Carmichael concluded, unless conscious efforts are made to acknowledge those dif-

ferences, today's girls will "reach womanhood in the 1990's
. . . confronted with a new generation of perfectly preserved
1960's males."

Dr. Oscar Christenson, professor of psychology and education at the University of Arizona in Tucson, echoes our
view of this book this way: "The reputed problems of single
mothers rearing boys are mythical. We've been oversold on
Freudian psychology. During my lifetime, I would like to
explode two myths. One is that every boy needs a dog. The
other is that every child should have two parents. All he needs
is one good one."

The first step for mothers is to decide what kind of men
they want to populate the next generation, rather than rely
on what past generations have to offer. The second is to adopt
and use proven strategies to support that decision.

Raising Sons, Part One, emphasizes what behavioral parenting is and how mothers rearing sons can make the best
use of it. Part Two continues and expands these themes, but
with an additional emphasis on how the principles of behavioral parenting can be adapted as sons grow up and are increasingly on their own.

PART

ONE

Don't Sing in the Streets: What's Going on Here?

Joann, a veteran of "car wars," recalls this exchange with her son Adam when he was fifteen. It occurred minutes before she set out on a round-trip excursion as chauffeur to her son, two of his boyfriends, and their movie dates.

"Mom? Are you ready?"

"All set."

"Uh, you're wearing *that*?"

"What's wrong with it?"

"It's *red*!"

"I'm wearing a coat over it."

"The beige one with the high collar?"

"Uh-huh."

"Can we go now?"

In the car, en route to the first checkpoint, Adam launched phase two of his preemptive strike against maternal visibility.

"Mom?"

"Um."

"Are you going to say anything?"

"To whom and about what?"

"Anything to any of the guys."

"I'm not sure I get your drift."

"Well, uh, don't take this the wrong way, okay?"

"I'll try."

"Could you just drive and not talk?"

"That's weird, not to mention rude."

"What I mean is, it's okay if you say hello or whatever if *they* say it first, but don't say dumb things like how's their mother or are they planning to go to Harvard."

"Oh."

"And you won't tell any jokes, right?"

19

"Not even the one about the traveling salesman who . . ."

"Maaa-aaa!!"

"Only kidding."

"Mom?"

"Yup."

"What about the radio?"

"It's not on."

"Right. I know. So could you leave it off unless somebody asks for it to be on and then if someone does, play *only* 98 Rock forgodsake and not a Pavarotti tape or Barry Manilow or something?"

"Check. Any other instructions?"

"Don't look at me through the rearview mirror and smile."

Thousands of mothers will recognize some form of this "here's-how-mothers-should-act" exchange with their sons. The circumstances may vary with age—younger boys are less involved in dating but more intense about school, sports, and camp activities. But the need to control mother is consistent and universal to mother-son relationships.

Typically, single mothers interpret such "orders" as the son's need to keep the mother's profile low enough to get his ego mounted. Without dad or some other man around to keep the insult level down, the son will, she believes, exercise his budding macho whenever possible, especially for the benefit of friends. He really pours it on in this kind of situation because he can't very well demonstrate his "cool maturity" when a smart-aleck mother asks such absurd questions as "How are you?"

In calmer moments she understands. The sensitive mother recognizes her son's fears and insecurity, the embarrassment he feels at his witless failure to have been born a slave owner or at least old enough to drive.

On the other hand, she cannot help but resent the "hired-hand" treatment. After all, she is a person. Sensitivity does not mean having to hide her shine under a beige coat.

Even so, doesn't mom want to show off just a bit in front of son's friends? To prove what a good-natured, responsive, ready, cheerful, competent Girl Scout she is, able to ferry seven adult-size persons around in a five-passenger vehicle and willing to drive around the block during good-night-kiss-and-grope sessions at the door?

Single mothers especially want sons to accept and welcome them into their circle. Joann recalls another classic conversation with her son Jared, age twelve, during a walk through a shopping mall as "Never on Sunday" wafted through the piped-in music speakers.

"Mom?"

"What, babe?"

"You're humming out loud again."

Joann turned to see Jared's eyeballs roll into his upper lids. The look clearly said, "Shut up." The mouth was only slightly more diplomatic.

"When you sing in the street," he said, "I look like an idiot. I can't take you anywhere."

What is all this? Is anything going on here the single mother really needs to pay attention to besides her growing irritation?

There is. In interviews with dozens of mothers and sons we found that the issues raised in these kinds of mother-son exchanges are the real concern of most mothers rearing sons. They are verbal covers for patterns of behavior that govern family life. Such exchanges are, for those who learn to read and to use them, powerful tools for teaching and learning between mothers and sons. And they are the subject of this book.

The following discussion puts the kinds of exchanges described above into a *social* and *behavioral* context. It is not always easy to do. But if the goal is to use logic and order in the business of raising sons, it is essential.

So, let's begin.

First, to see such encounters as confrontations, as evidence of lapsed discipline, as battles to be won or lost, is not only commonplace but understandable.

Suddenly, or so it seems, mom is no longer the center of her son's universe. In the past, her son may have sought outings with her; met her suggestions for shared projects with enthusiasm and smiles or at least with assent. Now that she is alone and has the task of rearing him, her son is critical, openly resentful, or even contemptuous of things they once shared without question and even with fun.

Single mothers, as a consequence, may see the contest as a falling apart of their disciplinary structure, a sign of incipient delinquency, or the tip of a deeply resented chauvinist iceberg rising in the sea of family tranquility.

"I've begun having a terrible time getting my sons to visit their grandparents," one mother told us. "They become nasty at the suggestion, and try to wheedle out with one excuse after the other. Here are two people who would happily die for them, who stepped into their lives after their father left, and whom they used to adore. Now I insist they go with me once a week, but there is always a fight and threats and tension."

This mother, like so many we spoke to, perceives disagreements as the beginnings of a power struggle she is determined to win.

In stark contrast to that view, we think there is a much better and more useful way to look at what goes on when mothers and sons meet and tilt. Our view and how to focus it will be described in detail in future chapters. For now, let us just say that if we look at the actions and language of these sons within context of their ages, we see their behavior as a normal, reassuring drive for adult independence. And once we look at behavior this way, we have the chance to influence it by design instead of wasting energy trying to clobber it by chance.

Throughout these pages, the reader will find this message put forth again and again: By learning to fit the things sons say and do into a rapidly-changing field of possibilities; by using what sons say and do as cues for predicting what they'll do next; by preparing for situations and even rehearsing responses to them, single mothers can learn the art of raising successful sons successfully.

In the normal course of growing up, there are always lags between what sons are able to do and what mothers will be willing to let them do, and there is no single more touchy issue than a boy's desire for privacy, independence, and time safe, free, and away from mothers. Touchy, because this desire usually arrives on the developmental scene at just the time when parents are struggling to reconcile their own apparent loss of power and importance with respect to their sons; when parents begin to realize they can no longer delay putting their actions where their philosophies have been.

In a single-female parent home, there are added dimensions to deal with. Quarters may be cramped, time overscheduled, and priorities based on the more obvious and more easily met needs of younger children and the ever-present nagging fear that any misbehavior is due to the breakup of the marriage or some other cause of a woman's single status. Sons want to spend more time with peers outside the home, and mothers want to keep watch for trouble. Every refusal of car keys or permission to roam is viewed by sons as the revenge of a domineering witch who "never was a boy and can't understand."

Although sons still need their mothers for shelter, food, clothing, money, and love, every rein on behavior is a reminder that mother is the primary barrier in their leap to independent manhood.

In the drive-don't-talk scenario, Adam is not trying to put Joann down, but to keep his emerging manhood afloat. Adam is worried that Joann's behavior will be that of a mother with her child at just the time when he is trying to be like a man with his friends, particularly those of the female persuasion. Because *he* is uptight in social situations and likely to say or do something childish or dippy, he fears *she* might, in a moment of social stress, regress and opt for the comfortable role of Mommy.

His instructions not only reflect his frustration about having to rely on Joann for transportation, but for a whole lot more. He doesn't have a driver's license, but wants the freedom to get around, make his own decisions, and be a grown-up. He is trapped by a conspiracy of the Motor Vehicle Administration to keep all youth subjugated to parents.

He's in a classic Catch-22 situation.

He wants to be a man with his friends, but to do so he needs wheels, which at the moment only his mom can provide. On top of that, he is afraid she'll embarrass him by treating him like a child—a not unreasonable fear, because for most of his life that has been her practice and responsibility.

Looked at in this context, Adam's instructions and Jared's comments are strictly defensive, not offensive. And they shouldn't offend.

Adam and Jared both have an agenda, but it isn't to antagonize. Nor is it very likely that it has anything to do with the fact that their mother is without their father. Sons do not get up in the morning and devise ways to torture their mothers. But they *will* torture them out of desperation. The problem for both is that sons won't or can't always explain that they are desperate, and moms can't read minds.

To turn these events into opportunities for satisfying both the son's agenda and the mother's intentions (to rear a responsible, competent, happy, male, remember?), the first step is to recognize that the developing boy is a moving target. It's easy for a mother to get stuck, especially during her son's teenage years, looking for him to act on one level (the level she is accustomed to), when in fact he has moved off into another stage and is marching to some other beat. This is going to happen a great deal. Sometimes the shift is trivial; other times important and painful for both.

One of the painful shifts, for instance, centers on a mother's kiss. Suddenly, the son begins to avoid or draw away from mom's kisses once eagerly taken and returned. This behavior is often coupled with a refusal to let mother in his room, see him undressed, or tuck him in at night.

What has been one of the most sought-after and positive experiences for the young child is now awkward, strange, and embarrassing for the boy. There is no one to blame for this. It happens with most children. The problem is that the single mother is likely to perceive all this as a rejection of her and relate it to a divorce or other factors in her single parenthood, instead of to the fact that her child is growing up.

A mother laments: "I know Sammy is unhappy and needs affection now more than ever. So do I. But he's so angry about the separation, he won't let me near him."

Although that could be the case, the chances are that if other signals of maturity are occurring at the same time, mom should be rather pleased.

Refusing a mother's kiss is often part of the drive for independence, a boy's way of "trying on" adult male roles as he perceives them.

For instance, Adam, in the exchange about the car, is doing what comes naturally for his age. His behavior shows that he is starting to find his peer group to be very important to him. He likes it and respects it. Why? Because his friends are beginning to view *him* as important, as a man. As long as his friends are responsible and don't sell controlled substances for a living, this is a situation mom should recognize as a good sign—even if the specifics are a bit hard to swallow.

It should be clear by now that don't-sing-in-the-streets episodes are also fortune's smile, if not fortune's kiss.

In this case, for example, Jared has given Joann potent

clues to track that moving target, a long peek at what makes him feel good, and most important of all, what or who turns on good feelings. When a mother knows this, she has found a powerful way to teach behavior.

The approval of friends and desire for independence are not only important instruments of reward for sons, but ones that at certain times will rival mothers' approval as the big payoff. In the best sense of the word, take advantage of that. The method is not mom versus peers in fifteen rounds. She accepts her son's need. She just wants him to accept some limits on his behavior. She might try this during the car ride (or in the shopping mall or wherever):

Mother: It seems that what you want me to do really is very important to you, but I have a little bit of a problem with it. We can't solve it right now, since we'll be picking up your friends soon, so how about if this time I keep the beige coat on, play 98 Rock, and speak only when spoken to. (A concession, to be sure, but how bad is it?) But here's the rest of the deal. On Saturday morning, before soccer practice, we sit down for half an hour and talk about tonight. Okay?

Son: Sure, fine. (His concession. He'll agree fast because the last thing in the world he wants right at that moment is a heavy discussion or an argument. His stomach is already in knots thinking about how to get his arm around Pikesville High School's answer to a perfect "10" when the lights go out.)

Incidentally, having a regular, neutral time, one without noise or distraction, to put critical stuff in the family discussion hopper is a must. (See Chapter Nine, "Making It All Work.") Too often, talk sessions fail because mom tries to start them when son is already late for practice or is studying for a math test the next day. Also, it's best to declare a set amount of time and not extend it. Otherwise, the discussions become endless. Children are not noted for their patience. Having a formal ritual keeps the lid on it and lends a certain decorum that reduces the temptation to shout or bolt for the door. It is no accident that international diplomats put a lot of stock in such factors as size and shape of the negotiating table and length of sessions.

Okay. It's Saturday morning. A sure way to begin is to bring up the issue in the context of other problems that need solving. For example, the items for discussion might include settling how late son can stay out next weekend at the school dance or whether the budget can manage the jacket he wants.

It's also a good idea for mom to say, *out loud*, that she knows his friends' approval is very important. That makes it clear she is not coming into this discussion to argue her rights versus his. She might even admit that perhaps in the past, she hasn't always recognized changes in his life fast enough, that at times she has trouble running in the fast lane.

Mom could add that his behavior is on track for his age and that she's glad he wants to be regarded as an adult. That's her wish, too.

Mother: I really feel left behind. I need to have some idea about what you want to do *before* I get run over. It would help if you could tell me well ahead of time if you want me to do certain things a certain way. Then if I don't see it your way, there is time to say so and work it out.

Son: I can't always do that, but maybe sometimes I can.

Mother: Fine. (Know when to take a profit.)

Son: What else?

Mother: I'd like to know whether this is only a problem because I'm a female-type person?

Son: Maybe.

Mother: Okay, when Dad drives you on a date, does the same problem come up for you? Do you worry about the same things?

Whatever the son's response, this much is certain: If dad is not around often to be chauffeur or reassure his sons about their worries, there is little either mother or son can do about that. If he is around occasionally, dad is more likely to be malleable about do's and don't's situations than mom, who spends more time behind the wheel than a Manhattan cab driver and has to do her food shopping between shifts.

Mother: Well, I think you can understand that it might be easier for Dad to do things the way you like under the circumstances. Unfortunately, Dad can't always drive, but we can change the circumstances under which I drive so we're both happier.

Son: How?

Mother: Suppose you tell me what things you like and don't like that I do when I drive you and your friends around and I'll respond.

Here, you may have to prompt your son and you will probably get a mix of useless generalities . . .

Son: You act like you know everything.
. . . and helpful specifics:
Son: Brad gets uptight when you ask how his parents are because they're not getting along.

Now it's time to negotiate. Mom might agree to give up the questions and keep the chatter down. Or she could ask what topics should be brought up. If mother is going to give sons advice about appropriate social behavior in circumstances *she* is expert about, why not have son return the favor for her?

Her son might agree that wearing red does not mean she's the village whore and that beige coats are uncomfortable in August. She might agree to scowl when she has to check for cars in the rearview mirror if it will make him feel better. He might agree that they both will feel great when he can drive himself to the movies.

The bottom line is a contract both can live with, forged with dignity and (please!) a sense of humor. Both give in—and up—a little. Most mothers and sons won't easily operate this way. The strategy won't always work, either, and it will take some practice to even have a shot at success. But to the extent that it will work, those who negotiate behavior are accomplishing a lot more than getting through the next triple date without angst.

As son—and mother—learn to negotiate, both will find that this is clearly how they prefer grown-ups to operate the world.

Mother can always lower the boom on behavior that is intolerable. But she'll do it with a clearer conscience and a lot more credibility if she has given her son the chance to behave like the adult he wants to be. Also, *he* can lower booms, too, and drive her out of her tree.

As in a war, you can always escalate and it's almost guaranteed you will at times. But the goal of behavioral parenting is to negotiate as long as reasonable.

Whenever mothers and sons negotiate, by the way, mothers have to play fair even though they have the power to do otherwise. This is especially true as sons grow older, larger, and more able to get along without mother. It is not fair, for instance, to change the rules without renegotiation. If some issue comes up that hasn't been thought of in the contract (Brad suddenly begins to talk about his parents' fights), mother shouldn't abandon the agreement. Instead, she should try to err on the side of discretion. The best negotiators always try to *think what the other person would want done* and then do it as well as possible. Later, they can talk about it.

Mother: I didn't know how exactly to handle Brad's comments in the car, but I did what I thought you wanted me to.

Son: Yeah, I know what you mean. It was tough for me, too. I didn't know what to say.

Mother: I guess I didn't do too badly with it. Maybe your friends feel comfortable talking to a grown-up when they don't have to look at her face!

Son: Well sure, if someone brings up something like that, you should say something. (*Ole!*)

Some mothers and sons to whom we have described negotiation sessions complain that there is too much talk already. "We're so damned verbal around here, that I find myself ready to scream," said a forty-two-year-old divorcée with a ten-year-old son.

Some things are tough or even impossible to discuss. Many times no one wants to talk, and "talking something to death" can be a way of avoiding action.

As with any other kind of behavior, negotiating, too, can become a trap if every time there is a problem its solution is delayed by promise of a discussion. The delay then becomes the payoff, the way for the son to get mother's attention. When mother catches on, she feels used and the purpose of the negotiation is often forgotten.

A good way to avoid overtalk is to deal only with specifics and keep away from generalities such as "I don't like your attitude." We have found that a son's behavior and the circumstances in which it occurs can tell mom a lot about what is important to him. If what is important is at all reasonable, and the behavior only moderately troublesome, the goal is to "fine tune" the behavior, not trample it.

Newly single mothers are surprised to find that although troubles with their sons have an I'm-a-female-you're-a-male component, they may have nothing whatever to do with the absence of an adult male around the house. There is no solid evidence to support the old chestnut that mother-son or family tranquility requires a testosterone referee (see Chapter Five, "Who Am I?").

In any case, if the goal is a smooth family course, the key is *what's* happening, not *why*.

Time and again, we were told by single mothers and their sons, teenage boys especially, that as soon as they settled down to really negotiate some changes, the facts of divorce or widowhood and absent fathers rarely entered the picture. "It got to the point," said a thirty-six-year-old mother, "where if one more person implied that I needed to remarry to get my son to clean his room or do his homework, I was going to commit mayhem. Even if it were true, what am I supposed to do, advertise for a father-figure? I don't want a husband. What was, was and what is, is. I need to get some changes made right now."

We couldn't agree more.

In taking you through this analysis, we hoped to show how our approach to raising sons in a single-female parent home works. We also wanted to get you quickly used to new parental geography.

Joann, who has done a lot of traveling, finds the process of parenting something like getting to know an unfamiliar foreign country. There are two basic ways to do it. One is to rely on the hotel concierge, the cab drivers, and places where only English is spoken, to step slowly and carefully into the life of the place. The other is to dive right in, picking up the language, the color, the vitality, and native customs as you go. We obviously prefer the second option.

Now that you are (we hope) immersed and comfortable with the new surroundings, we are ready to give you a detailed map for planning your own outings and reaching destinations of your own choosing.

CHAPTER TWO

What You Do Is What You Get: The Principles of Behavioral Parenting

A popular cartoon shows a mother and her female guest sitting on the living room couch. A little boy is on the couch, too, with his hand inside the guest's blouse. The mother is saying, "If you just ignore them at this age, they stop behaving inappropriately."

From the casual grin on the child's face, "ignoring" his behavior is clearly not going to do the trick. That's what makes the cartoon amusing.

What makes it pertinent is what it says about the need for knowing something about the principles that underlie the relationship between mothers and sons and what to do about it. The mother in the cartoon is clearly on the wrong track, but is going to be the last to know.

In this chapter we introduce a set of guidelines, all based on behavioral psychology, that will put mom not only on the right track, but the inside track. They are designed to help mothers focus on specific behavior in the relationship with their sons and to avoid the social and emotional traps so often set for both of them.

All are based on the observation that the relationship between behavior and its consequences is the key to everything we do as mothers and sons and therefore to all changes in behavior, both desirable and not so desirable.

Each guiding principle we offer below has its roots in a precise scientific term. In order to avoid technical jargon, however, we will present the scientific term only in this chapter. After that, the principle will be referred to by a practical, easy-to-remember term or short descriptive phrase whenever strategies for mother-son relationships are discussed.

Although drawn from a long and complex series of experiments and observations with broad, parent–child implica-
tions, the only guidelines we have listed are those we believe
are the most important to mother-son relationships. We call
this collection of ideas *behavioral parenting* and they are as
follows:

Times Are A-Changin'

There are very few things we can be sure of, but one of
them is that everything changes. The only successful way to
deal with unavoidable change is to adapt to it. In the past
hundred years, there have been two major advances in thought
regarding adaptation to change. One of them is based on the
Darwinian scheme of evolution. The explanation is that living
things adapt by genetic selection to changes in the environment, and maintain the new traits across successive generations. It says that those species which do this best continue;
those which do not, become extinct.

The other major advance related to adaptation and change
is the recognition of day-to-day behavioral adaptation to
changes in the environment. Mothers experience such change
and the need to adapt to an exquisite degree when they first
encounter single parenthood. Such a change in their role and
status is often sudden, dramatic, and to say the least, wor-
risome and painful. This kind of change is a prod for action,
and that action—adaptation—is the key to success. Those
mothers who adapt to their new status are successful; those
who do not often become "extinct" as viable parents.

As we have noted before, this process is especially true for
the single woman raising a son today because of the additional
emotional and social male-female issues that charge her environment. Her family set-up is probably radically different
from the one in which the mother herself grew up. It is also,
literally, undermanned—just when the boy is going through
rapid biological, social, and psychological changes en route
to manhood. And the concern over what *kind* of man she
wants to raise has been changed by feminism and the sexual
revolution, among other things.

There is another reason the principles of behavioral parenting are also compelling for single mothers who wish to
rear sons sensitive to feminism and other social change: These
principles offer sons a neutral, nonsexist language that has

special appeal to women. Tomorrow's women are even more likely than today's to be sensitive to verbal and behavioral dominance and power games played by men. By definition and function, boys who grow up on behavioral parenting learn how to avoid those games.

There is nothing a woman can do to prevent her son from growing up and growing older. There is often nothing she can do about her divorce or widowhood. What is flexible is her and her son's behavior. Behavior is not poured in cement. It is a response or an action that depends on both the doer *and* his or her surroundings at the moment. To the extent that mothers understand the nature of that connection, they can influence it in a very powerful way.

The process by which adaptation takes place is outlined in the guidelines comprising the rest of this chapter.

Simply put, success occurs through learning. Learning, or knowledge, is gained through experience. As a single parent, mothers try different things until they discover what is successful. This process requires not only trying different actions, but also experiencing the consequences (good or bad) and then adjusting one's future actions to reflect what has been experienced.

The first of our guidelines, to sum up, is to look at the mother-son relationship as a process of adaptation, which takes *time* and results from experiences.

Talk Behavior

Usually, the more precise and clear we are about any particular matter, the easier it is to be understood and to get things right. It is tenet and hallmark of behavioral psychology and therefore behavioral parenting, that we set up very precise *response definitions*, which we have renamed *talk behavior*.

This book is about *behavior*, such as making the bed and picking up the clothes from the floor before leaving for school, taking out the garbage, and mowing the lawn on Saturday (or not doing them), about hitting a brother, coming home after curfew, dating the girl next door, loud-mouthing mom. What this book is *not* about is anger, aggression, laziness, not caring about how mother feels, disobedience, misunderstanding, or any other general traits used to categorize an entire class of very specific actions.

We experience the world and thus have the chance to learn how to adapt to it, through each individual act in which we engage. Of course, the sum total of all these acts is important. But if we are to do behavioral parenting, it is essential that we talk *behavior*.

Notice that we are not saying "think" behavior. Thinking is not observable, or measurable. To raise the son she wants, a mother will need to guide and change her son's behavior, actions she can observe. Unless she is a mind reader, what he thinks about something is a private event to which she is not privy. She is only able to see what he does, not what he thinks. Therefore, she should talk behavior. And the behavior she should talk about is the behavior she can watch.

We can demonstrate the practical wisdom of this approach with the case of a mother who brought her preschool son in desperation to psychologists. She and the boy's father told the professionals they were worried about the child's "lack of independence," that he never "let them alone" and "always seemed to need us every moment." The lack of independence in a boy was already viewed by this mother as "unmanly," and she blamed herself for this "horrible" state of affairs.

What the mother did not mention, but the psychologists drew out in interviews, was that her son was throwing twenty to twenty-five full-blown tantrums a day. The psychologists ignored the "independence" issue, which they could neither evaluate nor measure, and concentrated on extinguishing the tantrums. The issue was intolerable behavior not independence. This mother did not know how to talk behavior and therefore was sidetracked for months in useless worry about independence and her own value as a mother.

The Pot of Gold

Behavioral approaches to human relationships have as another basic tenet that objectives—or requirements for those objectives—must be specified and a clear path identified for achieving those ends—the pot of gold at the end of a rainbow. The rainbow marks the path to follow to achieve the treasured objective. Because everything changes (including your son's rainbows and rewards), the conditions that produced the rainbow may change over time, and the rainbow may even disappear. Mother must be aware that this might happen and watch for it to occur. When it does, she will need to follow a different rainbow to find a different pot of gold. When things change, so should her goals and her path for achieving it.

For example, she doesn't just want her son to be nice to his brother. Her specific objective is for her son to get through the day, week, month, without landing a punch when an argument rears. Similarly, it is not that she wants him to be neat. More specifically, she wants him to make his bed each morning and clear the floor of his clothes and Oreo cookie crumbs before he leaves for school. That's the pot of gold. The rainbow, how she gets to these and far more critical and desirable pots of gold, is the subject of the rest of this book.

What You Do Is What You Get

These notions about adaptation and behavior change follow from the exhaustively documented observation that behavior is a function of its consequences. Put another way, what you do is what you get. (And what you get is what you do.)

This is not to say that behavior is exclusively the outcome or function of consequences. Other things count, including genetics, biology, biochemistry, hormones (the bane of an adolescent's existence), and so on. What's important to remember is that *all* behavior is in some respects connected to some outside event or influence.

If mothers remind themselves to always think of behavior in this way—as a step-by-step operation and a process, not a finished product—they will be able to find imaginative ways of dealing with and changing it.

Here's how it works. After decades of psychological research, we know that a particular behavior or action can be increased or decreased by a consequence. A good way of thinking about these consequences is adding or removing certain forms of "encouragement" or "discouragement." The famed psychologist B. F. Skinner popularized the concepts that form the foundation for such strategies. With time and use the concepts have been modified to fit a variety of situations, including those we deal with in this book.

For example, if mother wants son to continue a certain behavior, or even increase it, she can add something that will bring that about. Psychologists call this reinforcement of the behavior, and it is usually achieved by some action on the mother's part that is rewarding or pleasant for her son, something he likes, something that makes him feel good.

At first the good feeling will be linked to the reward. If the reward continues, however, the good feeling will become linked to the behavior itself. And later, the good feeling, banked in the son's personality, will draw interest that can be applied to other, similar, kinds of behavior.

Now of course, no one, not even mothers, can see the feelings. All one can see is the behavior. This doesn't mean feelings don't exist, but that we only have a method for altering *behavior*, and so it is the behavior we must pay attention to.

Another way of encouraging a particular kind of behavior is to remove, or subtract, discouragement, or what psychologists call "aversive stimuli." This is the theme played out in Androcles and the Lion. In the fable, remember, Androcles removes a thorn (the aversive stimuli) from the lion's foot, an act that initially does little more than guarantee Androcles his life. But over time, as Androcles continues to ease the lion's pain, the lion's newfound gentle behavior toward the man (he doesn't eat him) continues to be reinforced. This culminates in a repeat of this man-lion interaction a good deal later in time when good Androcles is thrown to the beasts in the Coliseum. The lion he is thrown to is the one whose gentle behavior toward humans has been previously reinforced. Even after passage of time, the lion's behavior remains intact.

Encouraging behavior through consequences is an enduring process affected much less by the passage of time than by what other different consequences occur in the interim. This is an especially important guideline to remember when later on we discuss the influence of past experiences, or personal history, on the way mothers and sons act and react.

To discourage certain behavior, or eliminate it altogether, reverse the procedures by subtracting rewards or adding aversive, or punishing, events geared specifically to the behavior in question. Here's a familiar scene drawn from an interview:

Mother: It's seven o'clock and time for bed. What book do you want me to read?

Son (age five): I want to play. I never get to play. You don't love me.

Mother (walking him up the stairs to bed): Okay, you have

a choice. If you take off your clothes, brush your teeth, and get in bed, we'll read a book. If you continue to cry and say mean things, I'll just put you to bed with your clothes on and you'll have to go to sleep with no book or snuggle time.

Son (screaming now): You don't want me. I want to go and live with Daddy. You hate me.

Mother: You know you have school tomorrow and that's why you have to go to bed at seven. I do love you and would be sad if you didn't live with me.

Son: I won't go to sleep unless you read to me. Will you just read one book?

This mother, like many we spoke to, spent up to an hour each night going through this same frustrating ritual. "I spent at least half an hour explaining that I want him with me and that he isn't a burden to me and every night I'm exhausted and depressed by the whole ordeal."

Many single mothers confuse what their sons say with their sons' actions. The important thing here is to get son in bed at a healthful time without aggravation. He has learned that there are things he can say ("I want to live with Daddy" and so on) that will, every time, pull mom's strings and get her to pay attention for another half an hour or more. It's insidious. He'll keep trying things to win time and escape bed, and she is priming him for it by trying to deal only with *feelings* and not with *behavior*.

The result is a late bedtime, and the lesson for son is that his repertoire of endless talk works.

The behavioral mother would set up a reasonable amount of bedtime ritual (story, snuggle, drink); apply immediate consequences for noncompliance (leaving the room without a story or any conversation); and letting her son know that if he wants to live with daddy, that is a subject they will take up in the morning but not at bedtime.

Unfortunately, mothers rarely see sons' behavior in such clear terms. They tend to pay attention only when extremes of behavior are involved and they often fail to understand that for sons, the biggest, dearest payoffs come from something that is not extreme.

The way to help sons sort things out is to remember that they want to be among the best and that they need certain information to do that. To get that information, they look at those getting the social payoffs they want and focus on what those individuals are doing. Some of those things may be all right, and mothers can help him concentrate on these.

Son: What's the big deal about pot and booze? Everybody does it sooner or later and few get into trouble.

Mother: It's true that anyone can take drugs. It's no challenge and it certainly earns a lot of attention. (Here mother is talking behavior, explaining the appeal of taking drugs as she sees it. Those who take drugs are sometimes very popular and very nice people.)

Son: You just proved my case.

Mother: I've discounted the other payoffs, though, such as the fact that drug use is illegal and an arrest could mess up your school and job plans, as well as your health if there was an accident or you got some bad drugs.

Son: I'm not stupid. I'd be careful.

Mother: I think we agree that your goals are good ones, to make friends, learn to experiment safely and evaluate the world around you, and so on. There are things, however, that you already do that get the same results with none of the problems of drugs.

Son: Like what?

Mother: Making varsity, dating Linda, trying out for the school play.

No one says this kind of conversation will work like a one-shot inoculation against drug abuse. The resolution of differences of opinion doesn't usually come immediately. The reason is that in such cases there may be no immediate consequences, good or bad, for the boy who has or has not taken drugs.

Moreover, mothers cannot always levy on-the-spot consequences, the kind that count most, for a quick fix. But by talking behavior, pointing out possible consequences, and providing consistent consequences when and if the occasion arises, she can track the moving targets of her son's behavior and deal with it.

One other caution: Consequences can shift quickly for adolescents and one of the biggest problems mothers have is that they may assume that one kind of consequence is working when in fact some other, or even several others, is more important. Mothers get stuck, especially with teenagers, expecting their sons to act at one level, when they are already acting at another stage.

To sum up, in this guideline, we want you to know that what you do is what you get. If adaptation is the process by which behavior changes, and if behavior changes as an outcome of consequences, then what mothers need to do to change their sons' behavior and ensure that they adapt is to arrange the environmental consequences linked to or dependent on the actions in question.

The Traffic Light

In behavioral parenting, the most important and powerful influence is the consequence for any given act. There is, however, another very important element in behavioral change that can make life easier and more pleasant for most mothers and sons, and for everyone else around them. It is that certain events can operate as *signals* that a particular behavior will result in either encouraging or discouraging consequences.

Such signals are very helpful when we want to adapt to the changes that take place in our family or the larger environment with the least amount of pain and problems and the greatest amount of gain.

In technical terms, psychologists call these signals *discriminative stimuli*, but we ask you to think of them as an ongoing series of traffic lights, which indicate that it is okay to go ahead with the behavior (green light); that it is best to stop it (red light); or that there is some degree of ambiguity as to what the consequences might be (yellow light).

The traffic light principle is especially useful in three areas of the mother-son relationship.

The first is in the case of what is technically known as instructional control—telling your son what to do. These instructions should not only signal whether a son's specific behavior will result in an encouraging or discouraging consequence, but also provide information about what that behavior should be and what the consequences should be.

Mother: Johnny, I want you to take out the garbage. It's one of the chores we agreed on, and your allowance is partially dependent on it.

Son: I don't have time now.

Mother: Then it's your choice to give up your allowance this week.

It's important to understand that when instructions like these are given, the traffic lights for behavior are only effective as signals if mother applies encouraging or discouraging consequences. Without them, the signals lose their meaning and they won't work. In the case above, mother had previously taken away allowance for failure to do other chores. So the son knew it was not an empty threat.

An important bonus: Boys treated this way learn that because mother's past instructions have so often resulted in important consequences, they will pay attention to new instructions even if they have not had the consequences spelled out.

In terms of time and energy, this is efficient and economical for mothers, and far less troublesome than having to provide consequences for every single behavior in order to establish control. If behaviors are clearly stated and consistent consequences applied, then instructions and signals will be very effective and sons will learn that mother means what she says.

Another application of traffic signals occurs with what psychologists call modeling, or imitating someone else. In this case, the instruction is not "Do what I say" but "Do as I do."

For example, little boys learn early that it can be very rewarding to imitate what the important grown-ups in their lives say and do. "Just like his dad" or "mother's little helper" are phrases heard in any home. The satisfaction of imitating may extend later to areas mother is not so enthusiastic about, such as imitating less-than-law-abiding peers.

Modeling can also, as this next example shows, be so powerful a draw, especially for very young boys, that signals can get crossed and cause problems unless mother is alert.

Dorothy recounted the time her son, age three, repeatedly threw his kiddie car into the street in front of their home. This was especially distressing to her, because she had tried hard to teach him not to play near the street and not to damage his toys.

Several times she retrieved the vehicle out of the same spot in the gutter and told her son that such treatment would soon break the toy and was therefore unacceptable. Her talk was to no avail.

"He would ride it half a block, turn around, come back, get off, and shove it in the street again!" She was on the verge of taking the car away as punishment (a consequence that worked in the past) when she saw the next-door neighbor pull up and park her car at the curb.

"It was like a light bulb going on in my head," she says.

"Jeff was just at that age when he wanted to imitate everything his father did. He was parking the car in the street just like Dad."

Clearly, this mother was tuned in to shifting consequences. She needed to alter her rainbow and her traffic signals. She would want to do this in a way that would tell her son she approved of his efforts to imitate dad's role as a preeminent parker of cars, but not her son's efforts to destroy his toys. She might, for example, suggest that kiddie cars are too small for the street and block out a safer parking area near the garage or on the walk.

Rule systems are an even more elaborate and exceedingly more helpful way of assisting mothers and sons to track and follow their rainbows.

For instance, boys are rewarded for following certain rules of behavior adults feel are right for them, whether it's "never hit a girl" or "boys don't cry" or "it's important to do homework." Over time, and given sufficient rewards and reinforcements for following rules and instructions, boys begin to follow other, unrelated rules without specific instructions and without specific rewards for doing so. Law-abiding people don't have to break a law in order to understand consequences. A mark of maturity, from our standpoint, is *not* having to test every consequence.

The same principle explains why most of us don't have to burn our hands on a stove to learn that hot stoves can burn. Or that once we have been burned on a hot stove, we know not to put our hand on a hot iron to learn the same lessons.

But it may also explain how some individuals learn to follow rules blindly or to bend to instructions automatically when they are offered by intimidating or authoritative individuals outside the home. That is why it is so vital for mothers to carefully consider the rules they impose and reinforce and to understand how they may be generalized in ways they never intended. In short, reserve this principle for those kinds of behavior that are truly critical.

A psychologist, divorced and rearing three children, provides this example from her personal experience. Her sons would visit their father for weekends and come back with a whole new set of behaviors that defied the rules of her household.

Her ex-husband allowed more leeway than she in some

things, less in others, and it took days to get the boys "back in shape" after one of their visits to dad. Consequences had shifted and the traffic signals changed.

Her way of handling it was 24K-gold behavioral parenting:

Mom: Glad you're home, fellows. Remember now, this is Mom's house, not Dad's. My rules, not his, are in force. Let's get our bags unpacked and get ready for bed.

Sons immediately get specific signals. Consequences, as they have learned, are swift if they ignore them.

The problem is not mixed messages. Sons can handle them *if* mothers make their own signals clear and help sons resist the temptation to sample contrary consequences too often.

Mother: It's okay to roughhouse in the family room, but not in the living room.

Mother: I don't mind if your table manners slide at home, but when we have company, you must use your knife and fork, not fingers. Let's pretend we're having company and see how you would do with this dinner.

Practice Makes Perfect

If behavior is an outcome of its consequences, then one must experience the consequences before behavior is likely to change. A change in behavior, or adaptation, is a process that takes place over time, or, to be more precise, over the course of experience, which takes time. Setting the occasion for experiencing consequences is just another way of saying "practice."

To illustrate this principle, consider this tale of woe from a twenty-nine-year-old single mother of a five-year-old boy.

"Whenever we go to the 7-11 store after school he just has to buy something. Whether or not I let him depends on how I feel that day really. Other times, I'll decide ahead of time, before I pick him up from school, whether I'll let him. If I say no, he might agree, but when we get in the store, he still works at it.

"His teacher says he can't respond to reasoning, but he's very empathetic really, so I can't believe that. But I get worn down with the stress of taking him shopping, even though he loves it."

A behavioral mother would sit down with her son, make up a shopping list with him, let him help choose things for the house, for her, and if budget allows, for him. She would discuss money and define rules for the shopping trip: Stay with mom, don't pull things off the shelves, no screaming and running off.

Instead of arbitrarily deciding, on the basis of how she *feels*, whether to buy him something or not, she can establish a consistent pattern.

Son: Can I have this toy?

Mom: We have discussed this and you know the rule is that on after-school trips, you can only get something that's on the list.

By letting her son practice appropriate shopping behavior at the 7-11 store with her, he learns several things. Shopping is fun, it does not have to end in tears, and there is benefit to planning ahead. Mom is likely to take him more often when there is less stress.

This guiding principle contains three important ideas. First, behavior change is going to take time. It won't happen instantly. Behavioral parenting is not what psychologists call a "stimulus/response" or a push/pull situation. You don't do something and get a quick change very often.

Second, mothers should set the occasion for tracking and providing specific consequences for behavior they want to change or maintain, with consistency and patience. Remember, behavior change is more related to the *number of times* consequences are experienced than to how long it takes to experience these consequences. That is, judge your patience not in terms of the passage of time but in terms of how many occasions have occurred for learning to take place.

Finally, arranging practice works for everyone, mothers included. If mothers wish to change sons' behavior, then mothers will need to change their own behavior. Specifically, mothers will need to change the way they react to their sons' behavior, and that will require rehearsals, tryouts, and practice.

Mothers should specify what behavior in themselves they want to change and try to arrange some consequences for themselves to encourage or discourage their own behavior. Often, just noting objectively what they are doing and whether it is on that rainbow course toward the objective, or taking notice of how some things they have worked on together have changed for the better, is sufficient. One young mother of a preschool son keeps a diary "of all the changes we have been through together" since her separation. By recording impressions and actions, some of which might not seem relevant at the time, this mother may detect patterns that will give her important clues to what consequences are operating for her son. It will help her discover what works. In short, the diary can help her figure out where on the rainbow she is.

But whatever it takes, mothers must realize that practice is an important activity for them as well as sons.

Money in the Bank

This last principle is the one we like best because it has the biggest payoff in the long run for everyone. It relates to the fact that knowledge gained from experience—behavior changed by a history of consequences—is enduring. It is changed only by *contrary* consequences.

This means that what mothers decide to teach their sons during childhood and adolescence is an investment in the future. We do *not* mean this in the Freudian, psychoanalytic sense, but rather that the positive and adaptive behaviors that mothers help their sons to learn will in very large part determine what type of men their sons turn out to be.

Simply stated, the two things that drive this principle are the prevailing consequences at the time, and the consequence history the individual brings to each new situation. The job of the single mother (and all parents) is to provide that history.

For sons, there is an added reward beyond the benefit to be derived from the reassurance and resolution of conflict with their mothers. It is this: Most boys, drawn to models of authoritative adults (they desperately want to be one of these), will at some point begin to recognize the pattern and purpose of their mother's parenting style and adopt it in their own lives. They will be able to use the principles with their peers, teachers, and, yes, their mothers. They will begin to realize the value of talking and tracking their own behavior as well as others', a mature step toward avoiding conflict and reaching their goals.

Joann's son Jared, age fourteen, for example, used some behavioral parenting principles in this exchange with her, which concerned his desire to purchase a seven-hundred-dollar electronic piano.

Joann: I understand how important it is because you have been invited to play in a real band, but seven hundred dollars represents half of your savings and you already have a smaller electric keyboard. You have also talked about saving for a car.

Jared: I've thought a lot about that. There are some other things I'd like to bring out, though. Is this a good time?

Joann: Yes, I guess so.

Jared: I've looked into second-hand keyboards in the classified section of the paper and learned that most of those for sale are too large for what I need. But I also learned that resale value is very high. So if I should lose interest, which isn't likely, or need the money later, I can probably get a good price by placing such an ad.

Joann: That's a good point. But what about the band? How serious an enterprise is it?

Jared: You've said a few things in the past that make me think you have some wrong ideas about the band members. They're all good students, in a private school where my stepbrother goes. They're seniors who'll graduate next year, but think I'm good enough to play with them. Dad's checked them out, too. They play for school dances and make some money. Rehearsals are on weekends, and I'll make all the arrangements to get there myself.

Joann: You *have* done a lot of good thinking about this. I'm really impressed. Have you priced the instrument in several places?

Jared: Could you come with me to check them out. I've called several places close to each other. Can we work out a time to do it?

(P.S. Jared got the keyboard and has now organized his own band. He has also learned a lot about negotiating and compromising.)

There are special rewards for mothers when older sons learn these lessons. Michael travels a lot and his "consequence history" has taught him that his mother worries a good deal when he is away and cannot call at regular times.

He has also learned that his phone calls can create worry if they come at unappointed times as well. ("Why are you calling? Is anything wrong?")

When he phones at unappointed times, he therefore always begins his conversation by saying, "Hi, everything is fine." When he is traveling and hears about an accident or air crash, he phones to say, "Hi, everything is fine. I thought you might have heard about the crash (accident) and I didn't want you to worry."

Here is a case where Michael has generalized consequences to preempt worry by his family.

We have said a great many things in this chapter—we hope in a clear and understandable manner. There are also many things that we have not said. We have not talked about the love, kindness, and caring mothers give to their sons, even in the most difficult circumstances. That is also the nature of parenting and parents, single and otherwise. Because we have not discussed it here does not mean that we underestimate its importance. We don't.

But much of the selfless behavior of mothers toward their children can be explained by how *rewarding* (in the strict, behavioral sense of the word) the children are for mothers. Regardless of how one wishes to characterize the sum total of mother/son relationships, the fact remains that the guidelines we have set forth are real. They are also well documented from basic principles in the scientific literature for a whole range of animals, as well as humans. Finally, these guidelines should not exclude but be used together with all the other techniques that characterize good parenting.

The major objection we have heard to the idea of behavioral parenting is that it is too controlling. The fact is that the principles we discuss here do not become inoperative, or invisible, simply because mothers don't consciously set out to use them (or don't know about them). On the contrary, behavior is *always* a function of its consequences and this is true whether mothers plan for that to occur or not.

Realizing this, then, isn't it better to make sure that what is occurring anyway is used to the best advantage of families and in the interests of rearing our children in ways that please us? We think so. Gravity exists whether we intended to fall off the roof or not.

We might add that consideration of these guidelines is helpful not only in planning the right course of action, but also in recognizing and analyzing when and how things go wrong. Knowing the basics helps us to handle unique situations and troubleshoot. Just remember, the principles don't fail, only the way we use them.

A last word: Behavioral parenting is for optimists. It is not for those who argue (and many do!) that the way boys behave with their mothers (or with anyone else) is rooted in genetics and therefore immutable. One of the authors has a friend who insists her thirteen-year-old son was "born stubborn" and therefore all contact with him assumes the need for confrontation and a winner and a loser. Predictably, their relationship is awful.

If we believed as this woman does—that nothing can ever change—we wouldn't have written this book. We believe that, by using the principles of behavioral parenting, nothing is foreclosed or doomed.

CHAPTER THREE

Who Owes Whom:
The Concept of
Basic Due

Mother: Don't forget to take the garbage cans down to the curb on your way to school this morning.

Son: Why do I have to do it? Why can't you?

Mother: Because we all have our jobs around here. This is yours. You know that.

Son: Well, I'm busy now. Get Danny to do it.

Mother: It's your job, not his, and anyway he's still in the shower. I don't want to tell you again.

Son (caustically): Big deal.

Mother: Did you hear me? I said do it now or you can forget the movies this weekend.

Son: You have a maid to clean the house and you've got me to do everything else. All you do is read the paper in the morning.

Mother (enraged): How can you say that? After all I've done for you and your brother . . .

Son: Great. Now you can lay the guilt trip on me.

We'd all like to have a dollar for every time that conversation or some version of it took place between single mothers and sons.

Mothers who are really "good" at this exchange extend it with a litany of all the things they have done for their sons. Joann's list is typically creative: a lifetime supply of alligator shirts, lakeside summer camps, allowances, vacations, three squares a day, movie money, color TV, typing term papers, nursing care, career guidance, the "very fact that I'm here," and, of course, overlooking the knee-deep debris and litter they leave everywhere when anyone with a shred of common sense would have grounded them for life.

Depending on the size and age of the son, an episode like this may be accompanied by threats, promises, tantrums, multiple bargaining sessions, and statements such as "You can't make me," or "Who cares?"

Although all parents get into flaps like this one, single mothers with sons are especially prone to the "who-owes-whom-what" trap.

"Sure we have rules, but there is an endless stream of small breaks in them that require nagging, cajoling, or renegotiation," says a thirty-seven-year-old high school teacher. She is rearing two sons. "Most of these have to do with things that need doing around the house and for the family. He does well in school and has nice friends. But after all we are a family and we all need to pitch in to do things for each other if this household is going to work. My son's tactic is to wear me down like a Philadelphia lawyer. And the truth is, it works."

A Boston writer with a sixteen-year-old son: "His best strategy and tactic is to wear me down with delays. Oh sure, he says, 'I'll do it,' and three weeks later it isn't done. He weasels very well."

"I have lists of my lists there are so many details I have to remember every day," a mother of two teenage boys complains. "After all I've done for them to keep this family going, it's time they did a few things." Says another, "If I ask Todd to take out the garbage on Wednesdays, he'll do it, sometimes even graciously. But it burns me that I have to ask. After five years, he should know it needs to be done and take this item off my shoulders. Why can't he be thoughtful of my needs? It's hard for me to haul heavy cans around or mow the lawn, and I detest having to remind him all the time. And while I'm on the subject, it wouldn't hurt if he occasionally put dinner on when I have to work late or vacuum the living room without being told."

A son's response to this kind of complaint from his mother is often "I'm not her husband or her servant. Why is it my job to do all this stuff? With school and everything else I don't have time to keep track of everything. What's the big deal if she has to remind me?" Or "I have a sister. Let *her* do it!"

There's not much mystery about why sons and single mothers behave this way. Boys who are growing and seeking freedom want to be in charge of their own time and energy and will inevitably balk when confronted by a woman demanding things that interfere with both. And if boys fail to see the link between clean dishes and washing dishes, it's often a carryover from the mother-father households where mother was in charge of domestic operations and dad always took out the garbage—when he was asked.

Mothers are traditionally the parents who bark domestic orders, and without a father in the house, these are certain to increase. Moreover, the immediate aftermath of a separation or divorce often sabotages established rules and discipline. A mother with any insight at all will quickly see the need to take control, and chances are excellent she will fix on what she perceives as an easy way to do that: by giving more orders for more household chores and responsibilities. She has reality and guilt on her side.

Mother: I can't work all day and come home and do all the meals, wash clothes, and clean your room too!

Son: I work all day in school and I can't spend all my spare time on chores, either!

Mother: After all I've done for you . . .

There are two important things to say about getting out of the who-owes-whom-what trap. One is that it makes an end run around assigning blame and guilt, which is a generally unproductive parenting strategy. And two, it is essential if single mothers with sons are to avoid psychological sex-role wars of long duration.

The way to get out of the trap is to embrace the concept we call *basic due.*

A major contingency in any mother-son relationship is the total resources of a given family unit. Financial, social, time, energy, and health resources must all be divided in ways that satisfy the needs of each member involved in the mother-son and family contract.

The size of the basic resource pie, of course, may vary. In some households it may mean swimming pools and live-in maids. In others, a two-room apartment and spaghetti three nights a week. But the method of dividing that pie need not vary if basic due is operating.

The notion is a simple one. It holds that certain parts of the resource pie, such as meals, clothing, shelter, medical care, some leisure time, and privacy are the "due" of everyone in the family, regardless of who is the wage-earner or who is in charge. And beyond that, nothing else is "coming to you" without some investment of resources.

The rationale here is that children did not choose to be born; they cannot yet earn enough to support their basic needs (the economy couldn't even find jobs for forty million teenagers without putting adults out of work), and they must accept dependence on those who can supply them for long periods of time in order to attain the skills they need to take over.

An important hallmark of twentieth-century society is that children remain in infancy for a period of time unprecedented in history. Thanks to child labor laws and a postindustrialized, high-tech society, we don't encourage self-supporting kids but superbly educated ones. The message we give children is to delay gratifications—financial, sexual, social—generally until our sons are past the age when their grandfathers were already rearing families.

Therefore as a tactic for rearing sons, basic due is especially valuable because it considers the current social and political environment in which single mothers must do their parenting. In a long conversation, Oscar Christenson, a University of Arizona psychologist, described modern parents as

> the first generation that doesn't know how to raise their kids because their traditional American approach to the job ignores the last thirty years of history, particularly the civil rights movement. Traditional child-rearing principles, particularly where boys are concerned, are fundamentally rooted in European, Middle Ages practices driven by a superior-inferior concept of human relationships. Everyone had a rank in the social pecking order. Nobles were better than peasants, men better than women and adults better than children. The child had to learn to knuckle under and bow and scrape, because that is what he would have to do as an adult.

But since World War II and especially the 1960s, the civil rights movement has won social equality, in theory at least, for all minority groups, including children. Children are the last minority to see themselves as having equal rights, and any technique based on autocratic power-drunk behavior won't work. In a society of equals, for example, if parents have the right to punish kids, then kids have a right to punish parents.

The child seeks to escalate his power to demonstrate not his strength but his equality, and the parent then escalates her power so she can be on top.

"The show-em-who's-boss school of parenting just can't work with today's kids," concludes Christenson. "I have yet to hear a child tell a parent who just spanked him, 'thanks, I needed that.' What he does say instead is 'O.K., I'll fix your wagon.' And believe me, kids are a lot better at wagon fixing than parents are at punishing and showing who's boss and winning battles."

Christenson suggests (only slightly in jest) that mothers take a tip from kung fu specialists and the power of other martial artists and "take your sail out of your child's wind." The essential strength of this approach to control rests in disarming power, not outstripping it. If someone is about to punch you in the mouth, the best thing to do is move your face. Yet most mothers faced with a physical or verbal power play will thrust their jaw straight out and create an instant war that requires a winner and a loser.

Basic due is an excellent way for mother to take her sail out of her son's wind, for encouraging behavior she does like and turning aside behavior she does not. And as a bonus, it works exquisitely well at just that point when mothers want sons to begin to take charge of their lives in some ways and to take a bigger role in her life and family life as well; that is, to take some of the family responsibilities as his own.

This does not mean, necessarily, major responsibilities such as earning a living or caring for younger children or providing emotional support as a husband would.

More often, and more appropriately, it includes day-to-day and mostly trivial details of running a household smoothly. Keeping track of overdue library books, making arrangements for rides to baseball practice, remembering to buy lunch meats, and the seemingly endless stream of trivial chores can be enervating to everyone.

Using the concept of basic due, all of these items are negotiable.

Moreover, if it is clearly understood that beyond basic due everything is negotiated, two things will happen. First, family responsibilities will be more evenly divided. It will become clear that although it is not the highlight of mother's day to drive her son to the orthodontist, it's part of her responsibility to her family. Equally, it will become clear that though it does not thrill her son to take responsibility for the yard work, it is a necessary part of family life. All of the principles of behavioral parenting, including conditioning, can be used to enforce the beyond-the-basic-due contract. And the basic due, so closely tied to the son's sense of belonging and security and equality within the family, is never threatened because it is not included in the negotiating process.

Second, every time an item outside basic due is successfully negotiated, the experience will reinforce several desirable kinds of behavior. Sons will learn that far more of life's rewards and privileges can be won through the art of compromise than through pitched battle or inflexibility. They will see more realistically what adult life often entails and why behavior that forecloses choices is self-defeating.

Behavioral parenting, as we've said, asks mothers to deal with practical needs and practical responses. It does not ask mothers or sons to read each others' minds, fix blame, discern motives, or apply guilt. It requires only a reasonable set of goals and a plan that is rewarding enough for all concerned to guarantee implementation.

The use of basic due, incidentally, does not require mothers to give up their leadership role in the family or let sons "do their own thing." In a democratic society, there must still be order and leaders. Mother need not abdicate her parental role. With basic due, all individuals in the family have equal value and equal worth, but equality need not mean sameness. Sons are not the same as parents in experience, resources, or power.

Basic due and all the principles of behavioral parenting form a framework in which to rear sons to be self-disciplined, instead of sons who behave solely because of outside forces or the threat of outside punishment. To accomplish this, mothers must give sons more opportunities to make decisions and choices, and to live with the consequences. Mothers, particularly single mothers, should stop doing everything for their sons once they are out of infancy and should give their sons a chance to be helpful, useful, and needed at home, even if sons don't appreciate it at the time.

Behavioral parenting accepts the fact that in a family, and in a mother-son family in some unique ways, all members need to behave responsibly for reasons of practicality and fairness.

Mothers must drop the guilt over needing sons to perform tasks that "he wouldn't have to do if his father were here." In the first place, that is not true. In many well-run and well-ordered mother-father-son families, chores are distributed among each family member.

Mothers can use basic due to maintain or restore their position of control, in order to create a secure environment in which sons will learn what they need to know as successful men.

Mothers can use basic due to counter everything from sexism to whining.

To begin the process of basic due:

- Make a list of family resources. For sons, resources include such things as time, strength, agility, outside income from part-time jobs, and talents ranging from carpentry to embroidery. (One fifteen-year-old boy we know sews hems better than most tailors or seamstresses, for example. He enjoys knitting as well.) For mothers, resources include earnings, time, access to the larger world, transportation capabilities, and individual talents and skills. For mothers and sons, together, resources might include child support, alimony, visits from dad, support from relatives and institutions such as the church or synagogue, family friendships, and household help and babysitters.
- Make a list of responsibilities to oneself. These include time for work, school, personal hygiene (one mother included "long, hot bubble baths"), adequate rest, privacy, recreation, and personal relationships outside the home.
- Make a list of collective family needs and responsibilities, and needs voiced by all members of the family. These include household chores, outdoor chores, emergency care, care of the sick, care of animals, repairs and maintenance, meal preparation, financial stability, peace and quiet, time to be alone, time for the extended family (grandparents particularly), and so on.
- Mothers make a separate list of items that are appropriate for males and females, which provide opportunities for her son to learn what she believes is important in male behavior and female behavior.
- Make a list of rewards and desired activities each member of the family wants.
- Get everyone familiar with the lists. With younger children, these can be talked about rather than read. But set

aside neutral time to discuss them, add to them, and so on.

- Assign (with some negotiation) the amount of time everyone should have for personal and family responsibilities and needs.
- Agree (after negotiation) what the basic due of each member is. For example, basic due in terms of personal privacy during the week may include one hour of uninterrupted time watching a TV program of one's choice on a school night, or it might include one hour of time on the piano without an audience, or an hour on the telephone without comment. Basic financial due might in some families include a basic allowance given no matter what and never to be taken away as punishment, or it may include only lunch money or funds for school supplies.
- Make clear that in order to realize more than basic due, sons as well as mothers will have to deposit some of their resources in the family bank.

A bonus of basic due is that it allows mothers who accept it to reserve all things outside basic due as items for negotiation in the larger mother-son contract, and that is big money in the behavioral resource bank. The contract is explained in Chapter Nine.

Different Strokes: Setting Your Own Goals/I

Gladys is a thoughtful, well-educated divorcée with a teenage son, Jerry. Recently, she read in a newspaper article that excessive modesty is a mark of sexual inhibition and possibly plays a role in the development of childhood homosexuality.

Her preventive "solution" to this "problem" was to traipse around the house in the buff, in a show of defiant liberation. She felt especially courageous and selfless about her behavior, moreover, because she personally found the activity extremely uncomfortable. Public nudity, even in her home, was clearly not her preference, but she sacrificed her dignity for the cause.

Jerry's response? Withdrawal and anger, at her and others, and complaints to his father about "mom's behavior." Predictably, Gladys responded to his anger with her own, resentful of his apparent rejection of her "lesson" and her good intentions.

What happened to this mother and son illustrates what can happen when parents fail to set clear child-rearing objectives. It can occur in any household, but may have especially serious consequences in single-mother-and-son households.

Gladys missed her mark precisely because she failed to clearly identify it. She never defined the specific behavior she wanted her son to learn, but instead attempted to use her own actions as a vague prod to influence a set of values and beliefs she wasn't even certain Jerry had ever considered!

A key element in behavioral parenting, as we've said before, is that only behavior can be observed and acted upon. Thoughts, feelings, attitudes, and values are important, but

we can only assess them by observing the behavior they produce. Jerry's anger at his mother's actions, rather than his
sympathy for her intentions, is a case in point.

If Gladys had looked for some specific behavior of Jerry's
that fit into her concern about sexual inhibition (discomfort
around girls, for example), she might have found that there
was no "problem," instead of creating one.

Ironically, in one important way, Gladys was on the right
track: She concluded, properly, that a mother's behavior can
influence her son's actions.

But the goal she set (lack of sexual inhibition) is far too
broad and "psychological" to be met by a single show of
activity, no matter how courageous or dramatic. Moreover,
she never considered the other, possibly conflicting, messages
her behavior was teaching. Nor did she "talk behavior" so
that her son had a clear idea of her goal in this instance. She
almost guaranteed failure by assuming that her performance,
motivated by her own agenda, would automatically lead her
son to think and therefore behave the way she was thinking
and behaving. (As we'll see in more detail in Chapter Five,
behavior does not change this way.)

The final blow to her program consisted of behaving in a
way that was clearly (to her son) uncharacteristic and (to her
personally) undesirable.

All in all, this mother's assault on sexual inhibition was a
poor one, not just because of its behavioral naiveté, but, more
critically, because she lacked a specific objective.

By the end of this chapter, we hope to convince mothers
that the cornerstone of behavioral parenting is the willingness
to set objectives and take charge of their own plans for achieving them. Equally important, we will talk about what some
of the goals might be for sons reared by single mothers in
light of the special problems and experiences they encounter
when raising sons.

When she begins to outline her goals with her son, mother
will make some mistakes—they're inevitable. But if she reviews her objectives periodically, mid-course corrections will
be possible. She shouldn't be timid. The mistakes that occur
in a leadership void are worse.

Mothers can and ought to pattern essential behavioral goals
they set for their sons in ways that at least sometimes meld
with consistent behavior on their own part. In other words,

there are many "different strokes for different folks," and mothers of sons do best when they select those that are both *important* to them and *comfortable* for them. That way they can establish very precise, specific goals both they and their sons understand, before putting a plan in motion.

In Gladys's case, she needed to make an important decision before she tried to teach anything about how she wanted Jerry to behave as a sexual person. If he was in fact already behaving in ways she considered normal and comfortable, she might have found ways to encourage more of that. If he were not, she needed to identify *specifically* what it was about his behavior she did not want to encourage. Instead of overreacting to a newspaper story's theories about homosexuality, Gladys needed to think carefully about what she felt constituted a successful man.

Is such a man a libertine? A nudist? Hardly. Pressed, she would probably agree with most of the women we interviewed: that a successful male is neither sexually repressed nor an exhibitionist. The model she presented by her behavior was at least counterproductive and at best confusing. Boys at Jerry's stage of sexual development are confused enough by their own peers and sexual hang-ups.

We recognize that it is not easy, especially for single mothers with sons to rear, to set specific goals because setting them requires mothers to make choices about the kinds of men they want to rear. But mothers are often reluctant to even try to come to grips with what they like and don't like about men because they worry that criticizing anything masculine or male, or leaving out traditional male experiences, is a dangerous disservice to a boy without a father in the home.

Beth: "Ian was almost six when my husband one day announced he didn't want to be married anymore and just left. Ian is twelve now and okay, but I went through a lot of fears about homosexuality. It took me two years to realize that I would be okay just being Mom. I tried to be Mom and Dad because I thought Ian would be a mess. He was the first male child born in our family in fifty years. I never had a male cousin or a close male friend. I had never had anything like him, never seen a little boy grow up."

Evelyn, an actress, now remarried, about her first son, whom she reared alone: "Raising a kid in New York without a father, wow! One of the big problems was that I am quite a pacifist. When Seth was young, I played the ingenue as stock in trade. I liked stories about elves, not guns, and wanted everything sweet. I liked soft, sweet children. I liked men with those qualities, but I found out too late that Seth was just totally unprepared to be a male teenager on the streets of New York. If I had to do it again, I would send him to karate school. I was absolutely the wrong person to help him with manliness. If I were a single mother again, I would act differently."

"Lou (her second husband) loves sports. I never knew how to throw a ball. I throw all wrong. Lou showed me that. I taught Seth all wrong."

Patty, single mother of three sons: "My husband left me to sort out his personal identity crisis and I was very bitter about that. But I have tried my darndest never to speak against him in front of the boys because he is their father and they *have* to like themselves."

In other cases, mothers are too ambivalent to set goals for behavior they consider ideal.

Beth: "I see Ian growing up as a traditional man and that pleases me. But I see him as a marshmallow, too, and I like that in men. I absolutely love the femininity in him and the masculinity in (daughter) Lisa. Sometimes I don't know what to think. I know that men are crippled by the new life-styles just as many women are. We've gone a long way looking into the kind of women we need to be to make it in the world, but what do we do with our sons? What kind of man will do well with aggressive, liberated women? I remind Ian a lot that it's okay to make mistakes. I want him to have self-confidence so that if there's an aggressive broad out there it's not gonna throw him. Or an aggressive male, either, for that matter."

Evelyn: "This will sound strange, but Seth's sweetness was a potential source of embarrassment to me. Here I wanted this nonaggressive boy, but I would be embarrassed when he did things unmanly like cry in public. I loved it when he let his feelings out, though it gave me problems. Yet when Pat (her teenage son by her second marriage) shows aggression at times, I don't like it. I guess I really did enjoy the little golden-haired Seth, this little pacifist angel. At least until the real world came in.

"We play a word game called Boggle as a family sport.

And hearts. I've finally now allowed my own competitiveness to come out. Once I could never allow myself to beat a man at cards. Now I can beat the pants off my family and look forward to it. They love it when Mommy's on a streak. But when I look back—with Seth—I almost always let him win. I was afraid to show him a competitive woman."

It is little wonder that mothers raising boys often convince themselves that setting specific goals is a form of "smothering" or not worth the effort. They talk a lot about "spontaneity" and the fact that mothering sons is "an art, not a science."

Many of the mothers and sons Joann met and talked to, sought and benefited from professional psychotherapists when their sons developed serious behavioral problems.

But most of them told her over and over that their real interest and need was not to deal with major crises, but to get help with everyday lessons of life: meeting responsibilities, setting rules and realistic goals, achieving, taking disappointment, learning flexibility, tolerating others, and assuring the day-to-day behavior that keeps a family rolling in addition to rearing a praiseworthy son.

Behavioral parenting does that. It is not interested in cut-rate mind reading, having come to believe that overemphasis on why we do the things we do is often enervating and self-indulgent, and more important, unnecessary to the process of growth and development. Looking for ways to achieve satisfying relationships by staring at one's psychic innards smacks of the tail wagging the dog. The goal is to learn behavior that brings competence and success. That means acting and observing how others react. This is not to say that feelings, motives, and our "surround" don't count in how we behave. They do. But in the parenthood trenches, these are a given, which, with few exceptions, most people cannot alter significantly. It's where you go and what you do with what you've got that makes mothering sons not only a successful enterprise but an adventure in the best possible sense of the word.

As we explained in the chapter on behavioral parenting, a keystone in any learning system is not only to talk behavior, but to define the criteria you will accept as measures of success, plan the minimum number of steps to achieve them, practice, and use the right "traffic lights."

We rarely think about it this way, but even relatively simple, mechanical actions are learned step by step in a continuously building, intricate web. For example, making a bed involves at least twenty separate steps that must be performed in exact sequence from putting on the bottom sheet to cover all four corners of the mattress to finding the rounded corners of the spread and pulling the square end up over the pillow. Moreover, each step must form a clue and a prod to begin the next one, and the completion of the task must be worth the effort if the bed maker is to take all that time and trouble.

Therefore, efforts to change behavior must also be done in steps that are thoughtfully planned and patiently explained over a period of time. (As with all learning, there are ripple effects, the "money in the bank." In this case, mothers who take the time and effort to do these things are also teaching and demonstrating for their sons that the most efficient way to achieve objectives is to have a plan.)

To some readers, this may seem mechanistic and manipulative. But keep in mind that this is implicitly what happens in learning, whether we plan it that way or not. Whenever a mother does something with her son, she is teaching, from the time he is an infant. What you *do* is much more important than what you say. Setting goals is critical, and so are the steps involved.

Setting behavioral objectives requires four of these:

• Listing concerns about your son's behavior. ("He fights too much," "He tries to act like the man of the house," "He gets bad grades," "He isn't dating," are examples.)

• Translating those concerns into behavioral terms (talking behavior) instead of vague "mental" terms. For example, instead of talking about your son's "bad attitude" in school as a cause of his bad grades, find out (from the teacher in this case) precisely what that means in terms of his actions in the classroom. Does he skip school, fail to turn in homework, ignore reasonable requests? Instead of describing your son's troublesome drinking habits as "a need to rebel," note specifically what those habits are. "He drinks beer all weekend, but never during the week." "He drinks before driving." "He loses jobs frequently because of drinking."

• Choosing only one or two target behaviors to start dealing with at a time. You can't do everything, so choose carefully. Select them either because they are at the moment the most important behaviors to change or get going (a drug-taking crisis, excessive overeating, or cutting school), or because they are relatively easy to change (and will give your son and you the confidence necessary to tackle bigger problems).

• Getting a fix on every aspect of the behavior question. How should it change (start, stop, moderate)? When does it occur? In what circumstances do you notice it? How often does it occur? Is it getting worse? What comes before and after the behavior? Which principles of behavioral parenting are best equipped to change the behavior? How will you know when it has changed? (What will look or be different about your son?) Is the goal appropriate for the son's stage of development as well as the chosen audience? Is a behavioral goal you choose one that needs to be achieved immediately? Does it depend on other behavior that must be learned earlier or at the same time?

In what context will the learning take place? What else will be going on at the same time? What other messages may contradict, influence, or support the goal? Are you on track with the goal or have interests shifted? Have you anticipated what and how circumstances will change in the short run and over the long haul? Has anything changed outside to warrant a shift, such as health, growth, new friends, remarriage? Is achieving the goal in question a good use of time and energy for you and your son? How important is the behavior you want or the behavior you want changed?

Michael, a bright eight-year-old, was subjected to weeks of training designed to get him to turn his clothes right side out before putting them in the wash. His mother claimed it saved her more than an hour of handling on laundry day. Was it worth it? For this mother, yes. For others, maybe not.

Here are some tips to get the job done efficiently and easily.

First, block out at least two hours of quiet, private time in which to begin, and have a notebook and pen or pencil on hand. We cannot emphasize enough the importance of this preparation. At first, the task will seem awkward and time-consuming, because it asks a mother to concentrate on what she and her son will be doing instead of on why things are done. Writing down your ideas and plans is essential. Not even behavioral experts can keep everything in their heads, but beyond the function of reminders, written notes help most people think clearly and learn well. This exercise also gives you a record against which to compare later events.

Leslie, divorced mother of a preschool boy, said: "I keep a diary in which I write down questions about Danny that concern me, about things he does and how I react to them. That has helped me keep my sanity. I can look back and say hey, things have really gotten better since then. But if I didn't have it in writing, I might not think so. I could see where the strength started to come in, where I stopped being desperate and started being creative and optimistic. It refreshes me to go back and look at those entries."

Next, in the context of your personal son-rearing objectives, draw up a list of desirable human and specifically male characteristics. Next to each, list those behaviors you believe best demonstrate the desirable characteristics. For example: physical fitness may be the characteristic; jogging, tennis, milk drinking, vitamin taking, and so on are some behaviors associated with fitness.

After you determine what son-rearing behavioral goals are important to you in specific terms, break them down into immediate, moderate-term, and long-range. Then rank these in order of priority.

Break these in turn into categories that involve behaviors within the immediate family, with absent parents or stepparents, in school, with other relatives, with peers, within other institutions, and so on.

Coming into the homestretch, think about how your parenting has changed since you became a single mother. How has it stayed the same? Under what circumstances do you find it most and least difficult to set goals for your son? The process of parenting is not sex specific; you may use the same process with sons and daughters. What *is* different is the goal content and context. Have you as a single mother changed the content of your son-rearing goals as a result of your single status?

Experts tend to err on the side of never asking what *positive* lessons and what behaviors are the goal, or of insisting that the why of behavior must be known before changes can be made. The mothers of sons are often, likewise, fixed either on what they think *causes* a particular undesirable behavior or on a constellation of behaviors too large to be dealt with on a practical level.

Michael recalls an eight-year-old child brought to him by a desperate mother because the boy had become extremely aggressive toward his playmates. He hit, bit, kicked, and fought at the least provocation. The mother, when asked what she thought her son's problem was, answered that he was "frustrated" because the father had recently abandoned the family and the boy had "no one to act out his feelings with in a physical way." She wanted the psychologists to "cure him" of his "frustration." Had Dr. Cataldo agreed to such a request, he might have been drummed out of the behavioral psychology corps. Worse, from the standpoint of this family, the boy might still be hitting, biting, kicking, and fighting.

The family had not identified the true problem behavior: the boy's aggression toward other children. Dr. Cataldo did, however, and persuaded the mother to work on that. He trusted his decision that regardless of what motivates it, violent behavior toward others is unacceptable behavior.

There are other frustrations that accompany the task of choosing the behavior a mother wants to influence. Even if the particular goal or the process is on track, something else may be interfering with her plan: outside pressure from friends, her ex-husband, or circumstances that are a direct consequence of divorce and the emotional upset that follows.

When we listened to the mothers we interviewed, however, two basic issues emerged that have a bearing on the selection of goals for mothers and sons.

One is that feminism and the impact of feminism on men is a major concern among mothers rearing sons. Most were unhappy about their failure to adopt a stronger feminist stance with their sons and equally worried about doing so. We'll talk about this in detail later in the second part of this chapter.

The second issue is that these women discovered both some distinct disadvantages *and* distinct advantages to being a single mother of boys. Having only one parent determining acceptable behavior can be an advantage, for instance. On the other hand, a mother's singlehood and the conditions that surround it may cause her to do some things she isn't comfortable doing. She may do inappropriate things or select inappropriate goals and strategies out of concern for her son's future. Gladys's nude encounters, for example.

Said a mother who left her husband, a junkie, when she was pregnant with her now twenty-four-year-old son: "I questioned every move I made with my son and never really enjoyed him. I was afraid to be fun and flirty and myself, even though I believe that boys need this kind of feedback from their mothers. All I could think of when raising him was that thanks to society he was going to be a homosexual. I had absolutely no confidence in myself and sought outside helpers for everything.

"His father was a drug addict, but a very charismatic character. Instead of letting my son know that his father had serious problems and showing sadness about that, I didn't want him to think he had a father who could do any wrong. So I never gave him an honest look. I protected his father's image. I was so scared of making him feel that any manly image was bad. It wasn't until my son began taking drugs and really messing up that I realized what I had done."

Beth: "Ian adores his father and considers him a saint. I have never interfered with that. When he asks why we were divorced, I just tell him vaguely that there were differences. I never tell him that the divorce was Bill's idea, that he didn't want to take responsibility for a family, that he was interested in other liaisons, which I didn't want. I have never expressed my true feelings about Bill's behavior."

A single mother may also run into problems selecting specific and appropriate goals because of her own loneliness, needs, and worries.

Diane, a widow, with sons fifteen and thirteen: "I thank God I have sons, not daughters. Girls their ages are so much more sexually and socially aggressive. I get so much support from my boys since my husband died. They tell me how nice I look and encourage me in my work. They see me cry and feel sad and I never want to lose that sense of acceptance from them. I want them around for emotional support and I always will. I want them to stay very close to me and I want them to make me a grandmother very soon."

An editor with a twelve-year-old boy: "The first person I consult about anything important is my son. He's my best friend and we are coequal in certain decisions. He has wonderful perspectives on things. He has taken on a lot in helping raise his sister, too. He is my first love. He angers me more than anyone and makes me prouder than anyone. The emotions between us are very intense."

Making a twelve-year-old the man of the house is a questionable goal to say the least.

The editor again: "He asked if he could sleep with me the other night. I would have liked that, but I didn't do it. He wanted to be cuddled, it wasn't anything erotic. But I didn't know what else to do."

On the other hand, single mothering of sons can lead a woman to do something different and perhaps better *because* she finds herself in that role.

For example, she is likely to be setting an imaginative, nonsexist standard for success in the face of adversity. Pam's sons have both talked about being like their mother, a psychologist, "so they can help people." Most important of all, she has a relatively unfettered option to choose goals and objectives that in her opinion will shape her son in the image of a successful twenty-first century man.

Diane, the literary agent: "In many ways it's a lot easier being a single parent. The two arguments we had in this house when my husband was alive were about children and money. He was a disciplinarian and felt I was letting them get away with murder. I felt they needed love and babying. The kids played us off. Now that doesn't happen. There is no tension. I hold the cards and I make all the decisions. I feel stronger about myself. Having another adult in the house gets you off the hook too much. Even deciding dinner was a big deal. Now the pressure is off. I have anything I want. I insist the boys take turns making dinner because I feel I work too hard. I encourage them to take care of themselves and they like it, too. I have this enormous feeling of power that I can do what I want to do and be in charge. They were very worried that we wouldn't be able to stay in our home because of financial problems. But I'm making it. I'm the one who is reassuring them and they see me as the strong one. I really like that."

Pam, the psychologist: "God, yes, but my parenting style changed after the divorce. Suddenly I developed a style that was mine, separate and apart from the compromise style that resulted from two people with quite different ideas, and I've seen this happen with a lot of couples when the marriage comes apart. As a married woman I gave in on almost every important area. I was the peacekeeper. If ever compromise was needed, I did it. I didn't listen to my own instincts. Now my ex-husband and I run very different kinds of households.

"I see my youngest son, Todd, for example, who is ten, as a very happy, relaxed, socially adept little boy who gets on well with peers and others. My husband sees him from a negative view, as lazy, as not doing well in school or not being active enough, and as being a very sad little boy. What has emerged is that he acts differently there than here, more depressed, whiney, and other things I don't reinforce around my house.

"It's great to develop one's own parenting, to carry it out without interference. It's a relief, one of the joys of divorce. My philosophy is one of responsible enjoyment, to be happy. In order to do that, you must be conscious of other people and be nice to them and do good things for them, or else they won't be nice to you and you won't have a good time. Therefore, the only rules I'm really strong about with my sons and daughter are those that say you have to be helpful, thoughtful, compassionate, empathic. I come down hard on that. My ex-husband's philosophy is that the main goal in life is not to enjoy yourself but to succeed, to do well in dollars and in accolades from others."

In the early stages of researching this book, we were both delighted and chagrined at the amount of previously published advice aimed at mothers. Delighted that the output makes a de facto case for the continuing importance society places on women's impact on her children. Chagrined that so little of the material addressed the mother-son pair and that when it did, it was often mired in outdated stereotypes, overly gloomy, limited by questionable or unsupportable attitudes and expectations, or imprisoned in pop-psychology platitudes.

As any parent hooked on these can testify, mothers (and fathers) are generally admonished to take charge and "be the boss" in order to "make children behave." An earlier generation's permissiveness has given way to parent assertiveness training and similar formulas for "taking charge." In some instances, the advice is sound and based on some of the same behavioral principles found in *Raising Sons*.

The problem is they are too often narrowly applied to "making children behave" in a given circumstance. Worse, they ignore most of the positive aspects of parent-child learning; they pay little attention to the inadvertent messages kids get from discipline-at-any-price parents; they leave little room for *kids* to learn some of the principle tools of manhood, such as assertiveness and the ability to negotiate compromises; they present parenting as an either-or condition in which kids either do this or that will happen; and they display an insulting lack of faith in a mother's abilities or her desires to set her own child-rearing objectives. (After all, one woman's discipline is another's nonsense.)

Experts, as we said, are generally very good at achieving ends. On the other hand, they often fail to ask what those ends should be or whether they are realistic for a given individual. That's not bad, because it is properly the mother's role. *You* must decide what behavior you want in your son and, most of all, what kind of male you want to rear.

Setting Your
Own Goals/II

Mastery of every behavioral parenting technique in the world won't be worth much to mothers uncertain about what kind of men they want to shape with those techniques, or too timid about applying them to that end.

All of the mothers we interviewed reported that their ideas about men, manhood, and male success have been drastically altered by divorce, widowhood, or unwed motherhood. What came through clearly was their reluctance to contribute to another generation of traditional "macho" males.

But even among those who had thought about the issues— What kind of sons do women alone want to raise? What kind are they in fact raising? Are there social and sexual tensions between mothers and sons that need attention and if so, what kind? What behavioral skills will young men of tomorrow need to cope in a world where men are denied traditional male roles?—few had tried to plug them into their son-rearing goals in a planned, thoughtful way.

Some mothers are so threatened by the idea they avoid talking about the subject. Time and again, women began our interviews with the statement: "I've never really thought about the issues you're raising. I'm not sure they're a problem for me." Yet when they were prodded and learned that other women shared their concerns, their relief translated into hours of tape-recorded statements that disputed their earlier claim.

The lack of assertiveness about encouraging nontraditional male sex role behavior is not especially surprising, even when a single mother has become assertive in her personal life or on the job. The emotional investment in "not screwing up," as one mother of three sons told Joann, "seems to send my will to act out the chimney."

Part of the problem is the collective shaking of sympathetic heads that continually fans an unmarried woman. In their ground-breaking book on how women grow up, *Beyond Sugar and Spice*, authors Caryl Rivers, Rosalind Barnett, and Grace Baruch note that "for women, the state of singlehood has usually been seen as nothing less than personal disaster." Being unmarried translates as being unwanted and "the behavioral sciences, with their insistence that only husband and family could fulfill a woman, added the weight of science to that notion." The situation is hardly conducive to instilling self-confidence around males.

An added difficulty is the burden of dealing with uprooted lives, new financial woes, new jobs, and new roles. Newly single mothers may have had precious little time to think through what they'd like their sons to value and even less time to work out ways of getting their messages across. This is especially true in cases where mother initiates the divorce and feels guilty about the possible outcome for her son.

As the authors of *Beyond Sugar and Spice* point out, a woman comes to believe early in life that others' wishes "take precedence over her own" and the overriding fear that challenges her independence is "I'm afraid of losing him!" That "him" may be a boyfriend or husband. It can also be a son.

Further compounding the problem is the confusion and anxiety perpetrated by many social scientists. Mothers of sons often misinterpret or overinterpret studies about male development, especially those that focus on male sex role identity and acceptance. For their part, the authors of such studies are too often guilty of tunnel vision and historically worn-out attitudes about sex roles.

They often fail to note investigations that dispute the "conventional wisdom."

Dozens of studies, for example, have shown that when single mothers take a strong interest in their sons' schoolwork, the "inevitable" rate of deterioration of school success among such boys, long attributed to "father absence," is offset. Obviously, it is not the presence or absence of father that's important, but what the mother does.

Still other studies focus on the negative impact of "father absence" when a more appropriate target is clearly "money absence." Financial power, that great and traditional mark of influence and status among men, works no less well for mom. Social scientist Norma Radin has found that the lack of a live-in father has little or no effect on school achievement in affluent populations where presumably mothers have enough support or enough of their own money to spend their energy on academic encouragement.

Many social scientists also take their hypotheses about what constitutes "normal" male development from conventional sources, ignoring current trends in human development. As Michael Lamb notes, the tendency for his colleagues to focus on "a traditional stereotyped notion of masculinity is . . . problematic. Many fathers especially today are neither 'masculine' themselves nor do they wish the sons to be (in traditional terms). . . . We need to take the parents' goals and values into account (in research) far more seriously than they have been."

At the very least, it can be safely stated that scientific ignorance on the topic of boys reared by women alone is far greater than knowledge. Most of the studies that attempt to link the absence of a father with sexual or other deficits in boys are seriously limited by two facts: they study the failures to the near exclusion of the successes (the squeaky wheel *does* get the oil); and they generally ignore the positive influence mothers may have when unfettered and unmoderated by the presence of dad in the home. Many studies would lead the unwary to believe that mothers are merely reactors, not actors in the parent-child drama.

The "available evidence" on standards by which we evaluate masculinity and the successful male personality, says Lamb, "with minor exceptions, concerns traditional fathers in traditional two-parent families." That's a serious shortcoming in view of the "steadily decreasing number of children . . . raised in such families. . . . We know little," he adds, "about patterns of . . . influence within the non-traditional family types now emerging. Where research has been done on nontraditional families," moreover, "it is plagued by confounded factors, poor measurement and methodological inadequacy."

Even if we were to give the benefit of the doubt to the suspect studies, and concede that boys without their fathers at home are less "male" in the traditional sense, is that necessarily something to wail about? Indeed, from our standpoint, it may be a real cause for celebration. Notes Lamb, no doubt in consideration of new life-styles, the new demands to be made on men of the future and the problems traditional males are having in society today, "some of the effects of father absence can be deemed advantageous, disadvantageous or neutral, depending on one's point of view."

We understand the ambivalence of single mothers about what kind of man to idealize. We sympathize. We ask you to fight it.

An educational psychologist earning a Ph.D. and rearing two boys, thirteen and eleven:

> As I gained prominence and professional self-confidence, I found myself increasingly irritated at the arrogance and anti-feminism displayed by some men in my profession. My ideas about successful men and manhood radically changed. In the past, I would have been reluctant to admit that for fear that my sons would suffer from any negative image I held of men. I did have some serious doubts about whether I would be fit to raise two boys as a result of my feminist outlook. Am I fit? You bet I am. Think what women can do to stop a lot of this nonsense if they just decide they have the right to do so. And you bet I have the right. At least as much as any father to make demands and set goals.

Only a few mothers, perhaps, will be as sure of themselves as this woman. Still, it is hard to escape the conclusion that many mothers fall into parenting traps not because they doubt their abilities, but because they are fearful of using them to shape nontraditional male behavior.

Mothers, like other people, need to trust their own experience, knowledge, and relationships when thinking about sexuality, aggression, violence, rebellion, or any other characteristic they associate with males. They also need to select an objective, work toward it, periodically assess it, and change objectives if later they judge themselves to have made a wrong choice. Otherwise, they will fall into what psychologist Bernie Zilbergeld calls the "therapy consumer" who psychologizes everything, and shops endlessly for some magic expert or expertise to change her life.

In his book, *The Shrinking of America*, Zilbergeld notes that parents "continue to be held responsible for all the usual things and new ones are continually added. A recent addition is sexism. If your son . . . grows up believing traditional ideas of what a man . . . is, guess who's at fault?"

By all means, think about what others recommend, but

take only what makes sense for you and your son. The fact is, as feminist Carol Gilligan writes, that women do speak, figuratively "in a different voice." They generally pay more attention to, or are told they should, such "feminine" qualities as empathy, nurturing, tenderness, and submission, whereas successful males should view the world and their role in it as an environment dependent upon assertiveness, individualism, dominance, sympathy, and toughness.

Acknowledge the differences if they exist for you. But don't apply the principles of behavioral parenting until you *define* and *clarify* your own, individually tailored, son-rearing goals and figure out how to add those you think are important but not uniquely yours to provide. Otherwise, you will be in the position of the mathematician who memorizes the formula but gets the wrong answer when he adds up the figures.

Joann recalls this example to illustrate the point: Her son, Jared, then twelve, commented as the two of them strolled by a well-developed young woman, "Now *that*," he said huskily, "is what I call an armful!"

Joann's response was to chuckle along, basking in satisfaction over her son's openness and the reassurance his comment gave her that he was "all boy."

Her behavior—words and deeds—decidedly reinforced his. The principles of behavioral parenting worked like a charm. But in truth, Jared's behavior did not please her. She personally finds such comments exploitive and sexist. Her laughter at his remark said more about her fears for his normal sexual development than about the kind of man she wants him to be. (One outgrowth of the episode worth noting is a persistent and periodic charge of "hypocrisy" from Jared whenever Joann criticizes sexist behavior.)

In many cases, unclear goals are the consequences of habitual triteness as well as uncertainty. "Why can't you be good?" is a common expression mothers throw at sons (and daughters). Or, "What's wrong with you?" "Haven't I told you fifty times not to aggravate me?" and "What am I going to do with you?" The questions are pointless and vague; the answers, even if they come, are just as vague and, worse, useless as "traffic lights."

Sometimes, unclear goals are embedded in a seemingly specific request: "I'd like you to think about what will happen to you if you punch your brother again." Or, "I don't ever want to catch you drinking beer in the car again." (Is it okay if she doesn't catch him at it?) Mothers will do better if they pinpoint and ask for specific behaviors from their sons: "I don't like what you are doing right now. Stop it immediately." "You will not punch your brother again. You are grounded for the day."

If everyday behavior triggers such uncertainty, how are single mothers to cope with the cosmic issue of rearing successful sons? The goal of single female parenting, both as we and most of the mothers we interviewed came to define it, is to ease a boy into self-confident, competent, sexually fulfilled manhood, to help shape a man with the capacity to delay rewards, maintain objectivity, lead an independent life, and be a caring member of his parent's and his own families.

But those are moving and shadowy targets. To do something about them, mothers need to pinpoint specific actions that represent their preferences.

Mothers raising sons, especially single mothers, as we suggested earlier, have a number of special problems and opportunities in setting goals.

Beth: "I have been physically frightened of my son. . . . He has a bad temper. He's a kicker. He doesn't verbalize, he gets livid and out of control. He's young now and I can isolate him. But it infuriates and worries me because I have never been like that and I don't know what will happen when he gets older. I already worry he might hurt his sister."

A divorcée with a twelve-year-old boy: "My son was six when his father and I separated and he tried to take over for his father. He would ask me if I was okay and tell me to take it easy. He was all of a sudden forty-two years old. . . . Now when (my boyfriend) spends the night, my son teases me about it. He says things like 'make sure you keep the door closed because I don't want to hear any noises.' But I know he's thinking that this man doesn't belong, that he (my son) is the man in the house."

Bernice, an author and college professor: "I'm ambivalent about my son's attitudes. On the one hand, I don't want him to be a patsy. I want him to be assertive. He is in ways that sometimes astound me. For example he will never hesitate to confront an authority he thinks is out of line. But the one thing that worries me is that I don't see in him real concern and passion for others. It's there under the surface, I know, but I can see some real selfishness, the kind of arrogant self-centeredness that girls get knocked out of them pretty fast as they grow up."

Diane, a widowed agent with two sons, fifteen and thirteen: "They don't want me to touch them or hold their hands or come too near, but they are sexually very curious especially the younger. I was wearing a bathrobe that pulled away and he quickly told me he could see part of my breasts. I just said, 'Oh, this flops open sometimes,' and closed it. But he looked embarrassed. One night I found him watching an X-rated movie on cable and my eyes jumped out of my head. I screeched at him and he was so upset he ran into his room without a word. I tried to reassure him it was okay and that I wasn't being critical of him, but I have a hard time talking about sex to boys. I want them to be able to ask me about wet dreams, boners, masturbation, and so on, but they haven't."

The professor again: "My mother was a lawyer, and my husband's mother is a housewife, but they are not close. My son will tease me about traditional mothers in a macho way sometimes. He isn't sexist, but I'm sure he'll pick it up from his peers."

Beth, the psychologist: "You may think you are a terrific communicator, a real askable parent and then when your kid comes over and says 'Mom, some white stuff just came out of my penis,' and you look like you're about to drop your teeth, you are communicating, all right, but not what you might like to. Parents have to get their own heads clear about their sexuality and male-female relationships before they can be good sex educators for their sons. If a mother is uncomfortable, that's her problem and it could soon become her son's."

Leslie, divorced mother of a preschool boy: "I know my son needs to respect his father, but there are a lot of things about this man and his feelings about males that I don't espouse. He's sort of outspoken about homosexuals and calls them faggots and he has these very prejudiced views about black people, even though he's an attorney. I've never belittled my son's father to him. I've told him he's a really nice guy. He isn't. The fact is I'm no man hater, but I sure as hell don't want him to grow up to be like his father. I would especially like him to grow up looking at women as people."

Bernice: "The lack of a man in the house may lead a single mother to overdo her power and her authority and either be overly strict or overly permissive because there is no moderating force in action. Women *do* act differently when there is a man around, they take on a more traditional feminine role and when you are single, a boy may not have the benefit of that."

The psychologist: "Single working mothers are more tuned in to women's issues than a comfortably married lady, because they are more hassled by inequalities in society, especially those between males and females. It would be an interesting study to survey feminist attitudes among children of single women. Such women are probably more articulate with their boys on such issues than other women. I know I am."

Several mothers described hairy battles over their sons' sexual relationships with girl friends. One said she preferred her sixteen-year-old to "make out" with his girl friend in her home. "It's better than the backseat of a car or a motel." Others are resentful: "I'm discreet about my affairs and he should be, too."

A widespread feeling among single mothers, we suspect from our research and interviews, is the hypocrisy of the double standard. The mother who let her son "make out" in the upstairs bedrooms has a preteen daughter "who better not do that kind of thing here or anywhere else at that age."

Leslie: "You get the feeling that as soon as boys turn fourteen all they want to do is have sex and there is no attention paid to the emotional aspects. I guess I'm going to let my son have his own space, but as a parent I also need to set limits. I'm not sure what I want him to be in this case."

And there is always the "ultimate taboo." As one mother put it, "There's no use pretending there are no erotic feelings between a mother and her son as he turns from a gawky kid into a gorgeous hunk."

An author, divorced with two sons, wrote about "discovering the man in my son" with a mixture of pride and grief: "Last year I lost two lovers," she wrote. One, a man with whom she had a long and satisfying relationship. The other, one who "listened . . . (who) knew me as well as I know myself . . . listened patiently to small tales of disappointments . . . (with whom) I didn't need to be clever or winning" and always remembered her on Valentine's Day and Christmas.

She got through the loss of the first lover, but mourned the second's withdrawal. "When I began to notice that there were fewer embraces, fewer absentminded cuddles, fewer touches, I could not speak of it to anyone. I could only mourn alone. It's only natural. He is my son."

"All that young male pulchritude around, not just in my son but his friends, is terrific to look at," says another divorcée. "What's not to enjoy?"

"To have an adolescent son," said the woman writer, "when you are already looking hungrily at the firm young bodies of men on the street, noticing and rejecting the pangs you feel at a movie or an ad showing romance or tenderness or sexual tension, is a particularly private pain. Here is a man who *is* flesh of my flesh, who anticipates my moods, shares my values and concerns, adapts to my career, and has lived with me for fifteen years. That (my son) is a caring, open, considerate, independent, helping human being is something I am very proud of. And something I must give up for myself, when there seems to be nowhere else I can find it."

Clearly, for single mothers and sons, everyday experiences, from watching a movie love scene to saying "no" to a request for the car, take on special meaning. Mothers who are insensitive to this situation, or ignore it, give up their options to mold the kind of men they someday want to see standing next to them.

On the other hand, the mother who sets her priorities correctly thinks about her "man for all seasons," about the kind of man she not only wants to rear, but the kind she believes will be best prepared to take his place in the world.

In a pioneering study published in 1980, Lawrence A. Kurdek and Albert E. Siesky, Jr., looked at seventy-four single parents and their ninety-two teenage children; they found that boys reared by single parents (mostly mothers) were more likely to be androgynous than a matched sample of children whose parents were married. These boys were able to blend traditional masculine and feminine characteristics into their personalities. This finding "greatly questions the prevailing view that boys reared in mother-headed families become feminized," the authors conclude. We applaud.

Most social science studies of father-absent boys have focused almost exclusively on the effects of the father's absence, rather than the role of the present mother. Generally, these studies have found that such boys demonstrate nonmasculine tendencies during their sexual development.

What Kurdek and Siesky did was ask whether the boys saw themselves that way and if such nonmasculine trends were the result of more "feminine" characteristics "incorporated into their sex role self-concept."

Previous studies had already established evidence for the fact that major changes in life, including marriage and parenthood, spark permanent changes in the way men and women perceive themselves in terms of masculine or feminine characteristics. They become freer to express the changes and more likely to do so. Kurdek and Siesky believed that divorced parents

> suddenly find themselves needing to demonstrate characteristics or behaviors that have been more traditionally seen as appropriate for the absent opposite-sex parent. Custodial mothers, for example, may find themselves needing to acquire and demonstrate a greater degree of dominance, assertiveness and independence while custodial fathers may find themselves in situations eliciting high degrees of warmth, nurturing and tenderness. Parents' adjustment to the divorce may, in short, result in a trend toward androgynous functioning.

Among other things, the Kurdek-Siesky study found that divorced mothers nearly tied with married females for the highest scores on tests of femininity, but far outranked any other group of women in masculinity. Cross-sex aspects of sex role increased, whereas those appropriate to biological sex stayed the same. In other words, divorced mothers were no less female than they ever were, but they were more masculine. When the boys of divorced parents were asked to assess their masculinity, they saw themselves as masculine but demonstrated lower levels of absolute masculinity. For girls, the same held true for femininity. Interestingly, the study used behavioral terms to assess sex role, such as "gullibility," "flatterable," "individualistic," "giving in to others," and so on.

The behaviors we associate with masculinity and femininity are not mutually exclusive. If you had a cupful of manliness, adding womanliness does not force the former out through the bottom. Although the contents might overflow, they mix.

There is no evidence that human behavior is finite in either quantity or character; our capacity to act can expand to form ever-larger containers for the qualities that drive our behavior.

Whatever the goals, mothers will benefit by periodically checking out both their "pots of gold" and their "traffic lights"—that is, the content of their objectives and the process used to achieve them. That way, if there is a desired shift in goals or a failure in process, new goals and approaches can be instituted before the old ones interfere with objectives.

A final word: There is always some danger in charting new territory and leaving the well-marked behind. If nothing else, a single mother who tries it will raise eyebrows among relatives, friends, ex-husbands, and others who may already have grave doubts about her ability to rear a successful male. Critics will also suggest that to adopt even moderate feminist-style goals for sons may be to instill in our sons a one-sided view of life. We agree that threat exists. Almost all of the women we interviewed emphasized their desire to give their sons time with "manly" things—cars, woodworking, rough-housing, dare-taking. They valued traditional masculine traits and had no wish to raise "feminized" individuals. They all recognized biological differences in sex as valid and were concerned about the bad experiences of boys who were perceived as "sissies" or "crybabies" or "wimpy" or "nerds." In the best of all possible worlds, where sex roles did not translate to life-style, mothers of sons would be off the hook. But in the world as it is, it would be both naive and foolhardy to ignore *all* the socially derived differences in status, expectations, and performance between males and females.

We have already taken note of the serious flaws in social science research on single mothers and sons. And as we will see in the next chapter, sons take on male models from outside the home with extraordinary ease. But that does not mean we can dismiss the need for mothers to actively encourage some traditional male behaviors in the home.

In *The Children of Divorce*, Linda Bird Francke extensively reviews the work of E. Mavis Hetherington, Judith Wallerstein, Joan B. Kelly, and others who have documented the impact of single parenting on children, and concludes with some justification that boys, overall, seem to suffer more psychological and social damage than girls when parents separate. These studies found that depression, denial, anger, low self-esteem, and guilt were more often present or more intense in boys than girls, and that family relationships produced more stress and depression among the mothers of sons than of daughters. Moreover, although daughters of divorce tended to become more sexually precocious and promiscuous, boys tended to become sexually insecure. Jerome Kagan, the Harvard psychologist who specializes in child development, has evidence that boys are more susceptible biologically to stress, including the stress of parental separation. Still other studies note that the tendency of fathers to desire sons more than daughters makes divorce or death of the father a double blow for a son. He loses not only a parent but a built-in adoration machine who has vested his son with the ego-building, symbolic mantle of importance.

We underscore, however, that these studies are inconclusive; that few social scientists have yet looked beyond the stereotypical father-mother-son relationships or asked whether similar problems occur in boys reared by single fathers; that few have controlled their studies for the mother's impact (or absence of her impact).

Yet collectively, these studies tend to support the need for mothers to encourage masculine behavior in their sons, especially if the sons are very young (preschool and grade school age) at the time of divorce, separation, or widowhood.

Our conclusion: Mothers who wish their sons to be compassionate and caring individuals carry a double responsibility—to rear a somewhat nontraditional male and one who can still live in a relatively male-dominated world.

Although rearing an androgynous (behaviorally, at least) male is seen by many mothers as admirable, and indeed may be achieved by some mothers, care must be taken so that this objective does not exclude other goals of equal importance. Evelyn, the actress, recognized this danger when she wished she had given her son karate lessons.

Mothers who encourage rough-and-tumble play, assertiveness, appropriate aggression; mothers who are authoritative, orderly, and present a structured environment are, says psychologist Henry Biller, mothers who are able to foster intellectual achievement and self-control in their sons. In addition, mothers who "reinforced sex typed behavior, encouraged independent and exploratory behavior, were low in anxiety and had a positive view of the child's father seemed particularly likely to facilitate the . . . boy's masculine development. In contrast, a combination of maternal fearfulness and inhibition, maternal discouragement of independence and maternal disapproval of the father were found to be associated with anxious dependency and a feminine pattern of behavior in some of the . . . boys.''

A balance can be struck and it will be up to each mother to set her objectives accordingly.

One way she can strike it is through the selection of a variety of workable, first-rate models whose behaviors she would like her son to copy, as our next chapter shows.

CHAPTER FIVE

Who Am I?: Masculinity, Manhood, and Models

Females don't understand males. So how can a boy learn to be a man from his mother? How can he learn to ask the question "Who am I?" and have a man answer?

Behavioral parenting answers by demonstrating that even if it were true that females don't "understand" males, it doesn't matter, and by providing a number of ways a boy learns to be a man from both men and women. Just as men may "mother," women can "father." A parent is not "born" a mother or a father, but learns to be one.

But let's back up a bit to find out, in specific terms, just what kind of behavior today's mothers (single and otherwise), and enlightened society as a whole, might want from sons.

There can never be agreement on what kind of behavior an ideal son—or ideal man—exhibits. But when we asked the mothers in our survey, and checked both social science and popular sources, a reasonable amount of consensus emerged on a number of things.

In pop-culture terms, the behavior of an ideal son, we were told, is a fine blend of John Wayne's macho, Dustin Hoffman's Tootsie, Gandhi's moral courage, Betty Friedan's determination, Florence Nightingale's compassion. He is both Officer and Gentleman. He swaggers . . . but shyly. He is masterful but vulnerable. When he fantasizes success in the jungle, he says, "Me Tarzan, me Jane."

He not only offers to do the shopping when asked on occasion, but remembers to write toilet paper and catsup on the market list when he uses the last of these items.

He takes up and fulfills a man's role with girl friends, boyfriends, school authorities, brothers, and sisters with self-confidence and self-discipline, but not arrogance.

He willingly delays rewards and maintains interest in the future. He competes fairly, is assertive, and embraces technological competency.

The ideal man, if we can rear him, will respect and participate in "nuturing, be tender and cooperate in family life," one mother told us. He will, said another, "be a father to the cat as well as the kids and sometimes his wife and his mother." He becomes part of society as a whole, yet retains a separate identity and comfort in a "man's world," maintaining a certain amount of conformity (essential for financial success in a still male-dominated corporate structure), but displaying a mature mix of flexibility and tolerance.

His feminism is "routine," but not knee-jerk or hypocritical. He knows how to be a good provider and might even join the Navy. But he is not threatened by being a "househusband" or by a take-charge wife when he is away at sea.

He doesn't confuse empathy and tenderness with lack of masculinity. He sees nothing unmanly or feminine about the male figures in history most associated with compassion: Christ, Buddha, Gandhi, and so on. He might know how to use a gun but won't ever want to. He might ride motorcycles but will wear a helmet.

He does not seek mothering from his wife or lover and is "secure enough to not need a woman to fill him up all the time."

The model son is "comfortable being intimate and sharing thoughts and feelings with men and women." He attempts peacemaking first, and "understands the difference between sex and emotional intimacy."

The successful male in the late twentieth century, our sources tell us, will ably compete with women as bright, ambitious, and motivated as he in almost every professional and white-collar field, and in traditional all-male blue-collar enclaves such as police and fire protection, construction, mining, and mechanical repairs. He will also manage to compete with assertive women in bed.

He will be among thousands of fathers able to juggle children and possibly stepchildren and stepparents, because it is estimated that half of all children born in the 1980s and 1990s will spend some time in a "blended family" or single-parent household.

Polls and surveys show that if he is like the majority of his peers, he will in fact prefer women who meet him on equal terms in their sexual encounters, want marriage rather than cohabitation because it offers companionship, stability, and regular sex.

The model male accepts a woman's right to have at least parity in the choice of having children or marrying. He seeks neither dominance nor submissiveness in his relationship with women or children. He does not need to "boss" women to assert his male identity, and he rejects the notion that men have a *de facto* right to authority, preeminence, and legitimate power in the family.

He would like to be a sex object to women who seem to need one, but he is just as likely to ask for what he would like (as opposed to taking it) as is a liberated woman.

He is neither a bleeding heart nor unemotional. He neither wears his heart on his sleeve nor on his fly. He is not afraid of failure or impressed with women who fear success.

He is compassionate toward, but not romantically beguiled by, Collette Dowling's *Cinderella Complex* girls, who never wean themselves from the notion that they will always need a man to take care of them.

Most of all, he doesn't accept the impossible expectations that society has traditionally placed upon men: to always be strong, never cry, never back down, never be passive, always dominate, always strive hardest to win at any cost, and always to view all failure as weakness.

When we asked sons what kind of behavior they felt most comfortable with, and what kind of men they wanted to be, the list was not that different overall from the one drawn up by their mothers.

"Sometimes," Adam told his mother, when she asked him for his rundown, "I want to be like Hollywood's male sex symbols, or John Wayne. Other times, I wonder what it would be like to be a monk, or a saint, or a quiet man. Mostly I think that there should not be separate sets of traits for men and women, separate buckets from which to drink. I think there should be one bucket and we should all, men and women, take from it what feels best for us."

Mothers and sons with whom we spoke did not select their ideal males from radical feminist tracts or antifeminist manifestos. The behaviors and characteristics they chose were, on the whole, reasonable for *all* people, men and women.

The pattern that clearly emerged in our talks with mothers and sons is their desire to bring sons full membership in a humane, if not unisex species; to open their eyes and minds to human, not just male or female, options throughout their lives; to provide them with repertoires of behavior that will carry them through the many changes they are likely to encounter as they age. Some present-day males were not prepared for current feminist attitudes, and there is no guarantee that the prevailing social norms of today will be the predominant norms when today's boys are men.

Mothers and sons, it seems to us, recognize that the kind of masculine behavior valued today is different than what was valued twenty, thirty, or forty years ago, and the definition of desirable masculine behavior will continue to evolve and change.

Boys are not little men. As children, males must do a great number of things on order of adults. As an adult—in theory at least—a male can choose to do whatever he pleases. But the process of becoming a man is a process of learning what has to be done and how to compromise the childish appeal of absolute freedom our society seems to hold out for men with realistic responsibility.

A century ago, it was arguably a lot easier for boys to learn successful manhood. Then, sons often had to be "fathers" and "husbands" to help support a mother and children in a fatherless home. Universal, compulsory education was absent, at least on the frontiers, so that young teenage males were soldiers, tradesmen, ranchers, farmers, factory workers, and often fathers themselves. They were therefore treated as the "equals" of adult males.

No thoughtful person would want to bring back the old days. Hardship, not adventure was the most frequent consequence of too-early manhood. But it is true that the opportunities for boys to progress easily from boyhood to manhood are fewer today. The boys are in school, and often dependent financially until their mid-twenties. Society frowns on mothers who expect their sons to provide a source of income or family stability or put family responsibilities on their shoulders. Boyhood is perceived in movies, books, and on television as a time that should be filled with friends, sports, school, cars, camps, and free time. That the ideal is often unavailable to single mothers and their sons only adds to the pressure to attain it. Thus, single mothers must be especially imaginative and attentive when they provide their sons with opportunities for developing "manly" behavior.

There are qualities we now divide into male and female camps that are in fact human qualities we may all embrace. In some cases that will mean the "masculinization" of girls, an end to child-rearing practices that give dolls only to daughters and footballs only to sons. It will mean a desire to give girls as well as boys self-confidence, self-discipline, the will to compete fairly, be assertive, and undertake competency in an increasingly technological age. In other cases it will mean "feminization" of males in the sense that we want them to value, respect, and learn nurturing, tenderness, and cooperation in family life.

The realistic goal may well be to prepare a boy to accept appropriate masculine *and* feminine roles. Sons need to become part of an increasingly unisex society-as-a-whole, yet retain a separate identity and comfort in a "man's world." A certain amount of conformity is essential for success in a society that has not yet eliminated—and may never eliminate—all sexist behavior, but success also will require flexibility and tolerance. Mothers will do their sons a disservice if they fail to think carefully about what masculine behaviors their sons will need to make it in the world.

It is the height of social naiveté to label violence, aggression, physical strength, and intense sexual drives as "male," and such things as compassion, gentleness, and sexual passivity as "female." We now know that these traits appear across genders and that tolerance for a diversity of life-styles is growing rapidly.

What the male-female contract of the future will contain is, uncertain, but surely no one suggests it would restore old divisions of male-female roles, or return to yesterday's definitions of male-female opportunities in the family or workplace.

We remember when a female speaker at a convention could count on chuckles from an audience with the observation that in the business world a woman who is insistent is defined as bitchy, whereas a man with the same quality is simply a tough executive; a woman is petty, whereas a man is good with details; a woman is bossy, whereas a man is an effective leader; and a woman who is irritable is premenstrual, whereas her male counterpart is merely overworked.

No one laughs at such jokes much anymore, not because

they have lost their sense of humor about the human condition, but because these observations are obsolete as social commentary. Not all mothers are likely to be comfortable carrying a sign that says "My gay son is terrific," as a New York woman did for TV cameras. But we have gone beyond the need to correct the obvious and begun to deal with the subtleties of male-female behavior.

Whatever behaviors mothers and sons idealize and find appealing, the big question is how sons learn them. Or, put the other way, how can mothers teach them?

The answer is by introducing models for their sons to imitate, behaviors the boys can "try on" and later integrate into their own way of doing things.

Casey Stengel, that astute if not always articulate judge of human behavior, once commented that "you can observe quite a lot about people just by watching them!" As usual, Stengel said far more than he knew he had. His statement aptly describes "modeling," the principal way we transmit new kinds of behavior.

There are many ways to teach behavior. The simplest, perhaps, for mothers, is to give instructions, to ask those we wish to teach to do as we say.

But one of the most effective means of teaching is the one that asks our sons not to do as we say, but to do as we—or others we designate—do. That's modeling.

Not all behavior will automatically or quickly be imitated and assimilated by our sons, of course. Because imitation, like all behavior, must be learned, what sons choose to imitate depends on how well mothers teach it. And mothers who want to recruit and use particular models must therefore make it worth their sons' while—that is, assure a payoff.

Modeling works well when a son not only gets to see clearly what behavior his mother wants, but when he is reminded and rewarded for imitating the model's behavior.

Mother might remember the way her son first learned to smile at her. She smiled at him. When she caught him smiling at her, she smiled back and perhaps reinforced the desired behavior—the smile—by petting, food, cooing, and so on. Thus modeling is a very special incentive for behavior; it not only tells her son what to do, but it is right there from the earliest stages to be copied and to be rewarded. Baby says goo and Mom says goo and that prolongs the attention and smiles. Baby learns from this another important element of effective modeling: that when he imitates a behavior which someone wants him to imitate, he gets rewarded.

All children *learn how to learn* from their parents, how to deal with their parents to get information that is important and relevant. They also learn how to interact with other authorities, seniors, and dispensers of information. Children tend to seek out people from whom they can learn things and get information effectively and efficiently. And they usually do it by imitating models.

Modeling, therefore, is a powerful tool. Experts who use it often illustrate with simple experiments you can try.

For example, for a whole day, speak only in a whisper, without explanation, and see how often people around you follow suit. Or look into the window of an empty storefront for fifteen minutes and see how many people stop to look, too. In contrast to these conditions, how many people do you think you would get to whisper or stare at an empty window if you simply asked them to do so? Not many.

Modeling is also one of the easiest ways for sons to learn. Even animals can imitate complex sequences of behavior. You have probably read of studies conducted over the years that demonstrated how chimpanzees reared in human families applied lipstick to their faces in front of mirrors, opened cans with screwdrivers, learned sign language, and sat at typewriters striking the keys.

Psychologist Albert Bandura, in *Social Learning Theory*, his classic on the subject, reminds us that learning would be "exceedingly laborious, not to mention hazardous, if people had to rely solely on the effects of their own actions to inform them what to do. Fortunately," he adds, "most human behavior is learned observationally through modeling: from observing others one forms an idea of how new behaviors are performed and on later occasions, this coded information serves as a guide for action. Because people can learn from example what to do, at least in approximate form, before performing any behavior, they are spared needless errors."

Modeling is used all the time by parents, but usually in an unsystematic way, to teach everything from dressing to language. Often we do not even realize that modeling is going on. Other times we assume it is when it is not, or we assume that certain models have more clout than others, or that we cannot overcome the impact of undesirable models.

A mother who understands the process of modeling, however, can avoid such assumptions and use modeling to her own best advantage by doing the following things:

- Deciding what skills are important to her and to her son.
- Selecting appropriate role models who have these skills.
- Clearly differentiating to her son between desired and undesired behaviors and traits (no one model is perfect in all respects, after all).
- Paying attention, setting the stage, and establishing a system that rewards her son when he imitates the behavior she wants him to and practices it. (Catching him, in effect, being good.)
- Seeking and being sensitive to new behaviors sons are imitating or behaviors you wish them to, those traffic lights we spoke of in Chapter Two.

Here to guide you are the key ideas you need to know about modeling in order to use it in steps one through five above:

- The most effective models are those individuals who are clearly important to your son, people with whom he associates or with whom he would like to; people who do things that are highly interesting but realistic and appropriate. Often they have a measure of charisma or charm. They are engaging and pleasant. Some of the most effective models are not "live," at all, but symbolic, or present in films, tapes, and photographs.
- With teenage boys, especially, one of the qualities most likely to be imitated is something that is different or out of the norm.

The unusualness of a behavior may be all that is needed to get modeling going. But a countervailing power to be aware of is that one of the tenets of adolescence is to belong, to be one of the group, even to wear the same clothes. When selecting models, keep in mind that most boys strive to avoid extremes of behavior because that jeopardizes their standing with the group, but they also strive to stand out in some way. In short, they want to shave the edges off the normal curve or create a little peak of their own.

- Models are uneven. They always have a mix of desirable and undesirable behaviors. But even a "bad" model can be an effective one for the mother who knows how to use it.

Consider this example involving both celebrities and drug abuse: In teenage society, taking drugs is often a way for a boy to gain the admiration of certain groups. He sees that drug users on a high school or college campus receive a lot of attention. Many boys fear them; but they may also admire their rebelliousness and risk-taking bravado. It may not be the drug use per se that is the attraction for the boy. The payoff is the positive attention of other boys and girls and in some ways the negative attention of parents, teachers, and other authorities. It is perceived as a "safe" way to challenge the establishment, particularly if the drug-taking models have never been caught or punished.

Moreover, the appeal of taking drugs gains added support from a variety of other sources. Every time a star athlete or entertainer is linked publically to drugs, the model and the message are reinforced.

Some mothers might conclude that a way to handle this dilemma is limit or stop exposure to the drug-taking models. That is the strategy behind many of the current efforts by certain reactionaries, some churches, and so-called pro-family groups to exorcise and censor news, information, and publicity. At worst, this is a head-in-the-sand approach doomed to failure. No one can pull the plug on all the outlets of such influence. At best, however, these influences can be recruited as a "hook" with which a mother can fish for behaviors she wants her son to model.

Instead of calling in her disciplinary and verbal juggernaut to blot out these sources, or uniformly condemning everyone who uses drugs, she can instead accept and teach her son to separate those qualities in such individuals that can serve as good models of behavior, while rejecting those that are not. This increases her credibility with her son as well.

Research shows that a mother's best approach is to promote some behavior and avoid promoting others, but not to try to exclude some models entirely—it doesn't work very well.

Joann recalls trying to ban toy guns from her sons' play. That was easy to do, but she soon noticed they used Tinkertoys, paper cutouts, or even their fingers to fashion toy guns.

A wise behavioral parent would also encourage their use in very restricted contexts:

Mother: It is all right to play with the gun in a game of cowboys in the backyard, but it is not all right to point it at me or at anyone who is not willing to play the game with you.

Mother (watching a shootout on television provoked by the villain and won by the law enforcement officer): The policeman must protect himself and has shown good sense in trying to avoid what is happening now. If this were real life, people would get seriously injured or killed and no one would be happy.

Mother can also take this opportunity to point out that damage done in real life is not reversible. Children "wound and kill" each other in play and five minutes later can do it again, or exchange roles. In real life, the finality of the act is what is so frightening. A good model for this lesson is to use the death of a pet to point out how final things are and could result when real guns are used.

This approach—pointing out different consequences of behavior drawn from similar models—is a practical one as well when your son's father has far different ideas about male behavior and values than you do. Trying to ridicule, override, ignore, or damn them won't work very well. The model—father—is there and probably powerful.

The message is that there are different ways to behave in the world and that a son will always have to choose some over others from his bag of skills. Although mothers can use modeling to influence the acquisition of skills, the most important skill of all is the one that enables her son not only to choose models and to imitate behaviors, but to assess the consequences—what will happen if I do that—beforehand.

Joann recalls this conversation with Adam after the drug overdose death of John Belushi, a performer whom Adam greatly admired.

Adam: Why can't they leave Belushi's case alone? He's dead now, so what does it matter whether he took drugs or not? Lots of entertainers do it. They are under a lot of pressure. Belushi wasn't a criminal.

Joann: There was a lot in his work to admire. He was a very funny man. His death was a double tragedy because the drugs not only ended a young life, but also a great talent.

Adam: Yeah, but now everybody like you thinks he was a punk because he was on drugs. They think all actors take drugs. But I don't blame him. I think Belushi was great.

Joann: One way to look at Belushi is that he was a complicated man. He did many things we can all admire and other things we don't. (Talking Behavior)

Adam: Well, he sure was successful. He made a lot of money.

Joann: Yes, he was popular and he achieved a lot in a very tough business. He must have worked very hard.

Joann's comments were designed to determine just what it was that Adam wanted to emulate in Belushi's behavior. Then, she could concentrate on and encourage those qualities she agrees are acceptable and worthwhile; show Adam how to evaluate his own response to what he finds appealing in others and set up a way to point out other models who manifest the qualities she wants to encourage.

Adam: Well, I wouldn't take drugs the way he did. That could mean death.

Mother: Exactly.

• Effective male-role modeling is not dependent on male presence.

More than twenty-five years ago, a husband-wife team of researchers, Sheldon and Eleanor Glueck, reported that 40 percent of a group of delinquent boys they studied came from homes without a father. Since then, more studies have echoed that theme, suggesting that without a father around, there is no model of self-control, no proper moral authority, and a breech into which overwhelming mothering slips easily to the son's detriment. Many of these researchers suggest from this that delinquent behavior such as the Gluecks found (aggressiveness, explosive tempers, unbridled needs for instant gratification) are an attempt to throw off "feminizing behavior," and find a masculine identity.

But as we saw in the previous chapters, many of the studies that purported to explain such behavior in terms of absent fathers were flawed. Moreover, numerous studies demonstrate clearly that the mere absence or relative absence of a boy's father is not a prescription for doom. Michael E. Lamb, in a review of such studies, concludes that "with fathers as with mothers, there is no necessary correlation between the quantity of time together and the quality of interaction."

Furthermore, he said, "important influences do not have to be direct."

In sex role development, moreover, studies suggesting that fathers have a major impact are "extraordinarily inconclusive and contradictory." To say the least. Even when psychologists investigated macho fathers—strict, punitive, limit setting, and masculine in the traditional sense—they often "failed to find any significant relationship" to masculinity or lack of it in their sons.

Other fieldwork has found that fathers who are *seen* as heads of their households have more masculine sons, and the masculinity of sons is lower when the father is passive, henpecked, or feminine in his at-home roles. But sex role identification has *not* been found to be affected by the degree of a father's involvement in child rearing. Ironically (and much to the point), where a father's influence is important in a son's sex role development, it tends to depend at least in part on the degree of his feminine or "mothering" actions with his son. These include nurturing and demonstrations of warmth and affection. As Lamb concludes, evidence suggests strongly that "warm, accessible, masculine fathers should have masculine sons as indeed they do. . . . Fathers who are warm, nurturant and involved in childrearing have masculine sons."

In a seminal study a decade ago of boys nine to fourteen, psychologists at the University of Maryland investigated how well the boys developed self-esteem while living in single-mother homes. They looked at such things as the frequency of visitation of the father, the quality of relationships between the parents, and the length of time the child spent without a live-in male role model. Results showed no significant difference in self-esteem between boys living with single mothers and single fathers.

Edgar Stern, in a study published in the *Journal of Divorce* in 1981, suggests that single mothers tend to magnify a father's importance in sex role development because of their own guilt over having separated from the father and deprived the son, and because of resentment of the father for not being around to help out with burdens.

In fact, Stern goes on to say, the "cultural notion that boys need men" may or may not be the case as sex roles become blurred by unisex conditioning. He comforts single mothers with the thought that they can learn to live with their hang-ups.

With effective modeling, we believe they can do a lot more. They can begin by remembering that even where divorce has not occurred and where the husband is around, fathers often are not. One study of middle-class men found that a father on the average spends less than forty minutes a day in "meaningful interaction" with a one-year-old.

One more item: Boys who learn to nurture will often be deemed to have feminine qualities. In fact they will have learned a human quality and are no more likely to become homosexual than other boys. The question is not what boys learn, but what they *don't* learn from their mothers or individuals their mothers expose them to. If boys don't learn to discriminate among behaviors that our society deems rewarding and normal—or not rewarding and not normal—they indeed have a problem.

- Behavior to be modeled must be behavior that is within the capacity of your son at his stage of development.

A teenage boy's dating behavior, model though it may be, is not likely to be imitated by a six-year-old. Introducing your son to a concert pianist as a desirable model is not likely to be effective if there is no piano in the house.

- Modeling is often best used in conjunction with physical guidance and instruction.

If you want to teach baseball, it is not enough to take Johnny to the ball park. Someone must place the bat in his hands, position him over the plate, practice with him, and explain the rules.

- Mothers should give positive feedback as soon after a desired behavior is imitated as possible. ("I like what you're doing.")

As behavior to be imitated is reinforced by mother, she will need to do this less and less frequently to maintain her son's interest in, and imitation of, the model. A well-placed, positive comment from a mother, regardless of a son's age, can be a very powerful weapon in the war of proper behavior development. Mother needs only to arrange for the behavior she wants to compliment.

- Try to remove other conflicting, or distracting, stimuli or models.

If you want someone to learn to recognize red, don't put

him in a roomful of red things or in a room with every color.
First, make sure he knows what to look for, and then limit
the choices between red and something else. Set up the environment so it works for you, not against you.

- People cannot be influenced very much by behavior they
  can't remember or that isn't memorable. Therefore, it
  helps to link a model's behavior with other activities and
  symbols that aid memory.

Sometimes those symbols can be verbal. ("That's a 10!")
Sometimes they may evoke strong images. (The mere reference to riding a motorcycle produces a picture of the activity
in the mind.) Linked symbols can include scents and sounds.
(One teenage boy said he could never "make a move" on a
date who wore baby powder!) Such tie-lines make it possible
to trigger the behavior without having the model present, just
by using the symbol or code word for the model. When "John
Wayne" is used to describe certain behaviors, most people
understood the reference is usually to his movie-macho persona.

- Allow for some trial and error during modeling.

Things don't always go well the first time. Sometimes that
is because it is difficult to observe all the components of someone's behavior at once, especially if they involve complicated
activities. Just as learning to bat a ball will require a lot of
misses, most people learn a new behavior by "getting the
idea" from the model but "getting the knack" by refining
their attempts as they practice. Effective modeling will help
your son be alert to what kind of learning works best for him,
and realize that making mistakes is an effective way to learn,
not a mark of failure.

- Sons are more likely to imitate a behavior that provides
  rewards of value to them, and that is positive rather than
  negative.

This might seem to belabor the obvious, but when mothers
say they can't understand why Johnny takes drugs ("Where's
the reward in that? He knows he'll get punished!"), it is clear
they don't understand that Johnny found some positive reward in that behavior.

- Models can be prompted.

One of the best bits of modeling we know of came from
the mother of two boys who asked her fourteen-year-old to
keep his clothes picked up so that his nine-year-old brother

would "get the message." The older boy, pleased with the offered role of "older brother and teacher," complied. Mother responded with warm appreciation. The younger boy, eager to "be like" his older brother and get the same appreciation from mother, did imitate his brother's behavior. Everybody won.

- Contrary to widespread belief, modeling does not make a mimic or a monkey out of a child.

Creative behavior can emerge from modeling. As Bandura notes, Beethoven imitated the classical forms of Mozart and Hayden, but adapted it to his own style. Science is a classic case of creative modeling: Neophytes reproduce others' work and experimental style, but the best scientists build from there.

- When models are punished for their behavior, people tend to avoid the behavior they identify with that model.

Robin Williams, the comedian, was a good friend of John Belushi and was reported to have engaged in the same drug-taking, mind-dulling behavior as his friend. After Belushi's death, acquaintances say, he stopped. At the same time, seeing others involved in forbidden or dangerous activities without suffering punishment can weaken inhibitions in your son. Sometimes that is not a bad thing. When a boy watches a friend jump in the swimming pool and not drown (no punishment), his fear of the water is often diminished.

- Sons will frequently take an interest in a model's behavior simply to "try it on" for a short period, or even experience it vicariously, knowing well that it is wrong for him or his circumstances.

A psychologist we know, for example, admits to "boundless joy" watching the popular television show, *Hill Street Blues*. Why? Does he admire cops? Which ones? The reason, he reports, is the occupational behaviors permitted policemen are not permitted him in his role as an academic, an intellectual, and a psychologist. "Those guys get to tell people off when they're angry or irritated. They can often act out their frustrations. I can't do that or I'd get blown away."

- Modeling's most significant contribution to raising sons rests in lifelong applications.

When sons learn to select models or tune in to those that are valued by society as a whole, they have learned to flex their behavioral and intellectual muscles and adapt even when mothers are no longer there to choose and reinforce attributes of models for them. If sons can achieve this use of models from their mothers, they will be well prepared to face futures that are vastly different from the present. Just as many adult males were not prepared for the new feminist society, today's sons may be equally unprepared for the future if all their preparation is based on present social values.

How does a mother find effective models for her son? And how can she best use them?

A first step is to be prepared to meet some resistance to these ideas.

There are still those who would bring back the old days, a time reflected particularly in popular movies, television shows, romance novels, and in genetic and sociobiological studies that explain the sex differences in behavior and social status as a matter of biological imperative.

Practitioners of this trade will point out studies linking high levels of the male hormone testosterone (dubbed the "take charge" hormone by some) and additional Y or male chromosomes to sex and violent crimes. They will also support their position with studies among animals lower on the evolutionary scale, and with anthropological data among those primitive tribes where male dominance over females is the order of life. Finally, they will point to the influence of natural chemicals and even nutrients on behavior to explain such behavior as hyperactivity, learning disabilities, and infidelity.

The works of E. O. Wilson, Konrad Lorenz, and others contain much of value in our efforts to understand human behavior. But they all beg the important question: Where does learning—and particularly modeling—fit in this scheme?

The answer of course is that it fits everywhere, and can be used to *overcome* biological or genetic influence by giving individuals adaptive skills.

That theoretical human who is free of all cultural and environmental influences (i.e., learning) simply does not exist. From the moment of conception, human beings are learning, subjected to the influence and expectations of all the people and things that surround them.

The issue is not whether biology influences behavior. It does, of course. The issue is whether we ignore what learning does to overcome or level that influence. If biology were truly destiny to the degree that some argue, it's possible the evolution of man as a thinking, social animal would never have taken place.

Consider dominant behavior, a hallmark of traditional male activity, which some still argue evolved as a biological response to the rigors of survival experience by primitive man, and remains in place. In her book, *Women, Men And The Psychology Of Power*, Hilary Lips notes that "although there *may* (italics author's) be an evolutionary basis for human sex differences in dominance . . . the evidence is certainly not unequivocal. Moreover, it is clearly impossible to accept the argument that because a characteristic may have had selective advantage for the species in the past, it is not modifiable under present conditions. Human dominance behavior obviously can be modified. Moreover, the process of evolution is a continuing one and different characteristics are favored as our environment changes.

"In studying dominance among human beings," she continues, "we would do well to remember that dominance, rather than being an unchanging personality trait, can just as easily be thought of as a behavior in a specific situation."

Much research, Lips notes, shows that the effect of male hormones on aggression can be mediated by experience. Indeed castration does not stop aggressive fighting behavior in primates. There are, she concludes, "strands of support for the idea that aggressive dominance behavior has at least some of its roots in social experience."

When mothers rear sons, all sorts of influences and resistors are present. They will help mold your sons, too. But they do not represent an irresistible force that cannot be matched or altered.

The second step in the successful selection of effective models and effective use of them is to accept the fact that modeling works whether we plan it or not. Nor do mothers need to understand precisely why modeling works in order to use it effectively, any more than they need to understand how a turbo charger is put together in order to prefer driving a car with the extra power it offers.

Third, mothers should let their sons know how they feel about male roles in a variety of ways. Be creative. Swing with it!

Mothers may emphasize behavioral objectives with a variety of models in a variety of ways. Sons could conceivably reject some or even all of the models and the behaviors at some time. But they will at least have given the behaviors in question a trial in the real world, what we call reality testing, before rejecting them. At the very least, such boys will have an additional skill to call upon when evaluating the world around them.

To the skilled behavioral parent, models are everywhere and she need only become sensitive to spot them.

Want to teach nurturing? There's the school coach who does volunteer work at the children's hospital or the man at McDonald's who feeds the infant while mom enjoys her hamburger.

The consequences of losing one's temper? Try parents at the local Little League playoffs, and call attention to the consequences for adults who behave like children.

The difference between violence and law enforcement? Try television. Some mothers may deplore the violence contained in police shows, but some of the occupants of the Hill Street precinct on the popular *Hill Street Blues* television series are nonaggressive, compassionate, and effective users of humor as a problem solver. In the guise of entertainment, boys might find a good model for disarming conflict by setting up non-threatening contexts. Johnny may admire prizefighters, but may be personally turned off at the thought of beating another human being to a pulp. He may find military heroes a source of admiration, but disdain military values.

The point here is that mothers who are sensitive and aware of the behavioral messages in the world can use almost any model effectively.

Joann recalls returning home from her office on the day John Hinckley shot President Reagan to find Jared, then twelve, casually doing his Spanish homework while reruns of the assassination attempt and the grisly scene of press aide James Brady, gunned down on the sidewalk, played on the television a few feet away.

Joann (looking at the television screen): Look at that awful violence. It's very upsetting to see. Brady is critically injured . . .

Jared (cutting her off): I know, Mom. I already saw it. I'm just waiting for something else to come on.

Joann (appalled by Jared's apathy at the bloody scene in front of him): You are treating this like some cop show. Those were real bullets and real people shot this afternoon!

Jared: No kidding.

A wiser behavioral mother might have turned the behavior

on the screen into a model for compassion and involvement in a social ill. Joann forfeited her chance by attacking Jared's lack of attention at the moment. She might have done a lot better. Later, she did:

Joann: Maybe one reason we still have so much criminal violence is that television makes it too real. It's too hard to deal with, so we shut it out and treat it like fiction, even though it isn't.

Jared: They show things like this too many times and it loses its clout.

Joann: Why do you think they show it so many times?

Jared: Maybe some people need to see it again and again to really understand that kind of violence. Maybe then we could find ways to stop it. I don't know why I watched it so many times, or even left it on. It's the kind of thing you do want to see and then you don't.

Modeling, as we said, occurs whether mothers plan it or not. Moreover, what a boy will choose to model out of a complicated environment is not always apparent to mothers— even sensitive ones.

A good example of this last point is to be found in all-male schools or camps foisted on single mothers raising sons.

This "good idea" is often recommended by owners and operators of camps, military academies, and one-sex private schools. The suggestion is made that all-male environments are a good hedge against homosexuality because they put boys in touch with so many he-man role models.

These institutions may be fine for your son, as they are for many boys, enabling them to enjoy the camaraderie, discipline, skill-training, and experiences of an all-male world for periods of time.

But there are potential problems of conflicting models here. There are multiple things to learn in any environment. Sending Junior off to Camp Tough Guy is no guarantee he will learn only how tough guys behave. He may learn things you distinctly sent him there not to learn. Although all-male enclaves may not be hotbeds of homosexuality, it is likely that some homosexual activity goes on. Sons who go there will be in a situation to imitate male behavior, but also possibly homosexual behavior.

Remember, too, that behavior is not imitated simply because the model is there; only modeling that is *reinforced* or *encouraged* by certain consequences continues to occur. Camp Tough Guy could have the opposite effect if assertive, aggressive behavior *fails* to get reinforced or is punished.

As a general rule, mothers can find and employ role models for masculine behavior from friends, relatives, teachers, neighbors, even public figures, celebrities, and fictional characters. They don't have to be male, either.

Beth: "I am very active in Kelly's Little League program even though I can't play baseball. As a parent, I make a point of praising the girls and the boys who behave in a sportsmanlike way and who practice hard to refine their skills."

Leslie: "Steven and I play a lot of tennis and I'm pretty good. I keep the conversation focused on athletic skills when we play, and I've noticed that is how he now evaluates others—how well they play, how well they concentrate, and so on."

Mothers may have to move Muhammad to the mountain. If you live in suburbia, certain kinds of models are plentiful for your sons. (Men who are involved with young families, yard work, household chores, sports, and responsibilities. But if you live in urban centers or on farms, they may not be.)

In our interviews, we found mothers who made excellent use of models by regularly including their sons on trips to their offices, out of town, on short excursions to novel environments, family get-togethers, shopping trips, and restaurants. The more kinds of models mothers seek out for their sons, the more opportunities they have to get their messages across.

For the preteen boy, mothers can also get a lot of mileage out of labeling male traits she prefers as good, bad, preferable, or not preferable. Thus, she may achieve her goal with a poor role model as much as with a good one. The young boy who wants to please his parent, and who is rewarded for doing so in some way, will frequently copy the behavior of the models she praises. There is often an immediate effect on a boy's behavior, in fact.

When boys are very young, they imitate parents because the parents, whom they depend on for love and comfort, reward them for imitating certain behaviors.

As the boy grows up, he begins to respond to more remote reinforcers, further out in time. Instant gratification is no longer so necessary. So now he both imitates and responds to more remote rewards and has begun to develop elaborate repertoires to help him choose which behaviors to follow.

As he looks for ways to choose, moreover, he is more likely to imitate behaviors that seem to provide the satisfactions or reinforcers he wants. Teenagers who are more under control of peers will tend to imitate individuals who are being rewarded in ways they want to be rewarded and whom their peers consider to be desirable role models.

Bill notices that his friend Andy is openly admired by the boys on the soccer team for his willingness to practice even when he doesn't feel well. Not complaining is often perceived as desirable masculine behavior. In search of similar admiration, Bill may imitate that behavior. Soon it may be second nature for him not to complain a lot when he is a bit under the weather. This process is known as *generalization*, and a mother who is aware of such processes can use them to encourage behaviors she favors.

Boys will often imitate the hero, because the hero gets all the rewards at the end. Through generalization, all the behaviors that result in heroic behavior can become reinforcing themselves. So a mother must make sure she has a method for encouraging her son to select reinforcers.

She could recruit some man to be around the house, but her son might not imitate what she wants to be imitated in him. For example, he may smoke and he may also be honest. She wants son to be honest, but not smoke. Be clear and label what you like and what you do not.

Mothers can also be sensitive to any positive or agreeable aspect of a man's repertoire that her son displays and reinforce it by saying such things as: "I like the way you did that. It was kind of like what he does."

At the same time, she can use things she does not like in a model to reinforce better alternatives.

Evelyn: "My son's biological father is dead now, but he was a drug addict, a young actor who died of an overdose when my son was eight. He rarely came to see his son and when he did he would tear the boy's world apart with a magical, charismatic day and then leave him flat again. The boy felt a tremendous loss when he died. The reason was that instead of saying to him, when he was small, 'Your father was not a good father, he was sick and sad,' I didn't want my son to think anything ill of him. I painted this rosy picture and held his father up as a role model. I never gave my son an honest look at his father because I was afraid to have him feel that any male image was bad. I covered for his father all the time. It should not have surprised me that my son took on the same kind of vulnerable Jimmy Dean persona his father had had, and have a bad bout with drugs, too."

This mother might have praised her husband's charisma, but been more realistic about his shortcomings. Then she might have found other "charismatic" models who were not drug abusers to hold up as standards for her son.

Mothers themselves can also, as we've said, be good fathers by imitating "fathering" behavior. Psychologists have found there are distinctive ways that fathers do the things that make them positive models for masculine behavior. Among them are physical stimulation in play, rough-and-tumble behavior, action as opposed to caretaking, or passive pastimes. Fathers introduce competitiveness into play and emphasize touching, and active participation rather than visual learning.

Mothers of year-old infants are more likely to do things such as tell stories, sing, play pat-a-cake and peekaboo, and read books, whereas fathers undertake "unusual" (for the child) activities such as physical play, loud talk and laughter, and activity "bursts" that are arousing.

Women who conscientiously plan "father-style" activities can fill the father role successfully at these times.

It's also important for mothers to give their sons a chance to practice behaviors they have modeled, even if it makes a mess in the house or takes longer to get chores done. Results may surprise you.

Diane (a widow): "My vacuum cleaner broke the other day and I can never fix that kind of stuff. My son Ray, who's fifteen, said he'd take care of it and he did. Ironically, his father couldn't fix anything. Ray is fulfilling masculine roles his father never did. I had some files delivered to the house one day that needed to be put together. When I came home, it was all done."

Sons also recognize the need to have masculine role models around and will let their mothers know if they feel deprived.

Todd, age ten: "I think when kids are real little and just beginning to grow up they should have mothers a lot. But later they need a father to show him other kinds of things like woodworking, which mothers could teach if they knew how, but usually fathers do. Working on cars is one thing my Dad is teaching me. My older brother teaches me baseball and now I'm a star. He's teaching me to play football, too. I play with a lot of boys. Mom teaches me a lot of things, but not everything."

A forty-three-year-old mother with sons twenty and eighteen: "I joined a family group at our synagogue where I was the only single parent, and a couple of the men were just fabulous to my sons. Larry told me that when he grew up he wanted to be a 'Daddy just like Mr. F.' and we had a long talk about that. Mr. F. had helped Larry build a laser for an eleventh-grade project. He was a fatherly man, but a skillful one, too. He loves children and is involved heavily with his own, always doing things together. I've given my sons a chance to observe a lot of good fathers and they see that not every father is like his own."

Grandparents make excellent role models and are easily prompted by mothers to point up certain behaviors for emphasis.

Here are some behaviors most people, including psychologists and the mothers we interviewed, identified as masculine or unisex. With each are either suggested models to recruit or guides for mothers who will provide the behavior to be modeled themselves.

Asking for a Date

Michael has remarked that teenage and older males are sometimes bereft of models from which to learn basic social skills and in need of "anti-nebbish" training. Garry Martin and Joseph Pear, authors of *Behavior Modification*, recount this example of modeling to teach a college student how to ask for a date.

The student is rehearsing his lines for the therapist, who in this case, is the model.

Student: By the way (pause) I don't suppose you want to go out Saturday night.

Therapist: Up to actually asking for the date you were very good. However, if I were the girl, I think I might have been a bit offended when you said 'by the way.' It's like your asking her out is pretty casual. Also, the way you phrased the question, you are kind of suggesting to her that she doesn't want to go out with you. Pretend for the moment I'm you. Now how does this sound: There's a movie at the Varsity Theater this Saturday that I want to see. If you don't have other plans, I'd very much like to take you.

Student: That sounded good. Like you were sure of yourself and liked the girl, too.

Therapist: Why don't you try it?

Executive-style Competence and Self-confidence

When complex behaviors are to be modeled, it is especially important to find out what skills are important and will have value to sons.

According to a study published in the *Harvard Business Review*, and confirmed by numerous surveys, the ideal manager is male, competitive, aggressive, dominant, firm, able to solve problems and make decisions, vigorous, and rational.

Leaders are people who are more likely to be comfortable in groups. They also tend to ask a lot of questions, give agendas, offer opinions, and use conversations to identify problems rather than solve them.

Men seen as competent in the business and scientific world engage in other visible behaviors. They smile a lot, use body language well, and maintain a certain physical distance from other men and women.

They insist on personal space, but they initiate touch more than women do (handshakes, arm around the shoulder, and so on).

To achieve these skills, mothers might provide sons with models who have experience in talking in mixed groups; who are skilled in negotiating, debating, using resources.

Dealing with the "Liberated" Woman

Role models should be men who by word and deed respect women and their work; who listen when women talk; who are experienced in handling routine and trivial matters without complaining; who are team players.

Mothers need models who demonstrate that men are important but not superior; who are independent, but not dominant and who are valued for what they do inside the home as well as outside of it.

Mothers need to move to a more direct use of interpersonal power without worrying about being labeled unfeminine. They can stop depending on lack of physical strength and size for attention, for example, by not asking sons to open jars or reach items on a top shelf. They can point out the difference between real and perceived differences in physical strength, and that they make little difference in a society where ladders and tools that overcome physical weakness are easily available.

If the goal is to help your sons attain a male identity that is a good fit with demands for equality between the sexes, mothers and the models they recruit can be more direct and assertive. They can refuse to allow interruptions when they speak.

They can value physical strength enough to seek it for themselves with exercise and fitness programs. They can show that power and gentleness, strength and vulnerability are not incompatible.

Fathering

The mother of a sixteen-year-old boy vetoed his plans for a summer job mowing lawns and agreed to pay her son minimum wage out of her pocket to help tutor hospitalized children. Camp counseling and baby-sitting offer excellent models for nurturing behavior, and the rewards (financial or social) can be attractive enough to appeal to many boys.

CHAPTER SIX

Truth and Consequences

Tim: I'm late for school and I can't find my car keys!
Mother (also rushing to get to work): If you would only put them in the same place each time you come home, you wouldn't have this problem.
Tim: I don't need a lecture. I need help finding my keys! Like all mothers you're always putting things 'away' so I can't find them.
Mother: All right, I'm looking. (Pause) Here they are, under the newspaper on the kitchen table. Where *you* left them.

Two things important to mothers are happening in this brief exchange, beyond the obvious flap over misplaced car keys and mutual irritation. One is that behavior is not changed by pointing out the truth of a situation (true, Tim would not lose his keys if he would put them in the same place each time he came home). The second is that Tim's mother could probably not have designed a better, faster way of making sure Tim will continue to misplace his keys and demand that she locate them in the future.

The important "truth" here is that behavior—all behavior, all the time—is a function of its consequences. Consequences may be immediate or remote. But in every instance, what you do determines what you get. In the situation above, Tom has misplaced his keys. One consequence for him is that mother immediately drops what she is doing and attends to his problem. (She also criticizes him, but that's not very important to him at the moment. He has to get to school.) By her actions, mother has ensured that Tim will engage in the same behavior again. Mother has basically "rewarded" him for his morning's work. And worse, she has done nothing to encourage him to alter his behavior one wit.

106

Even when we don't notice them, consequences are always there. Every single thing we do produces a response of some kind that, like the traffic lights we talked about in Chapter Two, tell us to "go ahead," "stop," or "ignore this."

When we use these consequences in a deliberate plan to condition or modify behavior, we have a very powerful tool indeed. Conditioning has been used to cure phobias and even, when societies as a whole are conditioned by events, start revolutions. It is a way of permanently altering, through specific steps, the way things are done.

More than thirty years of psychological research has shown that a particular behavior can be increased or decreased by adding or removing certain consequences. For example, if a mother wants her son to continue a certain behavior, she can add something that increases it, a reinforcement or reward. Or she can remove aversive consequences. To discourage behavior, or eliminate it altogether, she can reverse the procedures by subtracting rewards or adding punishment.

Among the more obvious important consequences mothers can use are praise, acceptance by friends and family, money, privileges, and power in the family structure. Even very young boys can respond to consequence control of a rather sophisticated nature.

The divorced mother of a four-year-old used subtle signals of sadness to correct her son's behavior: "When Walker did something that hurt my feelings, or if he was very rude and created a scene that ruined a meal when we went out together, I noticed how sensitive he was about that and how keenly he understood how he adversely affected others. He is very empathic. I was hurt and he would sometimes get sad after these episodes and cry. But it was not the kind of crying he does when he explodes with anger or pain or when he can't have his way. After a while, he stopped creating scenes."

In other instances, with other mothers and sons, the consequences of mother's crying could have had the opposite effect. Crying could reinforce a son's rotten behavior as in the case of a three-year-old, or teenager, who is busy testing the limits of mom's patience and tolerance. The point is that mothers can best determine how the consequences they apply can change their sons' behavior. And they determine this much better by the reaction those consequences bring about than by the particular consequence itself.

Other consequences are not so obvious and for sons beyond a certain age, a mother may be unable to control them or even know how they operate. If your son deals drugs or steals a car, the police are likely to control all the aversive or punishing consequences.

Like the laws of physics and gravity, consequences occur quite naturally whether we understand them or not, see them or not, pay attention to them or not, or deliberately plan them or not. When we do something that gets us something in return, we are more likely to repeat the act.

Many things affect consequences, however, and the message in this chapter is that mothers who understand consequences and how they operate can set up and use consequences—both natural ones and ones they contrive—to guide their sons' activities. In addition, when sons understand how consequences are connected to actions (or lack of actions), they are more likely to respond positively to limits mothers and others place on their freedom, and to accept some limits as a means of preserving this freedom.

There is one other important reason for mothers to understand how consequences work when they rear their sons. It is this: Ignorance in this area can produce many pitfalls that bring about undesirable behavior, as in the case of Tim and the car keys. With the best of intentions (mother really did want to help Tim find his keys; she did not want him to be late), mothers can encourage behavior they would rather change or lose a chance to substitute a behavior they prefer for one they don't. The "ignorance factor" may not be critical where car keys are concerned, but it takes on critical dimensions when the issues involve cutting classes, trying drugs, ignoring curfews, refusing to do family chores, and in general using rebellious behavior as a way of asserting a budding independence.

Teenage boys, especially, will challenge single mothers in these ways. Nothing is perceived so intensely as the "injustice" of limiting their freedom and power. "It's not fair" is almost the battle cry of the young male whose life is circumscribed by "women's rules."

If mothers can make it clear that at home and at large, what you do is what you get, however, sons will understand that adults are not entirely free to set their own rules either, and that most consequences they are likely to experience come from outside the home, by law enforcement agencies, the demands of the economy and job market, and others with whom they form relationships.

A lot of the behavior that mothers find undesirable in sons can be tracked to the reinforcing consequence of attention—from her, from their fathers, friends, teachers. Even if the attention is angry or unpleasant, it may be serving a "rewarding" purpose for many boys. If nothing else, bad behavior irritates and upsets mother, which most boys at some stages of development find is a convenient way to test the limits placed on their behavior and "try on" adult roles. And getting attention gives them a sense of control over their mothers.

Evelyn: "Seth's tantrums were really something. This gorgeous little boy was so clever. He would lie down in the street at age two or three and not move. He wouldn't scream or anything, unless I touched him. Then he would scream bloody murder. Once he began to yell that I wasn't his mother. I just picked him up and told him we were going home. He began to yell that I was kidnapping him and a policeman tried to stop me. It was really embarrassing. The policeman followed me all the way home. I didn't give in to him or show upset, but he certainly still got my attention."

Annie: "My son had this project due for school and since I am a teacher, he naturally asked for my help. I said I would help him. But his idea of help was for me to do it, and I told him that I would not do it and he just blew up. 'I'm gonna fail this and it's gonna be your fault,' he said and carried on to the point of hysteria. So, finally I just said to him, 'I can't deal with you now. When you are finished I'll talk to you again.' He continued to carry on for a little while. I just went downstairs. The next day, we did talk about it, but I did not do his project for him."

Before mothers can use consequences—positive or negative, natural or contrived—effectively, there are some operating fundamentals and influential factors they need to know about.

- It is always necessary to identify, select, and label very precisely the behavior one wants to encourage, discourage, or alter in any way.

The "pot of gold," the goal, is not to "stop Johnny from getting angry" or "help Johnny to be more mature" but to stop him from punching a hole in the wall with his fist when he loses his temper. The goal is not to "make Tony more responsible," but to get him to "pick his clothes off the floor each morning." The only way to measure whether a particular consequence is working is to see if a specific behavior changes. If mom is vague at this stage, it's hard to know when to step in with encouragers and discouragers. In short, she won't know what's happening.

- Consequences are not in and of themselves moral or immoral, or by any universal definition, rewarding or punishing.

What is a very positive, encouraging consequence to one person may be a turnoff to someone else. A cigarette is not a rewarding consequence for someone who does not smoke. Staying up an hour later may be heaven for a seven-year-old and a punishment for a tired teenager. Often it is very difficult for mothers to understand this. "How can he punch the wall when he hurts his knuckles and has to pay to repair the hole?" "How can he go out and drink when he knows he will get sick and be punished to boot?" a mother asks. The answer is that the consequences of getting drunk are reinforcing. He may, for example, get attention from his friends ("What a guy. He can really guzzle!").

These consequences may completely override a hangover or the kind of punishment he suffers.

- It is important and very helpful, although not absolutely essential, to determine what consequences, what "pay-offs" are maintaining a particular behavior.

This is because in many cases, the consequences that are maintaining the behavior may be very different than the ones that set it up in the first place. For example, Johnny may have originally punched the wall with his fist because he saw his father do it, or watched an actor do it on a television show, or read about it. Or perhaps he hit the wall to stop himself from hitting his brother when tempers boiled over. But the reason he continues to hit the wall on other occasions may be because of the reaction he gets from his mother. She may back off and become docile. She may cry or placate him, and he has learned that *now* one important consequence of hitting the wall with his fist is that he successfully avoids or escapes her anger or her demands. She may also feel "guilty" for "letting this go too far" and therefore eliminate whatever punishment she was ready to mete out. And so on.

When mothers understand consequences that keep an activity going, they are in a better position to change the behavior by altering just those consequences that are reinforcing the behavior.

This is not only economical and efficient, but it avoids trial-and-error approaches, and other strategies that may produce undesirable or dangerous side effects.

For example, in the case of the wall-puncher, understanding what maintains it gives mother the inside track in stopping it by not producing the consequences (in this case agitated attention from her) that pay off her son.

Without that knowledge, she may have to get the job done by calling out her heavy consequence artillery and heaving such unpleasant punishments at her son that he (at least immediately) stops punching the wall. She can counteract and override the rewards he is getting, but she is still giving him attention. She may still be letting him off the hook. She is certainly not giving him any substitute way to display anger without wrecking the house, and she has done nothing to interrupt the chain of behavior that produces the flying fist in the first place.

Remember Seth's temper tantrum? If Seth was performing to get his mother's attention, *any* attention she gives may be a reinforcing consequence for him. Even if she perfunctorily picked him up and carried him home without comment, later efforts to pacify him, console him, even wipe his tears and wash his face may be payoff enough for a while. Knowing this can help her break the pattern by not rewarding this behavior.

On the other hand, she might have chosen to punish Seth, to counteract his behavior with behavior of her own that was so painful or unpleasant that it made him stop his tantrum. The difficulty with this approach is that it may be a tough act to follow the next time. She'd have to get much more unpleasant to get the same effect, because the payoff for Seth to throw the tantrum—getting attention—will still be there and in spades! (There will be times when mothers are backed into a corner; when they cannot apply the consequences they have planned on to stop a tantrum, for example. In these cases, they should be as perfunctory as possible, and make their attention as low-key as possible.)

Extensive behavioral analysis is not easy and not always necessary. But with older boys especially, it can save time and tempers. One mother did this very effectively with her fourteen-year-old who suddenly began to gorge on snacks continuously. He was in the refrigerator, freezer, or pantry repeatedly, even after mealtimes. His weight began to balloon.

As carefully as she could, she began to notice and write down the steps that led up to his leaving whatever it was he was doing to come to the kitchen for food. She watched him getting the food and noticed that his choices were fairly indiscriminate. She spoke to teachers and friends about his recent experiences in school and socially. What she learned, in essence, was that her son was eating out of boredom. Eating simply gave him something satisfying to do. He wasn't hungry. His grades were dropping because the schoolwork was not challenging. He was growing faster than most of his best friends and finding their interest in some of his interests flagging. As soon as he came home from school with nothing to do, he ate.

She had identified the behavior to be changed (overeating), learned its history (the context in which it occurred), and then made her plan. By offering an array of consequences designed to end his boredom and challenge his imagination, he stopped these binges.

In sum, altering consequences that maintain a behavior is a lot easier on both mother and son if they know what they are in detail. It's a short cut and a correct cut.

Moreover, although we can never really know if we are correct in our analysis of behavior and what keeps it going, it is important to keep track of what seems to work to change behavior. Only with experience and this kind of tough "grading" can the consequences that work be applied to other activities and recognized by sons as well as mothers as handy tools, indeed.

On the other hand, as we noted earlier, it is not always essential to know what the precise consequences are, and sometimes it is impossible without professional skills and lengthy behavioral analyses. On other occasions, there is no time or opportunity to think it all through. If Billy, age three, lives near a four-lane highway and decides to play in the traffic one afternoon, the best solution is to yank him back to the sidewalk immediately.

- Selecting effective consequences is a job best done by the mother or someone else who knows the son very well. As we noted earlier, what turns on one boy may turn off another. The effectiveness of consequences also changes with age and circumstance and they may shift wildly.

As a general rule, boys under the age of eight or nine find their mother's attention the most powerful of all consequences. Later, privileges and bonuses given or taken away by mother are more important.

Evelyn: "In order to get his allowance, Bob, fourteen, has to clean his room, set the table, and do the dishes when I'm not at home. He also has to take care of the cats."

Annie: "Mark likes to do things around the house that he associates with being the man of the house. He carries in the groceries, changes light bulbs, and tightens screws. He considers these big treats when I ask him to do them."

Annie again: "I have told Mark repeatedly that I would not tolerate bad language in the house and that it is not acceptable here. He didn't listen. I noticed that one of the times he used foul language most was when he was playing his Atari (video game). So I told him if he used bad words again I would take the game away. I try to make the punishment fit the crime, or at least have some connection to it."

Most mothers, with a little thought, can create a list of things that appeal to their sons. Garry Martin and Joseph Pear, psychologists and authors, suggest a fill-in questionnaire with a variety of categories that can be filled in and changed periodically. Among them:

Food and drink the son prefers at home and out; do-it-yourself activities such as hobbies, crafts, cooking, running, driving, gardening; free activities away from home (swimming, camping, hiking); pay activities (films, plays, baseball games); passive activities such as TV, listening to records or tapes, talking, staying up late to read; manipulative reinforcers such as toys and games that require the presence of others, preferably mother; possessions and collections, including comic books, clothes, records and social, physical and verbal stimulation such as kind words, lullabies, hugging, kissing, wrestling, and so on.

Experiments with a variety of reinforcing consequences confirm that the best ones in general are those that are commonly available, that don't take a long time to be applied, and that are strong enough to retain their appeal over long periods of time.

Selecting the correct consequences is important, but so is the timing of their application. Sometimes, consequences are appropriate but applied too late, and although they may work, the price is high.

For example, Shirley, a sociologist: "My son has a history of being very bossy and aggressive like his father, and after the divorce, he (the son) decided it was his job to take over that function in full. I had no authority over him and he was big and strong by that time. He was being the father, the husband, the strong man around the house. When he finally hit me I did what I should have done earlier. I called the police and got some authority involved besides myself. He never hit me again. But he never forgave me, either. He says I treated him as if he were a criminal or parent-abuser."

The consequence of this boy's behavior—his mother calling the cops—worked, but was an extreme step, one that should not have been necessary if this mother had developed a behavioral solution for "bossy and aggressive" behavior prior to her son's becoming so big and strong.

- Positive reinforcers or consequences can create ill effects in the hands of those who are ignorant of it, because they are likely to be unaware they are using it to strengthen an unwanted behavior.

In the case of the car keys, for instance, mother may have helped Tim locate his keys with the best of intentions: to be helpful, to encourage him to get to school on time, to avoid a morning argument. But she has also positively reinforced his unreasonable demands for her help, demands that may make her late for work.

Another example: Mother is ironing and watching her sons playing when one hits the other during an argument. The mother stops what she is doing to comfort the one hit and play with the kids for a few minutes to "settle them down." The long-term consequence here is that the child is more likely to sock his sibling again to get his mother's attention.

- Whenever consequences are used to eliminate or change a behavior, it's important at the same time to provide consequences that encourage or reinforce the behavior mother wants in its place.

Replacement is a part of the formula parents too often

forget. If avoiding a chore is the reason for Billy's tantrum, mother can get rid of the tantrum just fine by not paying attention to it. But Billy still hasn't done the required chore. In this case, mom should ignore the tantrum and end the consequence that rewards the tantrum, but should then make sure Billy doesn't escape his job.

Mother should restate the rule or request after the tantrum and, more important, reward her son when he complies without the tantrum. The bottom line is to show him that tantrums are a no-win situation, and doing the chore gets positive results from mother. Whether he has a tantrum or stops the tantrum, he must still do what you asked. The message will soon get through that tantrums are a waste of energy on all levels.

Nagging and reminding aren't the answer. Nor is giving up or giving in. The consequence of this approach for Billy in the case above is that if he makes enough excuses and creates enough diversion, he can get out of anything.

Mother shouldn't allow escape. Instead, she should set up consequences that pay off Billy to do the chores. After all, the reason for doing them is to make his world a better place and make his mother and others feel good about him. That's a consequence everyone can live with.

Escape shouldn't be allowed, even if there are extenuating circumstances, or it may encourage the son to recruit those circumstances to his own ends.

Diane: "I took Ray's allowance away for two weeks when he went to a friend's house without my permissison. He knew I didn't like him going there because it is an unsafe neighborhood to travel in. He couldn't reach me the day he decided to go, and instead he left the message that he was going over there on my answering machine. That got him off the hook without talking to me. Then he came home two hours late. I attacked him the minute he got in. He told me there had been a bus accident and he had to wait for another. That was true, but it was beside the point. He had no business going to his friend's."

- Mother should select consequences that fit into their already established life-style whenever possible.

For example, most mothers give their sons allowances and most require them to do a few household chores when they are old enough to handle them. But too few mothers tie the two together, making the allowance the consequence of performing the chores. Use what you have at hand.

In the economic marketplace, effective use of any resource means not giving it away or asking too big a price for what you wish to sell. That's a good thing to remember about consequences.

A mother we know tells the story of her son's arrival at the dinner table each night with dirty hands. A house rule was clean hands at the table. She tried—and failed to win compliance—with reminding, threatening, and complimenting him on those rare occasions when he did wash before sitting down to eat.

Finally, she concluded that some unpleasant consequences were necessary. Her son just never saw the advantage in having clean hands. But she was careful to extract a price from her son that was just the right amount to buy what she wanted (clean hands). She did not ask him to overpay. She simply made having any dinner at all contingent on clean hands.

To keep a limited soap-and-water action from escalating into a global confrontation, she resisted her temptation to "get" him. She didn't ground him for a week, take away his allowance, or make him clean the basement.

Nor did she tack on "extra" requirements for earning dinner at the last minute, such as clean hair, tied shoelaces, and brushed teeth.

Save the big guns for the big issues and stick to the issue at hand when selecting and applying consequences.

- With some behavior, there is no advantage to having a boy experience the full-blown consequences.

Few mothers would wish their sons to fail a grade in school as the "natural" consequence for not doing their schoolwork. Few would want them to learn that LSD is dangerous by actually experiencing an LSD trip. Mothers should try to separate *how* consequences shape learning from *what* they want sons to learn. How sons learn is always a function of the consequences. What they learn is up to their mothers. If a mother wants her son to learn the extreme consequences of not studying, okay. But most mothers will want their sons to learn to succeed in school, not fail. The way to do that is to contrive or set up forces that let a boy sample consequences in mild form or to approach them without getting blind-sided by the full effect.

It's a good idea to let kids sample the consequences of their behavior if the only cost is inconvenience.

Beth: "Fighting over who sits in the front seat of the car makes me crazy when I'm out with my son. I remember once driving to Belair and Kelly and his eleven-year-old sister started up. I pulled over to the side, got out, and made them both sit in the front seat while I sat in the back. That's the consequence of both wanting the front seat. No one got anywhere. It broke the tension and we all laughed. It really was funny for them to see Mom sitting in the back seat of the car in the middle of Harford Road."

- Consequences can and do shift, and mothers often miss the shift unless they pay close attention to what is rewarding their sons.

Keep in mind that all behavior, all actions, have a history. Nothing occurs in a vacuum. We do things on the basis of experience, either firsthand or learned vicariously. It's a moving target, especially for growing boys.

Be prepared to shift or get left dangling in the wind.

- The best reinforcing consequences are those given as close as possible to the time when the behavior you want to encourage is taking place.

So, catch 'em while they're good, or you may miss golden opportunities for reinforcing a behavior you want. Worse, mom may blow her whole program if her son fails to see the connection between what he does and how she reacts. A corollary to this is that mothers need to apply the consequences long enough to make sure they aren't working. "Long enough" does not necessarily mean length of time, such as two or three weeks. It means the number of times the behavior occurs and the opportunities arise to reinforce it. It may even be wise to "fix" a situation so that the opportunities for applying consequences arise more frequently than they naturally would.

- More is not always better.

If chosen well and used consistently and often at the start, consequences, especially positive ones, can be "leaned out," that is given less often, or diminished over time without reducing their effectiveness.

This is because, after a while, children become reinforced not only by a particular consequence (a reward, say), but by all the steps leading up to getting the consequence and even the mere anticipation of it. Soon, the consequence itself becomes less important than the behavior in making a child feel rewarded.

But keep in mind that when mothers begin to apply a consequence, they need to keep it in effect until the goal is well established. It won't help to tell a boy that if he cleans his room every week for six months, he'll get to go to Disneyland in the summer. Son needs to taste more immediate positive consequences of room cleaning, at least for a while.

Mothers sometimes worry that if they constantly use rewarding consequences, sons won't want to do anything without a payoff in the wings. Books full of experiments have shown this not to be the case.

- Whenever possible, point out how whole groups of very different actions can produce the same consequences.

This process will help sons understand the value of having many options and of selecting which ones to use in a given situation to get the most desirable consequence for the least amount of personal cost. It will also help boys recognize behavioral wolves in sheeps' clothing, or situations where identical behavior undertaken in different circumstances will still have the same effect.

Without this recognition, even boys who have had a beer or two at home with their friends may go off to college and be surprised to get drunk and sick after their first fraternity beer bash.

Boys need to establish as early as possible a whole class of behaviors mother has clearly labeled "moderation." She does not need to use liquor to demonstrate the point, either. Boys can overdose on ice cream or fried chicken just as well. As long as mother points out the connection between the consequences for overdoing a variety of things, the strategy will work.

Now let's move on to a more detailed description of the types of consequences available to mothers and sons and show how they can be applied in specific mother-son situations.

Rewards and Punishments

A considerable amount of research has been done purporting to show that single (especially divorced) mothers with sons cannot adequately discipline (read "punish") these boys. That explains, these studies suggest, why such women "compensate" by demanding more obedience and sometimes becoming domineering harridans.

Such conclusions may or may not be valid. But, as we have said, both *reinforcers* (rewards) and *punishers* (aversive events) are effective, and indeed research shows that the use of both in combination is usually more effective than using just one.

A tenet of behavioral parenting is to always use a reinforcement if you use a punishment, but not necessarily vice versa. That is, you don't always need to use a punishment in order to use a reinforcement.

Side effects are a part of any activity, but there are certain specific ones you can always expect when you use punishment. One is that at some point, your son will fight back, and the other is that he will try hard to avoid it, but not necessarily by complying with your wishes. For example, when a laboratory animal is given an electric shock to punish a particular behavior, it can be counted on to attack other animals in the cage or try to escape.

Another problem that may arise with punishing actions is that if they don't work, in order to stay consistent, you may have to escalate the intensity. Once you embark on a course of punishment, the continuum requires more punishment. That is why it is a good idea to start with the smallest and least-aversive thing that will do the job. Don't set out to use a cannon against a flea. We find that immoral. And worse, perhaps, it may not work. The only reason for using too big a punishment is ignorance, stupidity, or a desire to hurt.

Child abuse is a good behavior modifier. If you lock your son in a closet, or hit him with a belt, the chances are good he will stop doing whatever it is you dislike—at least for a while. But the fact that the act sometimes works does not make it acceptable.

Remember that all behavior is a function of consequences. This kind of behavior by mothers is also teaching sons to stop certain behavior with violent means. If you think that is sometimes appropriate or necessary, go ahead. But do think ahead. Before you use a particular punishment, decide just how far you are willing to go with it and whether you are willing to go beyond that if your son holds out a few notches.

You are the adult. There is no shame in *not* hurting someone. Don't be afraid to quit and try something else. That's what behavioral parenting is all about.

There are also physiological effects and costs of punishment that mothers may want to keep in mind. The body reacts to stress and pain by shifting into high hormonal gear. Many studies have documented the ill effects of stress.

None of this is to suggest that mothers should not punish sons. It's a consequence with effects that are sometimes necessary. In any event, both mothers and sons need to understand them, when they are likely to occur, and have some experience with them. This is because the outside world does punish, does provide painful consequences whether mother does or not. Sometimes they are excessive and sometimes they are undeserved. But they happen. Without some experience, sons will be too vulnerable in the real world. One consequence of understanding punishment is that sons will (we hope) learn to turn adversity to advantage. If the experience is unpleasant, he is better off if he says to himself, "I don't want that to happen again, so I will work to avoid it and find out what I need to do to avoid it."

Sometimes, people perceive consequences to be punishments even when they aren't designed to be. Getting a bad grade in school or a poor review in the school play are examples. Grades and reviews are designed as teaching aids. They are a natural part of any institutional effort, from medical school to the theater to business. The successful man is one who uses an unpleasant experience as an immediate impetus to change his behavior when it is appropriate to do so, instead of fighting or blaming the "system" for his misery.

Inattention

Changing behavior by ignoring it or by paying little attention to it when such attention is rewarding for a child, is a process psychologists call *extinction*.

The rationale is that if a boy behaves in a certain way and does not get the usual payoff, or consequence, he is less likely to do it again. Danny comes home from school and complains about his homework.

Mother: "Gee, that's too bad that you have so much to do. I'm sure you'd rather be outside playing."

Her response is guaranteed to encourage Danny to continue complaining about his homework and to delay tackling it.

If mother simply ignores the complaint and asks him to set the table or how his soccer practice went, Danny is less likely to bring up the homework complaint the next night.

Sometimes inattention can backfire. Suppose that Danny came home every night and, without complaining, went off to do his homework. If mother ignores this behavior (which she may well do because most parents respond only to "problems" or to obvious situations), Danny may be less likely to continue his good behavior.

Inattention works very well, however, especially with tantrums or other kinds of gross acting out in younger boys. As with all behavioral parenting techniques, the extinction strategy avoids the use of escalated force and anger and makes it clear to a boy that it's the behavior his mother is unhappy about, not him.

The Snowball

Many things that mothers want sons to do require completion of a fairly long sequence of events. Examples include such things as mastering a piece of piano music, housebreaking a dog, improving grades, and completing half a dozen chores a week in order to collect an allowance.

To be most useful in these situations, consequences should, at least at first, be applied not at the end of the sequence only, but along the way. In this way, mothers not only help sons see how they are doing, but limited consequences can serve as cues to begin the next step in the sequence—a snowball effect. The more steps mothers identify, the more opportunities they have to influence the behavior with consequences that work. As the chain of behaviors is repeated, the rate at which consequences are used can be reduced until they come only at the end of the sequence.

Preventive

Both little boys and older boys try all sorts of behaviors; some mothers can live with, some they really like, and some they really cannot tolerate. If you can anticipate and/or be on guard for these behaviors, you may be able to apply certain consequences that quickly get rid of those acts in the latter category before they become established. These consequences include the almost casual use of inattention and rapid substitution of other appealing behavior, and the selective use of natural consequences.

For example, suppose Kevin arrives home from school one afternoon, approaches his mother in the kitchen, and begins to complain about having to do "so much" homework. A preventive use of consequences might have mother deliberately ignore the complaint, smile, tell him pleasantly how conscientious he always is about his tasks, and offer him cake and milk before he sets the table for dinner.

Tokens and Symbols

These are the very best kinds of consequences because they are the most useful and easy to use. They are powerful because they can be used to trade for or buy other things. Moreover, they are the kinds of consequences that most adults use throughout their lives. What's more, they can easily be given or taken away.

The most common token, of course, is money. But other items will do. For small children, it might be plastic checkers. For older boys, check marks or gold stars on a sheet of paper. For teenagers, IOU's for special trips or services.

A major advantage of token systems is that they knock satiation effects out of the box. Even millionaires want more money and like to watch their accounts grow. They also bridge time gaps between when a behavior occurs and when another reinforcing consequence can be delivered. They are easy-to-use indicators of continuing success or slippage.

Mothers who use the token system can create whole economies, in which sons can quickly count gains and losses. Tokens not only have trading value, but they can be inflated and deflated by mothers as conditions change. Boys at age seven may consider a quarter a week great wages for making their beds, but by age ten, would like a dollar for doing something more challenging in addition to bed-making.

The ultimate token system is one that approaches the ways in which rewarding consequences are often handed out in the adult world. When men do good deeds, the consequences are likely to be goodwill from others. These kinds of "tokens" can't be banked in a vault, but are considered just as good as gold by men who have learned to value symbolic as well as tangible rewards.

One way to establish this condition is for mothers to begin early using points, checks, and stars to mark the completion of desired behaviors each time they occur. Eventually, they can cut down the tokens to once a day or once a week, while simultaneously adding verbal or physical consequences, such as thanks, hugs and smiles, and privileges. Soon, boys are as satisfied with the latter as they were with the former.

With some practice, mothers will find the control of consequences such as those described above useful in a variety of mother-son confrontations and issues. Excessive crying is one, because our society still places a higher value on males who don't engage in this behavior.

Preventive consequences work especially well in these cases, together with inattention. Michael recalls a seven-year-old boy who had a habit of shedding waterfalls after every bump or scratch. A concerted effort was made to watch the boy in the play yard.

When he hurt his finger, Michael and others got to him (because they were waiting for the opportunity) before he had a chance to get his lungs full of air for that first watery yell. They quickly focused all their attention on his injured fingers, matter-of-factly and seriously. They did not look at his face, wring their hands, become alarmed, say things such as "Don't cry" or "That must really hurt."

Through a trip to the doctor's office, x rays, and a painful check of his digits, the child never shed a tear. Michael and the others let him know how impressed they were with his behavior, and that wrapped it up. Incidents of excessive crying dropped dramatically.

The use of foul language is another behavior that many mothers told us they disliked. Again, the use of consequences to preempt the practice is often the right route. Almost all boys (and girls) at some stage decide it's time to learn to swear.

A big part of the solution is to understand this, not assign too much significance to it, and not pay too much attention to it. The consequences of overreacting to first bouts of cursing are so well known they have been codified into jokes. One of our favorites involves the six-and-eight-year-old boys who decide they would try out some swear words on mother.

At breakfast the next day, when mother asks if Johnny would like some Cheerios, he responds with "How the hell do I know?"

Shocked, mother smacks him and sends him to his room without breakfast. "Now how about you?" she says sweetly to his brother.

Lips quivering, the boy answers, "I don't know but you can bet your ass it won't be Cheerios."

This mother defeated General Mills but not bad language.

Aggression in which boys attack others is a more critical problem for many mothers. It's especially tough to deal with this kind of behavior because aggression is its own reward: It does not need any other audience to provide satisfaction. All it needs is the victim, so that inattention is not likely to work. Other consequence-control methods, however, will.

Sandy is a five-and-a-half-year-old boy who fights with his playmates, especially his four-year-old sister when they are at home, in their yard, or at a neighbor's house. Sandy is a regular tiger. He yells, takes toys from his playmates, hits, kicks, and sometimes bites. Depending on how long he's allowed to play, these episodes occur two to eight times a day.

For Sandy's mother, his behavior is a source of constant irritation. She not only has to break up the altercations but also soothe the offended party. She is also fearful that one day Sandy will seriously hurt another child.

Because Sandy's mother has been careful to not pay too much attention to him when he fights, but only to the other child and to the matter at hand, she knows it is unlikely that his aggressive behavior is being maintained by her on-the-scene response to the fights.

So she didn't waste her time trying to "ignore" the behavior away. Instead, she periodically reinforced *all* the children and especially Sandy when they played without fighting—even if fight-free play lasted only fifteen minutes. The longer Sandy played without fighting, the more rewarding consequences she applied.

At the same time, whenever Sandy hit, kicked, bit, or otherwise misbehaved, she physically removed him two feet from the play area and made him sit on a chair for two minutes to watch the other children and think about how he ought to behave. If a toy was taken from another child, Sandy was made to hand it back. If the other child was struck, Sandy had to apologize.

Household chores are a chronic source of irritation and confrontation between mothers and sons between the ages of about seven and sixteen. What to do?

A big part of the solution is to label clearly such chores as laundry, room straightening, dishes, lawn mowing, and so on as things that make a family's life run smoothly. They should not be made a "punishment" or something that low men on the totem pole do, but as unisex jobs with a value for the group.

Then a good way to get chores done without nagging and threatening is to tie them to positive consequences, notably privileges and treats. But create an equitable economy, in which your son won't bankrupt his account if he messes up.

For example, if going to the movies with his boyfriends on Saturday afternoon requires him to do chores all week and he misses one on Tuesday, he has no incentive to do any the rest of the week because he's already blown it.

Instead, provide some reinforcement along the way, and enough "points" for doing four days' worth to keep him going. And have some remedial jobs available so he can gain ground that he's lost. If Tim forgets to take out the garbage on Wednesday, he should have a chance to clean out the garage on Friday and still get to the movies on Saturday.

In adolescence, especially, sons will come up with a whole array of provocative, rebellious, and refuse-to-do behaviors, including missing curfews, chucking chores, ignoring schoolwork, and demanding attention. The best consequences in this kind of situation involve a token economy. Rational conversation, and even indulgent patience, may not work.

Adam (walking into his mother's room after six changes of clothing): How do I look for school?

Joann (diplomatically overlooking color clashes and hair that looks terrified): You look fine, hon.

Adam (angrily): You're only saying that to make me feel better. You never say what you mean. I'm not that dumb, you know. My clothes stink. I really look like _____

This conversation took place the next day:

Adam: How do I look for school?

Joann: You really put the outfit together well. Your hair looks great, too. How about trying the new tie, the blue one.

Adam (angrily): What's wrong with the one I'm wearing? You're always criticizing the way I look. You think I'm ugly. I happen to think I look great and all you can do is put me down!

Joann's sanity was restored with simple, noncommittal "Ummm's" to all further questions about his looks. He stopped asking her opinion when he didn't really want it.

Tantrums in young boys are usually best handled with inattention and/or a combination of inattention and substitution of the desired behavior. Make up your mind to go through it with the understanding that things may get worse before they get better.

When Kevin throws a tantrum at bath time, mother can physically and verbally guide him through the activity of putting away his toys and taking his bath while ignoring his screams and protests. This is very punishing for mom, but eventually it will get better. When all else fails, she should remember that as hard as this is for her, it's much harder on her son. He is exhausted, hoarse, bruised, and unhappy. He wants a way out, too.

One mother we interviewed said she solved the put-away-the-toys-and-take-a-bath problem an "easier" way. How? She made the bath more appealing than the toy box by buying him a new rubber duck. That's wonderful. This mother has just instituted a consequence whereby she may have to buy him dozens of new and better bath toys. If her son is smart, he will use the same technique to get him new and better treats for *everything* Mom wants him to do. The time to buy the new rubber duck is *after* Kevin has taken his bath for two or three days in a row without a tantrum.

Finally, how can mothers use consequence control to improve poor school performance or, better yet, keep school performance from becoming poor?

One way to answer the question is to reverse an old bureaucratic corollary "Never let a good deed go unpunished."

Too often, parents "punish" good deeds by ignoring them or focusing attention on their children only when they mess up.

Concern for poor grades is understandable in a highly competitive society. But a sure way to reinforce your son's equal concern about that is to zero in *only* when he makes mistakes.

Why not focus more on all the things he does right in school.

Here is a prime opportunity to use the "snowball" effect. Think of all the things your son must do to get a good grade and learn a subject. Think about the long sequence of events involved in his learning. Surely in that long chain, there are things mothers can find to reward. The bonus is that by reinforcing one link in the chain, they are helping to support the others.

Some mothers we spoke to gave dollars for A's, or special treats for completing homework assignments each night. It's good to make the reward schedule very worthwhile at first. Later it can be spaced out.

Will mothers who do this rear sons who will always expect money for good grades? No. Used properly, they will encourage good school habits until sons realize the value of their education. For many boys, this does not happen until high school or college, when they can see the link between good jobs and a good life and their classroom performance. Until then, they can use a hand.

Rewarding school performance also bridges the gap between school and home, using reinforcements that are already familiar to sons and helping to establish classes of behavior that provide similar payoffs.

The mother of an eight-year-old recalls that her son was not doing his homework or classwork each day. She asked the teacher to send home each day a small piece of paper with a single word, "Yes" or "No" on it.

She had used the same system to encourage her son to dress himself on school days without being reminded and nagged. Very soon, her son was doing his homework. "It's just like home. I like getting 'Yes's' on the paper," he told her.

So did mom.

CHAPTER SEVEN

Do As I Say: Rules for What?

One afternoon, Jared appeared downstairs in Army fatigues from the local surplus store, high-top basketball shoes (sans socks), a Grateful Dead T-shirt under a Ralph Lauren Polo button-down, regimental necktie, and red bandanna around his long blond locks.

Jared: What time are we meeting Nan and Pop at the restaurant?

Joann: As soon as you change your clothes.

Jared: What's wrong with what I'm wearing?

Joann: It's making knots in my stomach. Your grandparents will have coronaries.

Jared: It's my body. I should be able to wear what I want.

Mothers may yearn for the days when clothes were worn to cover the body, not to make a political statement, but in any case these kinds of scenes are commonplace in the annals of mother-son confrontations.

Readers who have stayed with us this far might consider the exchange above and suggest that the best way for Joann to have handled it is by ignoring the outfit. She might also work at encouraging Jared to dress more appropriately by rewarding him whenever he wears something reasonable, and guaranteeing other consequences (no trips to restaurants, for example) until he shapes up.

Those strategies will probably work—eventually. But it may take weeks or months before Jared arrives via this routine at clothing combinations Joann can approve without blanching—what is "reasonable"? Socks yes and T-shirt no? Tie no and bandanna yes?

There is, however, a behavioral shortcut around situations like this one which, when in place, offers options and efficiency instead of head-on conflict and domestic fatigue for both mothers and sons.

Joann: When you go to school you may wear whatever you like as long as it is clean and paid for. When you go somewhere with me, I get veto power.

Jared: What about when I go out with my friends?

Joann: To parties and kid events, you wear your choices.

Jared: No hassles?

Joann: No hassles.

Although there is a certain amount of negotiation and compromise reflected in this conversation, the value of this approach for single mothers is its format.

Joann issued a set of instructions in the form of a rule. She let Jared know how he could expect to be rewarded (no hassles, smiles from grandparents, no problem with peers) if he agreed to her request. Jared complies with the rule (most of the time) because he knows from past experience that rewards are likely. He is also accustomed to following rules and instructions. Throughout his upbringing, he has found it rewarding more often than not to obey rules and verbal instructions issued by a variety of authorities. And he has seen others (models) complying with similar instructions. (His brother, his father, and his grandfather do not wear Army fatigues and red bandannas to restaurants.)

The use of verbal instruction to initiate and reinforce necessary rules is a special type of activity psychologists call *stimulus control*. In plain English, it means that mothers learn to signal or produce a certain response with more or less ready-made or readily available events, objects, or language. This technique—and the signals—will be discussed in more detail in the next chapter.

For now, it is important to understand how these signals operate and to realize, particularly in the case of verbal instructions, that their power is too often overlooked—probably because it is too often taken for granted.

"Saber-toothed tiger!" was no doubt one of the phrases uttered by cave mothers as a signal to their offspring to run for safety. The rule it governed was simple: Ignore the tiger or the warning and get eaten. "No!" is a wonderful all-purpose word, teaching more rules for safety and behavior in a child's earliest years than all the reinforcers and consequences known—at least until overuse makes it meaningless.

Used strategically and purposefully, instructional control

of behavior not only gets the job at hand done but sets the stage for a son to add rapidly to his behavioral bank all sorts of appropriate responses to people and events as he grows up. When sons experience the benefits of following rules, they will learn to initiate rules of their own to be followed in other situations.

If mothers had to wait until every response or behavior they wanted sons to learn arose naturally, child rearing would be extremely hazardous and take centuries instead of a decade or two. Without rules and a repertoire of followed instructions, everything would have to be learned the "hard way."

Complicated and lengthy chains of behavior, in fact, might be incredibly difficult.

Without the habit of following instructions linked to rules, the consequences for sons and mothers may be a great deal more serious than embarrassment in the local four-star restaurant. By far the major consequences for mothers are the fear of and loss of control over sons who become too strong and too big physically for her to handle; for sons, the consequences are fear over their own loss of control, pain, anguish, and sometimes severe punishment.

When the six-year-old, whom mom could pick up and put in his room, grows into a five-foot ten-inch seventeen-year-old who lifts weights for fun, it's daunting. He could, if he wished, put mom in *her* room. Or hit her. Or cause serious damage to property.

By the time this happens, outside intervention may be necessary.

Clearly, mothers need to establish the habit of instruction following early, and their sons must learn to be alert to society's rules (even if they aren't always followed to the letter).

In addition, especially as sons grow into adolescence and beyond, mother needs the security of knowing there is a one-to-one link between what sons say they will do in response to her instructions, and what they actually do. If the rule is to be home at midnight and Tom says he will be home at midnight, mother must be confident that he will be home at midnight. And Tom must be there at the appointed time or discuss a mutually agreed-to alternative in advance.

For the single mothers of sons, it should be obvious that this kind of behavioral control is absolutely essential, if for no other reason than it removes the problem of uneven muscle power and a system of authority based on force and strength. It is the great equalizer—and a moral one—both in the home and in society.

Just as important, we think, is that like all elements of behavioral parenting, this one saves time and energy. It is efficient. We all know that juggling the multiple responsibilities of single motherhood frequently reduces the amount of time allotted for fun and games. When mothers are pressed, they tend to use less positive behavior around their children, and are slower to respond to them. Anything that can free up time for the harassed parent is to be valued, and instructional control is gold. There are also many behaviors mothers have difficulty observing and providing consequences for.

For example, in the case of venereal disease, playing with matches, starting a fistfight, and taking drugs, there is absolutely no advantage to allowing those behaviors in order to provide consequences. Mothers don't want them to *ever* occur.

By the time they reach adolescence, sons will get many of their most influential reinforcements and approvals from those outside the mother's reach or control. The value of having rules in place and an efficient, verbal way of invoking and discussing them is immeasurable.

Joann and Adam discovered this when Adam, who had been driving a car to and from school for less than six months, broke an important rule of the road.

Joann: You are more than half an hour late getting home from school for the second time this week. You were already grounded Tuesday night after the first incident. (Consequence.) You are supposed to call if you will be late getting home. I don't like to worry about this. You will be grounded again.

Adam (angrily): What's the big deal. I *always* call you. Okay I was wrong to not call the other day when we stopped for a Coke. But this time it's because I was doing someone a favor by taking her home. I didn't think half an hour would throw you into a tizzy! Now I'm getting punished for doing a favor, right? I've been driving for six months almost and have been very responsible. I think I should have a little more leeway. I don't think it's fair that I have to account for every minute and be on such a short leash. My friends think I'm weird. I always have to stop and call my mother.

Joann: The rule is to call even if you will be two minutes late. As long as you are not coming straight home from school, the rule is to call. (Talking behavior.) Whether or not the rule is appropriate is not the issue here. We can talk about that at another time.

They did talk about it the next day.

Adam: I want to talk about the phone call rule.

Joann: Okay. This is a good time.

Adam: I agree that I broke the rule. And I agree I was wrong to do that. I know you worry. I should have talked to you about this first. But it's really getting me down.

Joann: You mean having to call me when you are going to be even a few minutes late driving home from school? (Clarifying and talking behavior.)

Adam: Exactly. I appreciate how you feel. I know you were worried when I began driving. But I am very responsible. I have pretty much followed all the rules, about seat belts, calling, letting you know where I am, and all that. Don't you think it's time to ease up?

Joann: You have been pretty good about the rules I set up when you began to drive and I appreciate that. You are also a safe driver. What do you think the rule ought to be? (Joann had already decided that she would give Adam some extra time before he had to call home—up to half an hour.)

Adam: I think I should be allowed to have an hour's leeway coming home from school. That will give me time to do an errand or stop for a Coke or take a friend home or just talk to people for a few minutes without rushing off to the nearest phone like some wimp.

Joann: I think some leeway is certainly possible. Perhaps an hour is too much though. What do you think?

Adam: All right. How about a half an hour and if it's going to be any later than that, I'll call. But not before that, right?

Joann: You got it.

A few days later, Adam called ten minutes before he was due home to say he would be an hour late.

Joann: "Thanks for calling. Take your time. I know it's not always easy keeping track of the clock."

Among the mothers we talked to, most depended on rules and instructional control for a variety of behaviors. They used them to establish authority ("You are not your father, you are their brother and it isn't your job to discipline the other children."); to assure privacy ("Sometimes I come home at night and it's bills, and worries, and they all jump on me when I come in. I need half an hour to just get myself together because a lot of the arguments started this way. So I go to my room for a half hour. I made a little rule about them not interrupting this private time."); to take up family responsibilities ("If anyone in this family is to be out late or not home on time, we deserve a phone call. We require some good manners and they must go to certain places and family events with me."); to assert authority ("Ian thinks I'm unusual. I'm real old-fashioned about him being places on time, being polite to others, and calling me if he will be late or I might worry. My son needs limits."); and to assure domestic tranquility ("He has to keep his room neat and feed the pets.")

Among the more imaginative, the lighthearted use of even a single phrase can control and mold a slew of desirable behaviors such as reasonable caution, acceptance of responsibilities, assertiveness, physical fitness, cooperation, and independence.

Mom: Where are you going?

Son (leaving the house after dark in a bad neighborhood): To Eddie's.

Mom: When pigs fly, fella.

Bernice: "With Alan (sixteen) the best thing in the world in terms of discipline (keeping him in line) is saying something isn't *fair*. That's the key word. We're not talking constitutional rights. He knows what fair means around here. Thank God. He's too big to throttle. Especially since he's taking karate."

These mothers have established instructional control for rule-governed activities.

As always, the first step to the successful use of instructions for rule following and rule setting is familiarity with how Do-as-I-say methods operate and in what circumstances they operate best.

- Early is best. Getting sons to follow instructions is a process that is best introduced in the preschool years, because mothers can take advantage of children's overriding desire to please them at this age and because sons are around a lot to be encouraged and reinforced. By the time sons approach adolescence, mothers will find it very difficult to pit their instructions to do this or do that against the now-overriding desire sons have to pay attention to their peers instead.

Early instruction following also allows mothers to start working on getting what a son says he will do and what he does to correspond.

Mothers who get instruction-following behavior locked in early have a way to exert remote control when their sons are no longer subject to direct control. They can reinforce what sons say—knowing it will have a fairly close connection to what they do—even when there is no one around to make sure they do it. Setting up this correspondence, this link, is critical.

Here is an example of a mother who wishes to establish correspondence between what her son says he is going to do and what he in fact does. Tommy is almost seven.

First, she chooses the setting—the lunch table, for example—for working on the behavior. (Tommy doesn't have an eating problem; that is not why mom has chosen this time and place. She is simply using the occasion to help her establish "remote control" methods for directing her son's behavior.)

Next she tells Tommy a range of things she has available to eat and asks him what it is he would like. (It's "easier" to just put lunch on the table, and he may eat it. But no learning about instruction following or rules takes place without a lesson.)

She knows what it is she wants to give him within a range of three or four things, say milk, peanut butter, soup, and peas. If he indicates that he wants one of the items available, she compliments him on his choice and then asks whether or not he plans to eat all of it.

If he does eat all of it after he says he will, she again compliments him not only on his choice of selecting the "right" foods, but also for doing what he said—that is, eating all of it.

If Tommy does not choose from among the foods available, she tells him that the one he has chosen is not a good idea and why. She may say she does not have it or it is not good for him, and asks him to choose something else. Or she might suggest again a range of things for him to choose from that she has available and is willing to provide.

In addition, if Tommy does not finish all that he asks for when he stated he would finish it, then she can comment on the fact that he has asked for food and has not finished it all and that this is not a good thing to do.

The point here is not that wasting food is "bad" (although many mothers may wish to make that point), but that here is a good opportunity to help a boy understand how important it is that he do what he says he is going to do.

An added reinforcement in this setting is dessert. If Tommy finishes everything he asks for and asks for the right things, then mother can ask him which dessert he would like as a reward. At the same time, if he does not finish all the food he asked for, she can point out that he cannot have dessert because he did not do what he said he would do.

• The effectiveness of instructional control depends on how quickly a boy can link his past experience with instructions to a current event. If you want your son to follow instructions, you need to have rewarded him for following instructions in the past.

If in the past, following a particular instruction about rules brought him benefits and failure to follow the instruction did not, he is more likely to follow the instruction again.

• The pot of gold is "generalized" compliance with rules, the prospect of a law-abiding citizen of the home and the community, and confidence that sons will do what they say they will do.

Mothers can start the process with very young children. Here is an example with a three-year-old:

Mother selects ten activities during the day, five of which she is going to work on and five of which she is going to watch to see if her son follows her requests.

The five that she chooses to work on she will ask the child to do twice. For example, putting his book back on the shelf, getting undressed for his nap or bed, washing his hands before dinner, and so on. These are activities she knows her son will usually do when she asks him.

If son complies with her request within five seconds, he gets compliments, a hug, and sometimes a special treat. If he doesn't comply, mother will show him what she wants him to do by guiding him manually to complete the request.

Mother will observe her son's response to the other five requests (which might include finishing his milk, putting his blocks away, sitting quietly for a few minutes), so she'll know if he is learning to generalize the idea that it is important to comply with requests which she does not specifically reinforce.

- Requests for instruction following are more likely to be met if there is some immediate feedback and if the instruction is simple and clear. The word "no" is a good example. It's an instruction that can apply to touching hot irons or taking the family car. It's unambiguous and nonnegotiable.

Even better are instructions that sons help construct. In this exchange, mother uses instructional control to reinforce her rule about midnight curfews on weekends. She might have reminded her son that the curfew is midnight. Instead, she does this:

Mother: David, what time do you think you will be home from your date?

David (aware of the curfew rule): I think about midnight or at latest twelve-thirty. I might need a few extra minutes to get my date home. The movie lets out late.

Mother: That's great, babe. That's reasonable and you'll be rested enough to get an early start on our trip to the beach tomorrow.

Or, it might go this way:

Mother: David, what time do you think you will be home from your date?

David: How about one or one-thirty?

Mother: That's not gonna make it. Do I hear midnight?

David: That might push it. The movie lets out late. I can make it by twelve-thirty, probably.

Mother: I'll plan on that, then.

Instead of indicating the curfew for David, mother has asked him to issue the instructions that follow the rule. Obviously, she would like him to come home sometime between midnight and twelve-thirty. She considers that an appropriate time for his age and it allows her the security of knowing that he is safe before she falls asleep on her feet. If he selects the right time, she can compliment him on selecting the right time and why.

If he selects a time later than the curfew, she can point out why that isn't a good selection and ask him if he would reconsider. She always has the option to specify the time for him to be home, but in this manner she allows her teenager, who is eager to be an adult, the chance to make a choice and exercise some independence.

Similarly, she provides the occasion for him to receive reinforcement for doing what he *says* he is going to do—that is, coming home at the specified time—and for her to start her attempt to influence more of his behavior by verbal instruction rather than direct consequence.

A mother who uses this approach gets a bonus: She will know that her son is paying attention to her instructions, a major step in the successful use of any of the principles of behavioral parenting. By telling her the instruction, he acknowledges that he has received the message.

- Once you get the habit going, it will continue only if you reinforce it. Following instructions related to certain rules is *not* like riding a bicycle. Boys don't get the knack once and never forget it. It is not reflexive. There is no inevitability about it.

Mother: "I've told him fifty times if I've told him once to _____! (fill in the blanks)"

That complaint arises out of ignorance of a fundamental fact about instruction following. Did the mother above follow through with a compliment or some other consequence after each of the "fifty times" she "told him"? Not likely.

- Just as mothers use models to get sons to do as others do in the interests of self-development, they can use models and consequences of all sorts to get sons to do as they say. The same principles discussed in previous chapters can be applied to teaching instruction following.
- There can be too much of a good thing. A major consideration for mothers rearing sons is how to have their offspring strike that neat balance between being an obedient son and an assertive man; how to encourage compliance without producing a mama's boy who never strikes out on his own; how to prod him into thinking for himself without running amok.

Most people love rules and instructions. They are easy to use, and they don't require a lot of thinking. The rewards for obeying instructions from mom, teacher, boss, and society are often considerable. The punishment for not obeying is often unpleasant. ("Get twenty out of twenty right and you get an A"; "Cut class, you get no allowance"; "Pass Go and Collect two-hundred dollars.") The presence of quick and easy instructions makes us feel secure. We invest them with a great deal of importance. They make the world go around, from the instructional "No smoking" signs in public elevators to the Ten Commandments.

Some people follow rules to excess, however. Military units that failed to question an inhumane order and whole nations such as the Germans during the Third Reich have been charged with that "crime." Just as we saw in the use of consequences in the last chapter, any event that is reinforced enough may begin to take on a life of its own. In the case of rules, people may feel obliged to obey them even without specific encouragement. Much of the time this is good, because rules are necessary to society. Law-abiding people are those who don't have to break a law or a rule in order to understand consequences, but they accept certain rules because they have learned the consequences of breaking family rules. To teach their sons to follow instructions associated with certain rules, mothers may provide a reward each time a request is obeyed. But sons may get another message from all this encouragement, namely, "always follow not just this rule, but all rules," or "always obey instructions from older people," or "never break new ground if the path doesn't run along old trails."

In short, rules that are followed inappropriately do damage.

Some people learn to follow rules blindly or bend to instructions automatically when they are offered by intimidating or authoritative individuals. They lose (or never find) a proper degree of assertiveness or a competitive edge.

This is why it is important for mothers to consider carefully the rules they impose and reinforce and to be aware of how boys may be generalized to some instruction-following habits in unintended ways. In the following scene, mother failed to get the desired effect.

Mother: Kevin, stop poking the cat.

Kevin (still poking): Why?

Mother: Just stop it, I said. It's not nice.

Kevin: It won't hurt him.

Mother (raising her voice): Did you hear me? I said stop that this minute. And if you do it again, I'll spank you!

Kevin stops poking the cat.

Mother: That's better, Kevin. I love you much more when you do what I tell you.

What mom has actually "taught" Kevin is that he doesn't need to pay attention until she threatens him with bodily harm. Her intended "rule" was completely lost on him.

Mothers should reserve instructions and rules for those kinds of behavior that are truly critical in their sons' relationships with her and the outside world.

The most creative individuals and the most successful individuals, those valued most by our society, often seem to be those who *break* some rules or at least know how to bend them. Mothers want to teach sons to obey rules at their request. But they also want to teach them to negotiate rule-governed acts without confrontations or the need for winners and losers in behavioral shootouts. People follow rules to excess for the same reason they follow rules: their history.

Bernice: "We have very few absolute rules, but we insist he do chores, take care of pets, and keep his room clean. He can't argue about that or coming-home times. Sure, he tries to finagle, but we don't have to do a lot of punishing because he accepts the rules and we can trust him to follow them most of the time."

Annie: "I'm a teacher and it's important to me that Mark have good study habits. I've seen what happens to boys who, because they tend to act up more in the classroom, have problems with teachers. We have some rules about classroom behavior and respect for teachers. He also has to do his homework before he goes out to play."

As we'll see in the next chapter, one way to prevent excessive or inappropriate instruction following is to establish conditions in which sons are induced and rewarded to *not* follow an instruction, just as you provide situations in which he is rewarded for following it.

As we noted earlier, it is easier to begin the process of instilling rule-governed behavior when boys are quite young, preferably preschool age, because it is easiest at this time for a mother to respond with her full attention. She can even physically guide him through an activity.

But mothers, particularly single mothers, don't always have the time and energy for total bodily commitment to such tasks. Moreover, as sons get older, the time necessary to provide all this guidance may in itself be punishing. Sons want to go back out and play, not stop for hugs and kisses and compliments.

Recent research and our talks with dozens of mothers and sons suggest there are some even more efficient and interesting variations in establishing the habit of following instructions. Moreover, these can be tailored more imaginatively to specific ideas and rules that mothers want to get across. For instance, one should take advantage of the fact that between the ages of four and six, children's use of language and their willingness to respond to spoken directions seems to flourish.

Let's go back to lunch for an example. If good health is important to the mother, she can begin in simple ways to classify foods into two general categories: healthy and not healthy.

There are a whole variety of ways boys can learn which is which. Mothers can tell them, show them pictures, tell them stories, show them what they eat, and so on.

And with small boys, they can do something else. They can say "Here, eat these alfalfa sprouts. They are healthy for you."

With older sons, she can ask "What do you think we ought to eat at this mall? That counter over there has fresh fruits and vegetables. The one next to it has tacos."

The goal is to get the boy to say that although he might prefer tacos, fresh vegetables are healthier so let's eat at the health food counter.

There is nothing so supportive and encouraging of any behavior—including instruction following—as the chance for sons to tell their mothers what the instruction should be. By giving them the chance and sufficient access to information, the son who chooses fresh vegetables over tacos is rewarded for his independent behavior, his selection of good healthy foods, and for complying with mother's requests.

A triple play.

According to the mothers we spoke to, boys beyond the age of twelve—beginning their break for independence—bristle at peremptory instructions. If by now, instruction following is "second nature," mothers have a "remote system" for reinforcing the right stuff in their sons, and sons have a safe and useful way to test limits.

Instead of rushing into an activity or event a boy suspects

or knows is breaking or bending rules, he can use the language taught him by instructions to test the waters and challenge mother verbally.

Son: I know you aren't going to like this, but I tried a cigarette the other day. It was awful. I don't think I want to try that again.

Mom: I'm glad of that. Cigarettes are lousy and as a former smoker I can tell you it's rough trying to quit once you start.

Son: I know you've always told me not to smoke.

Mom: It's a good rule to follow. And I appreciate your letting me know about situations you get into that you know I don't approve of. What led you to try it?

Son: Oh, all the kids were doing it. I know, I know, I don't want to do things just because others are doing it. When it comes to really important things, I wouldn't.

Mom: You're terrific. I believe you.

Hearing such reports, particularly *why* her son committed a no-no, helps mother to know how reliable his word is. It's one more handle on the controls. And for the son, he secures confirmation of rules and instructions that help him sort out difficult choices.

At a rock concert, Tony accepted a drink he knew had alcohol in it. But it had more alcohol than he could handle. At fourteen, he not only broke a cardinal rule of the house against drinking, but he also got sick.

Mother (the next day): I'm sorry you had to get sick, but I am glad you told me what happened even though you knew I would be angry or disappointed.

Tony: I know I shouldn't have had a drink.

Mother: That's right. You don't want to drink. You are too young. And you might have gotten some drugs other than alcohol in that drink, something more dangerous.

Tony: I guess it would be better to only take drinks from people I know very well or from a closed bottle.

Mother: That is always best for anyone who is drinking.

Tony: Okay. Next time I'll bring my own!

Mother: What?

Tony: Only kidding. Only kidding. It won't happen again.

Instructions and rule following are one of a whole family of behavioral principles of special value to mothers rearing boys. All of them help lubricate higher levels of learning between mothers and sons, and encourage independence.

PART
TWO

CHAPTER EIGHT

A Time to Cry and a Time to Laugh: Behavior as a Moving Target

Sometimes you need to fight to defend yourself. Don't fight on the schoolbus, and remember that boys never hit girls.

It's okay to interrupt mother's conversation if she is speaking to her boyfriend or to grandma. Don't ever interrupt when she is speaking on the phone or to her boss.

Necking with your girlfriend is allowed in the house. Necking with your girlfriend is not allowed at her house.

Mother has a right to privacy. Mother can enter your room whenever she wishes.

Drinking and smoking in moderation are fine for mother. They are not fine for son.

It's okay to roughhouse at dad's on weekends. Roughhousing is not allowed at mom's.

You don't have to open the car door for mother. Open the car door for other women.

Mom will listen to arguments about curfews on Sunday morning. She will not listen to arguments about curfews on Saturday night after son has missed his.

Jumping off the front steps is permitted. Jumping off the second-floor landing in the house is not permitted.

Taking narcotics after a tooth extraction is expected. Narcotics are bad for you.

These statements describe a few of the literally thousands of everyday distinctions between suitable and unsuitable behavior, good and bad conduct, and formal and informal rules that children must learn and parents must teach.

The behaviors they involve can be a particular trial for the

145

single mother worried about fostering independence and assertiveness in a boy without a dad at home. (And without hand-to-hand or head-to-head conflict.) Too often, as we've said, the single woman tends to blame her singlehood or her failed marriage for every lapse in her son's behavior.

Mothers also find themselves increasingly angry about what they consider inconsistent behavior as their sons enter adolescence and young manhood. "He knows better." "He used to be so polite and gentle. He never used to do that." "Why is he such a brat with me and so nice at his father's?" Sons caught in the crossfire often lie, become sullen, withdrawn, or depressed.

At such times, when a son's behavior is so distressingly wrong or cockeyed, mom needs to be able to tell if the failure rests in some lapse in her behavioral parenting and, if so, to identify it.

Is her son's behavior a problem because consequences—the single most essential ingredient in her parenting recipe—were not chosen or used well? Or is something more complicated and less under her control going on? Is her son unable to correctly interpret—and act on—the cues and signals that provide guides to appropriate behavior out there in the world?

Inconsistencies often reflect a child's clumsy efforts to deal with conditions in the adult world, a world in which successful men and women match their behavior to the needs and circumstances of the moment. So, if mothers want to rear sons who are both leaders and sensitive to others, who appear assertive but also flexible, they need to understand what circumstances trigger "wrong" and "right" responses and how people pick out the best triggers among the many that crop up.

Mother's skill in this department will help sons learn to discriminate, to be alert to what others are doing and to the fact that events, behavior, and conditions "outside" are always changing.

There is a good reason why this is *especially* important as adolescence gives way to manhood. Society demands that men, if they are to be successful and welcomed in society, strike out in some fiercely independent ways. They are expected to test the waters and challenge authority. It is as important for sons as it is for mothers to be alert to shifting consequences and to have the courage to try things that may not always work.

As boys mature, they meet more and more situations with unknown or fuzzy consequences. Therefore, the mother who can find efficient ways of teaching her son to sort out often confusing cues, to discriminate among conflicting signals of behavior and act on the one that will *serve him best*, will go a long way to helping him avoid or overcome discouragement, frustration, or fear of something new.

When men and women become sophisticated at picking out the signals, they can also successfully offer cues to others in order to get the results they want—from a good table in a restaurant to a job. We sometimes call this ability "charm" or "style" or "grace under pressure." Can these be taught? You *bet* they can. By being alert to behavioral tip-offs among colleagues, peers, and bosses that change is coming or is already in progress, people who are good at cue-reading can use their skill to sense the right moment for pushing ahead or backing off. Politicians, for example, are superb at sorting out cues and carefully timing their responses. The ability to discriminate quickly and accurately is also a hallmark of the adult who is sensitive to others' needs.

Readers may not realize—or if they do, not quite believe—that mothers can teach or that sons can learn such finely tuned behavior. They may insist that no one can train another person to see the appropriateness of his or her own behavior and to pick up nuances of behavior in others; they feel that such knowledge comes only by experience.

We ask them to believe that they can.

Behavioral parenting means accepting the premise that *all* learning takes place in the same way, whether the subject is learning auto mechanics, calculus, philosophy—or social skills. Our children are shaped, intentionally or otherwise, by complex and shifting events in their lives and by what happens—the consequences—when they behave in certain ways.

Next to consequences, the ability to rapidly "read" events and others' behavior for clues to what to do, is the most important technique behavioral parenting has to offer. Formally, this ability is known as *stimulus discrimination*, or SD for short.

If you behave in a certain way and get rejected or punished or put down for it, you feel hurt, angry, or puzzled and react accordingly. But if you have paid attention to the cues, to the way the person who hurt you behaved and spoke, you can learn something important about what you did to provoke the rejection and how to avoid it next time. In short, SD can help you turn a bad time into an advantage on the next go-round.

Why does it work? Psychologists know that if reinforcing or punishing consequences are used whenever people respond to some particular cue, such individuals can easily learn fine distinctions between correct and incorrect behavior. Equally important, people almost always want to try to figure out how they can tell ahead of time whether what they do will be rewarded or punished, accepted or rejected, encouraged or zapped. They figure they can avoid a lot of pain that way, and they are right. How people learn to anticipate what they ought to do or not do is the real goal of this sorting-out process. Therefore, awareness of the event (the stimulus) that serves as a cue or signal of a certain behavior is an important part of learning complex skills.

For example, by getting constant feedback to their performance, airline pilots in flight simulators learn very fine discrimination—fine enough to land a jetliner in extremely bad weather before they ever have the actual experience or face a crash.

Although most people don't think of that kind of formal training as a way to learn how to deal with others, it is a good analogy. Mothers can teach stimulus discrimination so that their sons learn to see very subtle distinctions in the behavior of our fellow human beings, to "read" them.

How often, after you have gotten to know some people fairly well, have you been able to read their mood or decide something is wrong just by their tone of voice when they speak to you, or by the way they carry themselves, or even by their failing to behave in a certain manner. You have probably not thought of it this way, but you learned this by paying attention in the past to how they behaved *before* you learned something was wrong. Whenever that behavior occurred—perhaps they talked a bit less or didn't make eye contact or slumped in their chairs—you found out later that something was wrong. You, in effect, learned how to detect the existence of a problem by reading the cues.

Mothers are often able to distinguish a cry of pain from a cry of hunger or fussiness in their newborns. We call this a mother's "instinct." But actually she has *learned* to read the cues by paying attention to what kind of problem her baby had when she answered cries.

The Pac Man video game provides another useful analogy for SD and how it works. Becoming skillful at the game requires the player to anticipate the moves of critters chasing Pac Man and make continuous fine adjustments in response. Each move the player makes and each response of the game's figures serves as a signal that the next move is en route and helps the player anticipate and execute the next action. Skillful use of this sorting-out process also allows learning to take place without having to provide consequences all the time.

It should be apparent by now that we believe the ability to distinguish among events that serve as cues for behavior is not only extremely important but something that can be taught.

When a mother is skillful at it, she can in some measure shape the environment to her specifications. That makes learning efficient, convenient, and easier for everyone concerned.

Keep in mind that SD has two different values for mothers and sons. The first is as a technique—a powerful one—that mothers can use to guide and mold their children's behavior.

The second, and just as important, is as a process—a way of learning to approach problems and deal with the world. Mothers who understand the process will probably find it easier to tolerate some inconsistent and improper behavior. They will be more able to turn bad behavior into an opportunity for change. And mothers who make the process clear to sons as the latter grow older give them more than just behavioral guides; they give them a lifelong skill for getting along and getting ahead.

Therefore, when mothers want to teach sons about doing the right thing at the right time in the right place, to quickly see that what may be the right thing to do in one instance becomes the wrong thing to do in another, that there is a time to cry and a time to laugh, they should:
- Become sensitive to the many stimuli or cues in their sons' world that can shift consequences for them. And point them out. (Talk behavior!)
- Take advantage of and set up as many situations as possible in which to reinforce sons who pick up the right cues and make the right responses and to not reinforce

them when they pick up the wrong cues or make the wrong responses.

The failure to respond appropriately to important behavior in others can be a prime source of difficulty in boys' personal lives and relationships.

Sally is a flirt at school in the cafeteria and has been batting eyes at Joe for three weeks.

Joe flirts back and by Sally's response is encouraged to continue this behavior. It evolves into playful pinching, patting, hair ruffling, and tickling.

But Sally is suddenly "Miss Frigid" when Joe suggests on a date that they go somewhere and "make out."

Joe (anguishing): "Either I did something wrong to turn her off, or she's a real jerk I should never have asked out."

Neither, of course, may be the case. What for Sally is acceptable boy-girl behavior in the safety of the school cafeteria is not acceptable in the back seat of his '74 Ford.

Perhaps she just had a bad day and is tired, anxious, or depressed. A batted eye and wiggled hip may mean far more— or less—to Joe than it does to someone else.

Joe can save himself a lot of grief if he pays attention to the many possible signals of Sally's "inconsistent" behavior.

The fact that Sally behaves in different ways with different people under different circumstances is one way of describing mature behavior. Joe clearly needs some skills for discriminating among Sally's "signals."

Mother can both ease Joe's immediate predicament and raise his sensitivity to behavioral cues and clues by careful statements and questions.

She can ask Joe what happened just before Sally flirted with him, as well as what happened afterward. Did she flirt with other boys too? Or just with him? She can suggest that in the cafeteria Sally has an audience that gives her security and makes it "safe" for her to flirt. She can suggest that he pay attention to how she behaves with other friends, to her interests and activities with others, and to anything he might have said or done that triggered her behavior during their date.

Mother might remind Joe of specific times when his actions did not accurately reflect what he wanted to do or thought he ought to do; when he clearly missed, deliberately or inadvertently, signals she gave him to do something—and of times when she missed his.

Finally, mother can point out that Sally's behavior, both in the cafeteria and in the car, might have been acceptable to her as a popular girl on a heavy date, but would probably change again in her roles as a daughter, a granddaughter, a Girl Scout, or a serious scholar.

The final goal for mothers who want to use SD is not to put out behavioral fires and "fix" immediate problems (although that can and will happen) but to make sons so aware of the idea that they will begin to fix problems themselves, to anticipate behavior by reading others' signals, and eventually to guide others' behavior by adapting their own actions to what's happening.

For example, Donny, seventeen, used SD and other behavioral skills to complete a project that was very important to him without provoking a social crisis.

Donny and two friends, Sam and Jack, wrote, produced, and directed a fifteen-minute film for high school follies. Toward the end of the editing process, with some serious raw edges still to be smoothed, nerves were frayed, tempers short-wired, and time running out. Jack, the cameraman and editor, was ready to "go with what we've got and forget it." Sam wanted the refinements but had very little time to spend on them.

Donny: I saw this coming. Jack doesn't want to spend anymore time and he's getting really ticked because I want to keep changing things.

Mom: How do you know he won't make the changes?

Donny: He's awfully quiet and the past two days hasn't called or had lunch with me and Sam.

Mom: He has finals this week, too, doesn't he?

Donny: We all do. But I know he's got problems in one or two classes.

Mom: How *few* of the changes you want to make can you live with?

Donny: There are three or four we really need. And one scene needs reshooting. I guess if I give up a couple of changes, Jack might go along with those. Maybe I can get Sam to help out in that case, too, since his time is limited. I think he's trying to be the peacemaker between me and Jack. One thing is sure, this film isn't worth breaking up a friendship.

Donny (on telephone to Jack): "Listen, I know you're up against it and ticked at all the changes. You're right. I could have planned some of the shots better to avoid so many changes. I'm running out of time, too. I know you care as much about the project as I do. If we just reshoot the one scene and dub in new dialogue in the other scenes, could we all be satisfied with that? We could do it Sunday afternoon and promise to spend no more than two hours."

Sam agreed two more hours was tolerable. A still reluctant Jack, faced with Sam and Donny's reasonable compromise, agreed to reshoot the one scene and hand over the final editing to Donny. Everybody won.

SD is most effectively taught when mothers find two kinds of occasions to demonstrate it. One (the easiest) is when the event they want sons to pay attention to is *present* to be reinforced. The second (harder to remember to do) is when there are clear occasions when the event or stimulus is *not present*. It's the contrast that makes the lesson more effective.

As we noted earlier, if you want to teach the color red, it helps to have other colors for contrast so that a child can learn not only what red is, but see it in contrast to, say, green, yellow, and orange—i.e., what red is *not*.

For instance, this approach can be put to work in a situation involving preschoolers and the telephone. Kid-phone combinations offer many opportunities for mischief. You know that if you have ever had three extensions on two floors left off the hook two or three times on a busy day. Playing with telephones is irksome at the very least. With a few SD moves, mothers can often preempt the mischief. It's all a matter of setting up conditions in which mom helps her son identify the right time—and the wrong time—to pick up the phone.

Mom (after the phone rings): "Billy, the phone is ringing. Do you hear the bell? When it rings it means you can pick up the handle and someone on the line will talk to you." (Do this often for a few days and, of course, find ways to reinforce the right behavior.)

Mom (when the phone is *not* ringing): "No Billy, you do not pick up the phone when it is not ringing. No one is on the line to talk to you. There is only someone on the line after the phone rings." (Likewise, repeat this message.)

Similar SD mini-programs can also be used to help small children learn such telephone skills as answering politely, not giving out potentially dangerous information (for example, telling an unknown caller that he—or the two of you—are alone in the house), calling you promptly to the phone, and so on.

Among grade school children, especially, there are many situations when SD techniques are helpful to mothers. Among them:

- To establish a mutually convenient "right time" for certain important activities such as discussing family rules, talking over problems, or settling arguments.

Too often, children learn to "tune out" a busy mother's numerous verbal requests because they find that frequently the requests are for relatively unimportant things that have little consequence either for them or for mom. The following comment from Leslie explains the value of using SD instead of simply a program of, say, reinforcers. Leslie is not only focusing her son's attention on the behavior she wants from Danny. She is also drawing Danny's attention to something *she* is doing: setting up a sort of universal signal that her son can quickly and clearly understand.

The signal not only tells him she wants his attention, but that she wants it for something truly important. Danny is learning that certain of mother's verbal demands, even if said in the same tone of voice as others, hold more importance.

Leslie: "When I have something really important to talk over with Danny (age six), I always wait until we are at home. I'll call him, usually to the kitchen, and hold his hands and get fairly close to him if he is distracted. I don't raise my voice, but I use more 'insistent' kinds of words or actions. I am very careful not to do this unless the issue I want to discuss is critical."

Discussing rules for behaving might best take place during a specified hour or two on the weekend rather than every time a problem develops.

The least effective time for either mother or son to dispute a point is in the middle of a busy day for her or when he has finally settled into a serious game of basketball on Saturday afternoon.

By setting up a family conference time—Saturday morning, for example—the conference becomes the stimulus, the trigger for bringing up matters for mother-son negotiation. Establishing a regular conference time also helps mother and sons distinguish between problems that can wait, and those that need instant attention and a quick compromise. This use of SD techniques will be especially important to mothers and sons negotiating the contracts described in the next chapter.

- To deal with unfamiliar and potentially hazardous events and uncertain (for the son) consequences.

A single mother will often find she must let go of her sons earlier and in areas she feels less familiar with and comfortable about—especially those involving dating, sexuality, physical risk, leadership, career selection, alcohol and drug use, and family responsibility.

In most of these areas, boys are expected to behave somewhat differently from girls, at least by society at large. For example, boys may be allowed a substantial amount of rebellion and "oat sowing" not tolerated in girls.

Here is where mother's goals must be clear and where she must point out what is and what is not tolerated in a variety of situations.

If mothers are to use SD principles for any one thing, perhaps it should be to teach younger children how to avoid danger.

For example: staying out of the street. To make sure this important behavior is learned, mothers must do two things: provide consequences (surprise!) and help her son learn what streets are.

As obvious as this second point may seem at first glance, it is not so for little children. Kids are not born into the world "streetwise." Especially if they live in a big city where heavy traffic threatens their lives and limbs, they must very quickly learn to sort out streets from sidewalks and driveways, and, as they get a bit older, to differentiate between streets they can and cannot safely cross.

In almost every case where street behavior came up in our interviews with mothers, we heard tales of tears and smacks and days or weeks of dragging Johnny out of the center lane.

A behavioral parent might say, after reading the previous chapters, that whenever she sees Ronnie step into a street, she will provide a punishing consequence to reduce the likelihood that he'll ever step into it again. She might also point out where the boundary is for the street. In the same way, our behavioral parent would reward her son if she sees him stop at a curb or avoid going near the street.

But why wait until these situations present themselves and go through the tedious, occasionally risky, and sometimes painful process of waiting for the chance to apply consequences?

A wiser behavioral parent could use SD for a far easier go, by recruiting a familiar game beloved by little kids: "Let's pretend."

Avoiding danger is not a lesson that has to be learned—or taught—the hard way. It can even be fun.

After a little planning, mother can set aside an hour or so on two or three days to teach the child about street behavior.

Mom (standing in front of the house): "Ronnie, let's pretend that I am not really here with you and you are here outside in front of our house by yourself. And let's pretend that your ball goes out in the street and there is Mrs. Jones (his baby sitter) on the other side of the street watching. Tell Mommie, what would you do?"

If Ronnie says he would run and get the ball, Mom can firmly and clearly disapprove. If Ronnie says he would run to the house to find her, he would get approval and a hug. If he says he would call out to Mrs. Jones to bring him the ball, he would also get hugs, kisses, and maybe a treat.

Mom should repeat the game a number of times, slightly varying the conditions and reinforcing Ronnie's recognition of the cues (the SD) and his behavior.

If possible, she might choose a quiet street with no traffic and have Ronnie not only tell her what he is going to do in each case, but show her as well.

By providing time for this important lesson, the experience will almost certainly be positive and pleasant for Ronnie, and one he is likely to remember. Mom will have some assurance that her son is able to control his impulse to run into the street in any number of situations.

This won't absolutely ensure Ronnie won't ever run into the street, but it will do a lot to help him avoid danger.

Single mothers may recognize a distinct lack of SD know-how among sons who stay with dad for visits and with them the rest of the time. Behavior that dad allows, mom doesn't, and junior seems to make the most—or worst—of it. Jumping on the beds is okay at dad's. At mom's it gets punished, but she has to punish it after every visit to dad's for months on end. She wants him to understand that different things happen in different households; that different adults have different rules for children. Two homes, similar behavior, but far different consequences for the same behavior. Sons need to discriminate and anticipate an often vast number of such consequences.

In the coming-back-from-dad's situation, mothers often engage in frustrating episodes of reminding-nagging for days after the homecoming. "Don't eat with your fingers," "Don't yell down the stairwell," "Don't jump on the bed." Previous chapters have outlined the stress and futility of this approach to teaching and learning.

A better approach is to use some element of your son's homecoming as a stimulus for helping him shift a whole constellation of behaviors from "dad's" to "mom's."

One mother of a four-year-old devised a brief "coming home" game (it involved his jumping across the threshold of the front door without touching it, coupled with a "Welcome to mom's house" message from her.) If it became necessary, she would remind him that her rules were now in force with a simple phrase such as "Mom's house!" or "You jumped over!"

The message helped reinforce his own skill at discriminating between behavior that was and was not allowed at mom's. Shortly after this mother began her weekly homecoming game, she noticed that her son began asking permission to do some things at home—or elsewhere—with the question, "Is this for mom's house?"

Bingo.

There are other situations in which mothers can help older sons use SD to avoid danger. As sons enter junior and senior high school, for example, there are certain groups of kids mothers want sons to avoid because they are both bad models and likely to pressure him into dangerous or even criminal activities.

By recognizing these situations as occasions for using SD, mothers can increase their chances of successfully teaching their sons how to avoid these groups. They might identify the groups, discuss the problems they are likely to get into if they hang around with them, and help their sons work on socially acceptable ways of saying "no" to such kids without appearing like a "wimp" or a "nerd."

Tony: It's easy for you to say I can't drive home with a

friend who's been drinking at a party. But I can't call my mother to pick me up. I'd be the laughingstock of the school.

Mom: If you think that might happen, then you be sure to drink nothing yourself, take the keys, and drive the car home. He can spend the night here. By the way, you might tell your friend that you're a lot of things to a lot of people, but not a damned fool for anyone. He'll respect that. Don't let him intimidate you.

A little later in their young manhood, sons also need to distinguish quickly and accurately such things as which bars, discos, and saloons they should avoid. As one son, a college student, told us: "By the time you get inside, order your drink, and stick your hand in the popcorn, it may be too late to realize you're in a leather bar or a neighborhood joint whose regulars have a real problem with guys from the local university. That could be dangerous."

Finally, SD techniques are extraordinarily useful for teaching sons to deal with distractions and to concentrate on the job at hand. Initially, mothers can set aside specific times and places during which certain jobs—and only those jobs—are done. Approaching such times and places provides a potent cue that becomes highly reinforced when the product is good or the job completed brings a good grade or other mark of success.

There are emotional consequences to all this. But in this book, remember, we are talking *behavior*, not *feelings*. It is difficult to be sensitive to feelings when your son is swinging from the chandeliers an hour after his weekend with dad.

Getting emotional or talking about emotions will not get Johnny to stop being upset for two days after he comes home from dad's house and is punished for jumping on the bed at mom's. Kids will only have problems if they can't make the discrimination. They can walk and chew gum at the same time if the cues are clear and consistent.

Making It All Work: The Mother-Son Contract

Jared: I was born much too late.
Joann: Too late for what?
Jared: To start living my own life at an age when I still have the energy and strength to do it!
Joann: Explain, please.
Jared: Like in the pioneer days of the old West or in medieval times. Boys my age (fourteen) were already earning their way. Some were even married. And they sure didn't live with their mothers telling them what to do all the time.

Joann can't vouch for what the lives of fourteen-year-old cowboys or knights-in-training were like, but there is no question that the appeal of independent activity grows apace with hairy upper lips and testosterone levels.

Theoretically, of course, as boys grow up, they no longer *have* to do anything any adult tells them to do—especially females and especially mothers. Coercion, nagging, hitting, yelling, demanding, and other unpleasant means of forcing compliance will work to an extent with young boys, but as sons grow bigger, stronger, and more independent, the only truly effective means of influencing what they do is through a system that uses positive means that are mutually rewarding.

Teenage sons usually outweigh their mothers and often have developed enough basic skills to escape death from starvation and exposure if they were in fact to realize their fantasies about independent living. Firm ground rules are needed.

Boys growing up in single female parent homes are especially eager to be free of "female" edicts and what they may see as feminizing, "overprotective" influences.

Society, too, contributes its share to male discontent and distrust of mothers by encouraging males to free themselves from "apron strings" and predicting dire consequences for male victims of prolonged mothering.

There are, however, two kinds of freedom. The easy one is freedom from restrictions. Most sons will achieve that kind of freedom from their mothers in the natural course of things.

The tougher freedom to attain is the freedom *to* do things; to make choices, recognize opportunities, keep options open, and live a rewarding and responsible life. In short, to be self-confident, to manage their own lives, to be able to plan ahead, anticipate the needs of others, put others' needs ahead of their own, and delay gratification for themselves when necessary in order to meet more important obligations.

To grow up this way, however, sons must give up some independence and learn about cooperation and compromise.

For mothers, helping sons to achieve that kind of growth offers some of the biggest challenges and some of the best opportunities for teaching negotiating skills.

A technique for accomplishing these things is for both mothers and sons to draw up or agree to contracts. The mother-son contract uses all that we have been telling you about behavioral parenting—most notably talking behavior, basic due, traffic lights, stimulus discrimination, modeling, rules and consequences, and token economies—to negotiate and maintain a wide variety of activities.

The process will, like the other principles of behavioral parenting outlined in earlier chapters, make the lives of mothers and sons easier, and make sons more amenable to the lessons and values mothers want them to learn and share.

And contracts do something else. They introduce techniques for dealing with important decisions in sons' lives, techniques that are used in mature adult society rather than in the closed, protected, "parent-child" "superior-inferior," "boss-underling" structure of the family. The whole technique is a model in and of itself for what adults, in the best sense of the word, do in the real world.

Contracts encourage sons to become more involved in managing their lives, setting goals, finding good models and reinforcing influences, imposing the consequences, and learning from experience.

Thus, contracts are useful in two ways. One, to help sons solve existing behavior problems and resolve thorny issues between them and their mothers, including drinking, smoking, lying, stealing, not doing homework, yelling, hitting, shyness, poor money management, failure to do chores, and the like. Two, they provide a foundation for succeeding in the outside world, away from mom and her parental authority.

The contract, designed by both, gives mother most of what she wants as a parent (a son moving toward a responsible, goal-oriented, sensitive, and tolerant life) and son some of what he wants (mobility, independence, and a chance to grow).

Contracting is a technique that, ideally, teaches self-control and self-management through negotiation, tradeoff, compromise, and standard-setting between sons and mothers and sons and others.

In terms of the process, contract setting is no different from any of the other principles we've discussed here. Everything else still applies, such as the need for specifying precise goals, as well as selecting and consistently applying consequences.

The difference is that here we are adapting the principles to a person in transition from boyhood to manhood, one who is experienced in rule following, talking behavior, consequences, modeling, shifting consequences, and delayed reinforcers.

These are merely prerequisite skills for preparing contracts. Whether a son is eight or eighteen, he needs to have been both the object and subject of behavioral parenting.

For most mothers and sons, this will not be a problem. As we've pointed out, a great deal of behavioral parenting is almost intuitive, such as instruction giving and modeling. But it is necessary to recognize the process, label it (talk behavior), and use it consistently in order to provide the history sons and mothers need to set up more sophisticated contracts.

It's important to say here that not all agreements between mothers and sons need to be written, but they still fall within the definition of a contract. What's critical is not always what is written on paper (although in some cases, that's going to be necessary, as well as easier). What's important is the approach—negotiation, compromise, and agreement—to solving problems.

Mothers should keep in mind that no issue or objective or problem is too trivial to make the subject of a contract if it is important in her family. She shouldn't be afraid to set her own goals. Mother-son wars are often fought over issues that seem unimportant to others. In behavioral parenting, we place a value on things because of their function, what they *do* for mothers and sons, not necessarily their content or meaning in some larger and vague sense. If something creates a problem, then by definition it can be approached and solved with behavioral methods.

In many ways, then, contracting is nothing more than mothers have done before; it just recognizes new developmental stages in sons as well as more elaborate behavioral skills and repertoires. It builds on all of these and it plugs into the fact that a lot of consequences are now out of reach of mothers. Contracts are now the best tool with which to direct behavior because they are more appropriate to where a son is and to where mothers need to be.

More specifically contracts do four things that are extremely helpful in the mother-son family. First, they avoid the "That's unfair" or the "That's your rule, but what do I get out of this" syndrome. Contracts involve mothers *and* sons in agreement on goals and procedures, and everyone knows in advance how much something is going to cost in time, energy, and even money. Therefore, contracts discourage blaming others for problems and encourage responsibility.

Second, because contracts spell out very specific objectives, they serve as a check on how far the contractees have come and how far they have to go.

Third, a written contract with signatures becomes a powerful encouragement to carry it out because, in our society, signatures signal a strong commitment. A contract is also open to very little after-the-fact misinterpretation. In developing a contract, mothers and sons learn to pay very close attention to each other's values and behavior, and to provide incentives for each other's responsibilities.

Fourth, good contracts increase freedom for sons.

Beth: "Ian and I have a contract about chores. The kids clear the table and set it. Ian has a lot of responsibility taking care of Lisa. He is paid for that, but half of his pay must go automatically into savings. He can do whatever he wants with the rest. It's his money to manage."

Mark, seventeen, and his mother have a contract which states that he may visit friends after school, but he must be home by six o'clock. Although this contract clause puts limits on his freedom to visit friends (he can't after six o'clock), it also gives him freedom to visit friends if he chooses. Without this contract, any visits to friends he makes might meet with mixed reactions from mom.

For instance, if he did not have to be home at six, he might come in at seven one night to a mother angry that he missed her supper; another night, late arrival might be met with indifference or relief when mom had to work late unexpectedly and never fixed dinner at all. Such responses are ineffective at best in teaching family responsibility or encouraging independent actions.

Before you set up mother-son contracts, here are some facts to guide you:

- Very simply, a contract is a clear statement of which behaviors will produce which payoffs and who will deliver those payoffs.
- The best contracts are struck when there is good communication on both sides. But even when contracts are hard won, they are effective when calm deliberation and clear language break down, as sometimes happens with older teenagers. Good contracts are unemotional, objective, and never nag or criticize.

"I can't understand it. I can't even talk to him. How can there be anything rewarding about taking drugs? I've threatened, warned, told horror stories, punished, and nothing seems to work," one mother complains.

How can contracting help?

By establishing a schedule of checks on the activities that encourage drug use.

Immediately, stop trying to read your son's mind. Read his behavior instead. Remember, sons learn to take drugs just as they learn to do anything else, and behavioral parenting is the way to help them "unlearn" or substitute better lessons for undesirable behaviors.

Successful contracts depend on the availability of consequences that make it worthwhile for sons to do what mothers desire and punishing to do what others oppose.

There are lots of incentives to take drugs if you think about it: attention from a group of people (other drug users) who are viewed as important, challenging, brave, and sophisticated; the promise of triumph over difficult situations that most people avoid (nausea, theft, danger, getting away with illegal activities); a sense of control over one's destiny ("I, not you, decide what's best for me"), not to mention the "high" or the freedom from anxiety, albeit temporary; and welcome into a whole "society" that gives approval.

It is necessary to understand how drug use—and abuse—

develops and what reinforces it, in order to prevent or reverse it before it has gone too far.

Mothers can, for example, apply a contract that involves meeting drug-free peer groups; that encourages physical fitness; that gives sons a chance to take control and behave independently in more socially acceptable ways; that helps find other means of relieving boredom and that points out ways for sons to recognize what circumstances signal the desire to take drugs.

If sons use marijuana or alcohol to lose inhibitions and anxiety, assertiveness training may be a major step in eliminating drug use. Helping sons develop skills for dating and making or keeping friends can help to reduce the need to "assert" oneself with chemical help.

With contracts, mothers can set up schedules for overseeing their sons' whereabouts. They can require check-in times and provide rewards only for situations and activities that avoid drug use.

• The best contracts go easy on responsibilities.

Mothers often tend to overload their teenage sons at just the time when teenagers have many outside responsibilities—school, jobs, peers, athletics, concern about future careers, and so on. "I don't know how he keeps up with all the demands on him," was a common wail from mothers when they finally sat down and made a list of their sons' required activities.

Joann recalls Adam's schedule during second semester of his junior year in high school: up at six-fifteen to make school by seven-forty. Classes until two-thirty included chemistry, English, trigonometry, Spanish, American history, and journalism; stayed after school until five-thirty, five days a week for varsity track; homework averaging three hours per night, not including term papers, studying for finals, and extra time spent on school paper for journalism class; career counseling in preparation for higher education plans on Saturday together with household chores, errands, and car care.

In between were occasional part-time jobs and visits with his father.

Jared's schedule, for second semester of ninth grade, was not much better: same school schedule, with courses including biology, English, Spanish, algebra, social studies, and choir. Jayvee track followed after school. In addition to homework, term papers, and finals, he was completing preconfirmation classes on Sunday and was a paid member of a rock group that played dances on weekends and required all-day rehearsals many Saturdays. Chores, errands, visits with his father, trips to the orthodontist were accomplished evenings and in between.

These are not unusual and mothers need to remind themselves that sons need "down" time just as much as they do, and in some cases, more.

- You can't have every end tucked in. The best contracts are those that have real significance for both mothers and sons.

Estelle: "Their rooms are their territory and if they look like pigpens, I turn the other way. They usually eventually take care of it. One night I went into Jonathan's room to answer the phone and almost broke my neck. In a fit of anger, I took everything that was on his floor and piled it on his bed. He came in at one A.M. and came into my room to ask where he could sleep. I told him on his bed or his floor, it was his choice. Eventually, he cleaned it up."

- The best contracts allow for some slips and have penalties that fit the crime. Don't fall into overkill or it will backfire:

Mother (listing terms of an inappropriate contract): Remember, if you are even two minutes late for curfew you will be grounded for a month.

Son (faced with growing roots in his room, thinks to himself): I'm bound to mess up once in a while so I'll break the curfew and stay out as late as I can. Might as well be hanged for a wolf as a sheep.

A better contract stipulates that if son gets home ten minutes late, he has to be in ten minutes early the next day. If he is late again the next day, the penalty doubles or triples. On the other hand, if he comes in on time for a whole week, he gets an extra half hour on Saturday night, an extra dollar in his allowance, or the privilege of throwing a party.

A single mother with three sons: "I praise them a lot. Punishment for not sticking to agreed-upon chores includes grounding and taking away the television or telephone. I put the phone or TV in the trunk of my car for a week, for example. I stick to it, but I try not to make the punishments punish me too much.

"Usually when I set down rules or assign jobs, they argue, they *'hondle'*. That's a Jewish expression that means wheedling. We usually compromise a little and it's kinda fun."

- Contracts are very economical. Mothers can save a lot of time and energy. Instead of figuring out what consequences work best by trial and error, they can ask and specify in the contract, a whole bunch of payoffs given prior approval by the payees—their sons.
- Contracts help avoid the pitfalls of satiation. Because multiple payoffs can be applied on a sliding scale that rewards every step in a mutually acceptable behavior, contracts avert the problem of applying consequences that may have lost their punch, or those that miss the mark because sons have developed in ways that require a whole different set of consequences and incentives.
- Contracts remind, in fact insist that mothers behave as adults, too.

That is one of the reasons teenagers often find contracts especially appealing: they acknowledge parity, equity, and emerging adulthood. Willingness to use contracts is a signal that mother recognizes the need to shift from an "I'll tell you what to do" mode to an "I'll work it out with you" mode with her son.

Mothers don't necessarily see this as an advantage because it makes explicit the process of toning down their expectations to more realistic levels. The process of negotiation not only makes mother's demands and expectations subject to modification, but also may point up where she has failed to spend adequate time and energy in her parenting.

But the behavioral parent will see that drawing up a contract is fair. For one thing, it makes intervention by a third person, such as outside authority figures (teachers, counselors, peers, fathers, siblings) less necessary. A five-year-old can't always point out his own needs for better parenting. But an adolescent in a contract situation can and often will do just that.

Adam: As long as we're on the subject of how we spend our time at home (the subject of the contract was television viewing schedules), you always seem too preoccupied with work to do anything with us.

Joann: You mean like watching a TV show, or something more substantial?

Adam: How about jogging with us or going downtown with us to a play or playing Monopoly or Scrabble—things that take some time. And not talking on the phone in between!

Adam's comments brought Joann up short. She learned a lot in that discussion about what consequences and incentives were meaningful for Adam and Jared: more time in family-style activities. She had assumed that they had outgrown those consequences, when in fact she had put them aside for more selfish reasons. They took up too much of her time.

Sons will always try to modify parental behavior, and negotiating contracts formalizes the process, gives a son permission, in effect, to modify his mother's behavior.

Understandably, mothers often balk at this, but it's fair to point out that mothers can be selfish or unreasonable in their demands, just as their sons can be. The need is there for both parties to modify and compromise as sons grow up.

- Contracts are a positive force. Mothers ought to look forward to the times when contracts are drawn up or reviewed. When the force is with you, it's heaven.
- The very process of drawing up contracts improves behavior in and of itself because it focuses attention on the behavior and thus is a consequence itself for the behavior. The contract becomes a stimulus ("Hi there, we are noting your behavior") and it formalizes the signals as well as the consequences.

Now that you have some facts, the following guidelines will help both mothers and sons avoid problems when they begin the process of negotiation:

- Don't renegotiate too frequently or on the run. Make appropriate renegotiation times part of the contract.

Mother usually wants to renegotiate at random when it suits her or when she forgets to include something. That's not only unfair, but it also negates the process. Better to let some things go. "A deal's a deal" cuts both ways. If she wants son to take the contracts seriously, she has to obey the same rules at least most of the time. There will of course always be emergencies when she will have to break the contract or force rapid renegotiation. But these times are—and should be—rare.

- Behaviors best suited to contracts are all of those that can be clearly spelled out in objective terms and checked afterward.

With older sons, especially, there are a lot of behaviors

that can't be watched. But their impact can be seen. If the garbage must be taken out every Thursday at eight o'clock and mom is home to make sure it is done and she wants to keep doing that, there is no need for a contract. If, on the other hand, she is not around to see to garbage toting or other behavior or rules her son must follow, contracts are the way to provide remote consequences, both positive and negative.

- Keep in mind that contracts are not made, primarily, because off the *kind* of behavior that must be dealt with, but because the consequences, the reinforcements, shift so fast with older sons.

Also, the amount of time she has access to her son has changed, and she is no longer going to be able to eyeball everything.

With older sons, there are a lot of behaviors mother can't observe or monitor. All she can do is see the impact.

- Basically, both mothers and teen sons should suggest behaviors and consequences, including those that involve issues or events outside the home.

Examples: relationships with friends and relatives and getting good grades.

John, fifteen, had poor study habits. He played Kiss tapes, watched television, and ate while doing homework.

He clearly needed help with stimulus sorting—choosing to do the right thing at the right time in the right place.

A contract in this situation might include establishing distraction-free areas of the house as the only places permitted for homework; designation of certain times when no interruptions are allowed from mother, phones, or anyone; imposition of a gradually increased study schedule; practice in the use of better study techniques, including "skimming" and outlining; and payoffs in the form of cash or privileges for taking better notes and performing well on tests.

Specifically, John had failing grades in physics. His contract with his mother had the cooperation of teachers and school officials.

First, John agreed to go to the library each day and leave all books except his physics text in his locker or someplace other than the library. He was to choose a special area of the library and could not study anywhere else. (This is stimulus discrimination, in which the place to study is not the place to talk, write letters, flirt, eat, daydream, etc.). To keep daydreaming in check, John was told that if he became distracted or lost interest in his work, he was to read or study only one more page and then immediately leave the library for a break, even if he regained his interest or wanted to stick with it. Behaviorally, this break gave John a positive option to stop studying. Stopping became an approved behavior, rather than an instant signal or reminder that he had "failed again" to be responsible about his studies.

Two weeks later, John was told to increase the number of pages to be studied before a break to two, but at no time could he study physics more than one hour day, even if he began to want to do more.

John's teacher's response to his work became more positive and his quiz grades improved. As a result, he was allowed to take control and it was made clear that the decision to go a full hour, or not, was his.

His contract called for him to keep a chart of his study habits and review them with his mother each evening. In the fourth week of his contract, he was permitted an additional thirty minutes—again at his option—to study physics, which he used to study for a big test.

For every fifteen minutes beyond one hour he studied physics, he received a thirty-minute extension of his weekend curfew or one dollar on his allowance, as he wished. These rewards were not contingent on getting higher grades, but on improving his study habits.

John's improved study habits inevitably led to better grades, which in turn provided a good model for maintaining the better study habits in other subjects.

The contract between John and his mother further called for a ski trip if, at the end of the semester, he had completed all assignments in physics and maintained a C or better average.

- *Always* put the contract in writing. It serves not only to check memory and details, but in itself acts as a signal or reminder for keeping it.
- Both should have the option to bring in a third person or arbitrator if negotiations break off or bog down. This person could be a teacher, neighbor, friend, counselor. Even an ex-spouse will do.

Many of the single mothers we interviewed brought the sons' fathers into the process, informally, by asking them to confirm demands the mothers felt were reasonable or oppose ones she felt were unreasonable. Sons may seek the same support for their position. The perspective of a third person will sometimes help a negotiation over a rough spot or suggest an option neither mother nor son had considered.

Joann recalls one heated contract session with Adam and Jared over doing homework. She felt it was best to do the homework right after school, because evenings became crowded with dinner and other activities such as television. Adam and Jared wanted to do it after supper and in between television shows or other activities.

Their father, recruited as arbitrator when he arrived to pick them up for dinner, suggested *no* television on school nights. That got the negotiations restarted and gave Joann's suggestion more appeal.

In the end, the contract was struck for homework when they chose, but no television until it was all completed. That gave Adam and Jared the option of doing it right after school if there was a show they especially wanted to see later, or doing it after dinner if they wanted the playtime after school.

Again, this kind of process has always existed, but contracting formalizes the process. It's usually appealing to kids because it holds out the potential for more control of mothers' behavior.

- Be fair. Don't use trick clauses in your contracts or load the dice with a precoached arbitrator. Contracts mean that both parties come away relatively satisfied and both parties risk penalties for breaking the contract. Although mothers will often be a little more "equal" in terms of power when negotiations begin, they need to temper it and agree not to use it unfairly.
- Don't abort a contract too fast, even if it seems to be falling apart. Sometimes when a contract doesn't seem to work, it means it is working all too well; that is, sons are beginning to experience consequences spelled out in the contract. Or it may mean that some fine tuning and consistency are all that's needed to keep it on track.

Estelle (mother of three boys): "When I started working full time, I had to do something to get the chores done. So I sat down with them and we listed all the jobs, such as emptying the trash, doing dishes, preparing meals, laundry, and cleaning. There were four of us, and I decided that each of us would take one week of doing the job, and we had a chart on the refrigerator. But it was always war about who didn't do his job. I would come home and find one of their girl friends cooking dinner or doing my laundry. It was trial and error. It didn't work very well.

"While we were fighting over who was to do the job and who didn't do it well, I could have done it myself ten times. When it came to laundry, they got all upset about it because they were older and each liked his laundry done a certain way.

"We renegotiated. Now everyone does his own laundry and ironing.

"The two middle ones decided to take a Cooking for Singles class. They love to cook and they cook for me. So now we've boiled it down to only two jobs we have to take turns with: the dishes and the trash. And I told them to alternate.

"At times in the beginning, it got really bad. The dishes were so cruddy you couldn't get into the kitchen, and the trash was all over the place. But since their allowances depended on getting it cleaned up, they came around."

Many boys have learned that if they violate a rule or an instruction to the limit of mom's patience, she will often give in and abandon it because the consequences for her are too punishing. There is also evidence that one way some children use to keep harder tasks from being imposed, is to make so many mistakes that mother or teacher will abandon the whole idea. In other words: "if you don't like what's going on here, mess up." So the message for mothers is "stick it out for a while." Things may initially go wrong and even get worse before they get better, but that may be a sign the contract is working, that son recognizes the consequences.

And always remember that consequences are not meant to change immediate behavior, but behavior in the future. If he doesn't take out the garbage today, applying the consequences may not change that; but it may well change it next Thursday.

- Multiple contracts can be in force, but it is helpful to start out with one for just a couple of behaviors or small things that are easy to do. Drawing up contracts is a lot of work, and an initial success is rewarding to all.
- If contracts should, at least initially, involve small or limited tasks and build to more complicated ones, so should the incentives or reinforcements. At first, they should be applied quickly, not too far down the line. Money and tokens that can be "spent" for privileges are often best.

- Contracts should reward the behavior that is achieved, not obedience to mother. The contract should say "if you do this you get that," not "if you do what I want you get a reward."
- Once the contract is signed and in force, no reminders or warnings should be used by mothers, even when the motive is to make sure sons don't break the contract and get in trouble. If sons break the contract, they must suffer the consequences or the contract is useless.
- Some "table" rules for negotiation should be set. Among them a time limit on statements and arguments (use a timer and set it for two or three minutes); no interrupting when it is the other's turn; a limit on the number of items to be negotiated at each contract session (one or two is enough); selection of the item by random draw or mutual agreement; a move to other topics only when the previous contract is established.

Now it is time to set up a contract following these steps:

STEP ONE: Make a clear statement of what behaviors are to be negotiated. Be as specific as possible about when, where, and under what circumstances they should or should not occur. If one is "no drinking" outside the home, does that include dinner at Dad's? Does it mean a beer is okay at Grandma's barbecue? If it specifies housework, does it mean the dishes have to be done immediately after dinner, or anytime before eleven P.M.? It's also best to state the goals in positive instead of negative terms: "Drinking beer is allowed at Dad's and Grandma's." Mother should take note of what she wants *more* of, not just what she wants to disappear.

STEP TWO: Clearly state what the consequences will be, how often, and who delivers them? Is this a token economy? Is allowance at stake or phone privileges or some more remote consequence such as a ski trip months from now? Remember, this is a contract, not martial law. Rewards and incentives must be identified for mothers and sons (what does he want, what can she give; what does mother want that son hasn't offered and vice versa).

Priorities must be set. It might be wonderful to have a son who gets straight A's, never misses a curfew, and is polite enough to impress Miss Manners. On the other hand, the practical limits of time and energy probably mean choosing to work on one or two items or trimming the objectives, a 15-minute leeway on curfews, and not grunting at his grandparents, for instance. Yes, it would be nice to have son fold his towel when he hangs it up in the bathroom or keep his bedroom neat. But getting the towels and clothes off the floor might be enough.

Is the behavior mother wants in the contract likely to create resentment? Is it too hard for the son? Is he willing to bargain and do it for a bigger reward even if he doesn't like the idea? What rewards does he really want?—not entering his room or going through his papers? giving him a private phone time? not reminding him about his homework?

Jared: I wish you would stop asking me whether I've done my homework. It really is annoying.

Joann: You think that it is a back-handed criticism.

Jared: Yes. It tells me you don't trust me. I really hate when you do that.

Joann: Okay, how's this. You show me your finished papers at the end of the evening and I won't ask the question anymore.

Jared: No, that's the same thing. You still don't trust me to take responsibility for my own homework.

Joann: I think it's important for me to know how you are progressing in school. Keeping an eye on homework is a good way.

Jared: The bottom line is not getting reports from school that I'm not doing my homework.

Joann: But they come only every eight weeks.

Jared: If after the first marking period there is any indication on my report card that I haven't done homework, I'll bring you my work each evening to let you see it.

Joann: And in the meantime, I'm not to ask you about your homework?

Jared: Right.

Joann: Okay.

Incentives for mothers can include help with chores, less talking back and arguing, improved grades.

It helps to play at walking in each other's moccasins when identifying incentives.

Jared: How would you like it if I always asked you whether you were making dinner on time?

Joann: I wouldn't.

Jared: See?

STEP THREE: Check for potential weaknesses or problems in the contract. Are there likely to be exceptions mother can or can't live with? Can sons (or mothers) short-circuit the contract by just opting out ("So what if I don't go on the ski trip? So what if I can't get away that weekend, we'll do it another time.") There should be provisions for troubleshooting and renegotiation.

Tim: You know, I earned eight hundred dollars this summer and I have decided I want to buy a used car with it.

Mom: What you need more is clothes for school.

Tim: Don't you want me to have a car?

Mom: The real issue is that I want you to have a sense of priorities and responsibility. What are our options for compromising?

Tim: What if I spend one hundred dollars on clothes and the rest on a car?

Mom: A seven-hundred-dollar car or an eight-hundred-dollar car might not be a good purchase in terms of safety and efficiency. You might have to spend a lot for repairs. How about if you spend two hundred dollars on clothes, put the rest in the bank toward a better car next summer, and we worked out a better deal for you to get regular use of my car on weekends?

Tim: Well, maybe I could get a part-time job and save up for a better car sooner than next summer.

Mom: I think that's a great idea.

STEP FOUR: Set up some bonus and milder penalty clauses for doing more than is required or just slightly less than required.

STEP FIVE: Decline to compromise on an issue you oppose ethically or morally even if you think it is one a mother "ought" to approve. You may become so uncomfortable with the consequences that you might jeopardize the contract at hand and future contracts as well. Mothers who unilaterally abort a contract in a fit of pique or upset have a tougher time setting up another.

A psychologist with two sons, sixteen and ten, states: "I do a good amount of sex therapy in my practice and the issue of sexuality is one I am therefore personally very comfortable with. My older son, who is getting ready for college, has had girls in his room. When he had his first serious girl friend, and they went together for over a year, they were allowed in his room with the door closed. We agreed he was entitled to his privacy just as I was entitled to mine.

"But I'm probably at an extreme in the population, since I am very comfortable with sexuality, in adults and kids."

Not all single mothers with sons will want to take this approach to sexual behavior. Some will feel much too opposed, for ethical or moral reasons, to be able to carry it off, and in that case, probably should not try without giving their own feelings a lot of thought and attention.

STEP SIX: Set up a time for review of progress and/or renegotiation.

STEP SEVEN: Get signatures and dates and have copies distributed or posted.

Here are two examples of contracts between mothers and sons, one between Mona and Doug, a high-school graduate still living at home, and the other between Jan and her son, David, twelve.

Doug and Mona

Events leading up to the contract were unpleasant at best. Every discussion about chores ended in a screaming argument. Mona said her son never listened and put off chores endlessly. Doug said his mother wanted everything done "this minute" and never understood "how hard it is for me to find time for things."

This mother and son constantly interrupted one another and their conversations had deteriorated to accusations, put-downs, and charges of irresponsibility (from Mona) and brow-beating (from Doug).

At the suggestion of a counselor, they negotiated a contract.

Mona suggested two household chores that she believed Doug should do without question: cleaning up the kitchen within an hour after dinner—Monday through Friday—and cleaning his bathroom once a week.

Doug agreed these were reasonable.

Mona then wrote down what "cleaning up the kitchen and bathroom" meant to her. A clean kitchen was not simply dishes in the dishwasher and pots in the drainer. It meant pots dried and put away, counter wiped and polished, and the floor swept. A clean bathroom meant clean fixtures, and also clean towels and an unspotted mirror.

A chart was drawn up listing all of the requirements and the definitions of clean with places for a checkoff each day for the kitchen and each week for the bathroom.

Doug's allowance of eight dollars per week was contingent on his cleaning the kitchen and bathroom. He received one dollar per day to clean the kitchen for a possible maximum of five dollars, and three dollars for cleaning the bathroom. Doug was not happy with this, but eventually agreed after Mona said he would receive a bonus of one dollar a week if the kitchen chores were completed as agreed for a whole week, and another dollar if the bathroom was cleaned.

For her part, Mona agreed not to remind or nag Doug in any way. To do so was to forfeit a half hour of her television viewing time.

Each evening that Doug completed his kitchen chores, he was to note it on a chart posted on the refrigerator. Each week he completed the bathroom job, he did likewise. Each time he failed to complete the chore, Mona noted that action. Similarly, her behavior (reminding, nagging, or not reminding and nagging) was noted.

All of these items were spelled out in a page-long contract that was signed by Mona and Doug.

One clause noted that after one month, progress would be evaluated and adjustments or additions made to the contract.

Doug and Mona's Contract:

> This contract is entered into by Doug and his mother Mona.
> Doug agrees to clean the kitchen within an hour after dinner each evening, Monday through Friday. Doug will rinse and place dishes in the dishwasher, wash and put away the pots, wipe the counter, sweep the floor, and empty any garbage or trash.
> Each time Doug completes this job, he will check it off in the right place on the chart kept in the kitchen.
> Doug also agrees to clean his bathroom once a week. This includes cleaning the sink, toilet, and tub; washing the floor, cleaning the mirror, and rehanging clean towels.
> Doug will check this off on the chart when he finishes the job on the day of his choice each week.
> Mona agrees to stop all reminders or discussion of Doug's jobs. If Doug does not complete the jobs as contracted, she

will say nothing, but will write "incomplete" on the chart and explain what was not done or not done properly.

Mona also agrees to pay Doug $8 per week maximum allowance contingent on Doug's completion of his chores and to cut her television viewing time by one half hour each time she enters into any discussion with Doug about his kitchen or bathroom jobs for the length of his contract.

The $8 will be paid out in this fashion: $1 per day for each day the kitchen job is completed as agreed in the contract and $3 each week for cleaning the bathroom as agreed to in this contract. In addition, a bonus of $1 will be paid for a full five consecutive days of properly cleaning the kitchen and an additional bonus of $1 for properly cleaning the bathroom and kitchen as agreed.

Signed

Mona_____

Doug_____

Jan and David

Jan decided that David's angry outbursts with his friends and sailor-style cursing at home and school were the two behaviors she would concentrate on in her negotiations.

She had to abandon her desire to "lower the boom" in a vengeful manner and negotiate a contract that encouraged a fresh start for her and David.

The initial contract would give David a certain amount of points each day for not fighting and not swearing. The points would "purchase" privileges. Ten points (the maximum that could be earned daily) bought a ten o'clock bedtime and two hours of television after dinner and homework; eight points bought a nine-thirty bedtime and one hour of television; six points purchased a nine o'clock bedtime and a half hour of television; four points, a nine o'clock bedtime and no television; two points, a nine o'clock bedtime and no television on Saturday; and zero or minus points, a nine o'clock bedtime, no television on Saturday, and one dollar off his weekly four dollar allowance.

A final word: You don't keep kids on contracts forever. In fact two to three months is usually long enough. After that, successful contracts should evolve into a more cooperative and informal agreement about responsibilities and privileges.

CHAPTER TEN

Older Is Better: Sons on Their Own

> The very essence of motherly love is to care for the child's growth, and that means to want the child's separation from herself. . . . The mother must not only tolerate, she must wish and support the child's separation. It is only at this stage that motherly love becomes such a difficult task, that it requires . . . the ability to give everything and to want nothing but the happiness of the loved one.
>
> —ERICH FROMM

> My mother had a great deal of trouble with me, but I think she enjoyed it.
>
> —SAMUEL CLEMENS

Mothers of successful sons have been known to invest their happy status with a certain amount of mystique. They will, for example, smile and nod when someone suggests they are the kind of women who "have a knack" for rearing boys, that is, possessed of some inherent combination of Fromm's insights and Mrs. Clemens's reputed love of pain.

We now know better. Behavior—welcome or otherwise—is learned over time and in certain situations. When boys grow up to please mothers, it is because mothers have been successful in shaping sons' behavior in mutually satisfying ways. We believe *Raising Sons* can help mothers do that.

But then what?

Here is your grown son. What happens next? What will it be like—from your perspective—to mother him at twenty-five? At thirty? At fifty? How will he behave toward you?

Women can look around and find many men reared in traditional, two-parent families and judge their personal, social, and occupational behavior, but the incidence of grown sons reared in nontraditional families is still limited. What

177

kind of behavior can we expect of male offspring reared by savvy and self-confident single mothers?

In the same vein, what do mothers want and need from their grown sons? What do their sons want and need? What can single mothers, especially, expect and where and how will they fit into their adult sons' lives as both mothers and sons age?

What's going to happen to the mother-son relationship when all or at least most of the opportunities for behavioral parenting disappear? Is it all over? Will mothers lose all of their influence? Will all the lessons from the past and all of the mother-son behavior both have practiced for so long fade away?

Absolutely not. And the reasons are as deeply rooted in the principles of behavioral parenting as everything else we have outlined in the book: People do what they have learned to do; what has been encouraged, supported, and rewarded. Though the behavior of sons is modified by whatever consequences are prevailing and dominant, behavior patterns that sons have learned at home are not forgotten simply because they are not continuously reinforced. What a son learned at mother's knee will be maintained, but will not necessarily be all powerful.

Just as behavioral parenting can help single (and other) mothers in shaping successful men, we believe it can also ease mothers and sons into adult relationships with each other by offering insights into sons' behavior and guiding their reactions to it.

Success for the mother of an older son depends largely on her willingness to pursue her own interests, to have something new to share with the man who is a unique and special person in her life. It also depends, however, on her understanding of some special problems and issues that influence sons as they move through young adulthood and even on through middle age.

For one thing, at about the time sons leave young adolescence and begin preparations for college, jobs, marriage, or leaving home, conditions that once placed control of the family in mom's hands rapidly begin to fade.

Continuous contact necessary for shaping and reinforcing behavior is no longer there. Physical and emotional dependency is diminished. Important payoffs in a man's life—status,

power, earning capacity, romantic love, children—are remote
and mostly out of mother's sphere of influence.

Consequences are more difficult to predict, and mothers
can no longer easily manipulate events that shape behavior.
Sons' behavior is now largely launched and maintained by
other forces.

Think of it this way: Mother has a history of doing things
that are now being placed on the "extinction" list. That is,
consciously or not, her son is no longer paying attention to
much of the behavior that he once did. It is not that he is
ignoring mom intentionally. Instead, he is concentrating on
other things, things that mother has long encouraged him to
focus on: career/achievement, mature friendships, and so on.
But intentionally or not, his behavior is going to upset her
familiar and comfortable mothering behaviors.

As a result, mothers' strategies must change. What worked
when Johnny was three, or six or twelve or seventeen will
not work when he is twenty or thirty or forty.

Many mothers, understandably, resist the change.

It is not unusual for mothers to regress—literally—to old
mothering behavior toward their grown sons when they are
challenged, because it is easier to do this than to come up
with a new and better strategy.

They fret at the prospect of becoming victims of nursery
rhyme verity in which a "boy is your son 'till he takes him a
wife . . ."

A mother of a preschooler told us: "I suppose I fear losing
him and I don't want to. I know that he is going to have a
life that I can't understand. He's going to go through these
mysterious changes that will separate us forever."

Another, Beth, was more specific: "I worry a lot about
what will happen to our relationship when Ian grows up. The
happiest days of my life was the day he was born. I once told
my (ex) husband that and he was really hurt. I have never
felt as good as the day he was born. Not even when my
daughter was born. I don't have a favorite child, but it was
my best day and my best time. Maybe in part because it was
my first and it was a difficult delivery. But I couldn't take my
eyes off of him from that first day. I will never lose that feeling
and I don't want him to be gone. He is such a part of me. I
worry something will happen to him or that he will grow up
and never need me again.

"Tradition and history say that sons are supposed to care for their mothers as their mothers grow old. But that role doesn't quite fit for the modern, liberated woman, does it? But I think Ian will be closer than my daughter to me. Maybe because we shared a particularly tough time or because he understands my special feelings about the day he was born and what we went through. We have a bond I will never have with anyone else in the whole world. It is absolutely true that he is my first love. He angers me more than anyone and makes me prouder than anyone."

Single mothers, especially, may fear the "empty nest" and the further loss of male influence in their lives. More than married mothers, they may be ill-equipped to stop mothering. Single mothers, therefore, may persist in their old roles and even intensify their efforts to "win back" what they perceive they have lost: sons who respond to all the principles of behavioral parenting and all the sophisticated reinforcements and punishments they can invent. Instead of letting go, some mothers work harder and harder to "win" back the ultimate reward—sons' attention—just as sons are beginning to concentrate more on friends, school, and career.

Most mothers—particularly if they are behavioral parents—understand the futility of such efforts. They do know better. They understand the need to shift out of parenting gears and retire their basic mothering manual to the attic. They know they must interpret their sons' clear, if not always eloquent instructions to "butt out" as proof of their success as mothers of independent, self-reliant men.

But how does a mother segue into an adult-to-adult relationship with her son, while still maintaining those elements of the mother-son association that she will genuinely need and to which he can respond?

A good first step is to set new goals for the mother-son relationship, and set them clearly. As mothers and sons grow older, if their relationships have been built on negotiations and mutual respect, it becomes not only inevitable but rewarding for roles to shift; that is, for a son to help take care of his mother, if necessary, and for her to accept his new roles (and a few of her own) without feeling or inflicting guilt.

What should be distinctly different about the application of behavioral principles, however, is mother's increased attention to those aspects of a grown son's behavior that significantly influence her *own*.

As boys become men and more aware of what influences adult behavior, they too begin to "play the game," to shape and mold the behavior of others with rewards and consequences.

Thus as sons grow up and begin to "parent" their mothers, they may ask, to paraphrase Freud, "What do mothers want?" For their own as well as their sons' sake, mothers had better know, so that there can be mutual understanding and growth, not simply a wholesale parent-child role reversal. Mother, after all, is not a child.

When we asked single mothers what they wanted out of their older-mother–older-son relationships, the most frequently mentioned goal was a shift from ties based on dependency to those based on mutual needs.

Pam, a psychologist with two sons, one a college upperclassman: "I would hope that my sons and I would form a natural backup that means someone is there who will always come through for you, even if you live apart. A sense that there is someone who will unconditionally accept you if you need it. For myself, I hope we will be good friends. I don't see parents as people who tell you what to do, or who are always doing things for other people. What I have worked hard to establish is that we are all equal in this venture, and we must all pitch in.

"There is a tremendous amount of respect that goes with this, and tolerance. We may not always be the closest friends and probably won't be. We are different people and will be at different places in our lives. But I hope we will always be able to share our lives."

Bernice, an author: "Do I want Alan as a caretaker? God, no. That's the one thing I don't want. I don't want him responsible for me. I'm very uncomfortable with the idea of dependency, of being a child to my grown child. Emotionally, yes, to some extent. I would like to be able to tell him if I have a problem. But I certainly wouldn't want to feel he should be obliged to schlepp me around. I don't want to be schlepped.

"There is nothing he owes me. He has already given me a great deal of pleasure. My attitude toward having kids was that I had them because I wanted them. Sure, I'd feel real hurt if he didn't write or if he behaved like a boor. But I don't feel I'm due something. I want to see Alan with work he loves, financially secure, and in a good relationship with a family of his own. That's pretty traditional for me. I would be very unhappy to see him as a swinging bachelor. But that's because I don't see bachelors as very happy people, not because I want him to live the kind of life I've led (married). We base what we want for our kids on our own experience."

Not surprisingly many single mothers hope their relationships with their grown sons will resemble the relationships they have with their mothers.

Bernice again: "I would like my son to be a really interesting friend, to whom I can talk. I'd like our relationship to be like the one I had with my mother. We really liked each other. She was my cheering section and always thought everything I did was wonderful. But I also liked talking to her. I always thought of my mother as the person I would choose to go with if there was anyplace I really wanted to go. I'd like to have that kind of relationship with Alan."

The mother who feared loss of her son described her hopes for their future relationship this way: "I would like to have the same kind of bond with him that I have now with my mother. We are very close friends and I know that no matter what happens to me, she will be there and I can always go to her. That no matter what I do she'll still love me and understand me. That's pretty much what I want."

A journalist with an eleven-year-old son: "I want him to need me when he is grown up in some adult way. I don't know what that will be. I don't want him to depend on me or be unable to get along without me, but I want him to need me."

A corollary to setting clear goals is for mom to resist mixing ideas about the behavior she wants from her son (various kinds of help and attention) with ideas about the feelings— affection, nurturing, sympathy—she wants to elicit from them.

Lynne shows some of that confusion: "I hope we can have fun together when my sons are grown, go out to dinner some night or out to a play or a movie and have a nice discussion. I keep hoping they are going to marry someone I'll like so that I can enjoy being a mother-in-law. I worry about what will happen if they marry someone I can't stand, how I'll feel about that.

"I want to be able to visit and have them visit me, but I don't have a clear picture about how that would work. I'd probably like to have found somebody (to marry or live with) by then. I don't look forward to living alone entirely. Ronnie is worried about that, too. He has told me he is upset by the idea that he will have to go away and leave me alone. I told him that's a long way off and that I might be married by then. I think it made him feel better. But if the times comes and I'm not, I would tell them I was going to be fine and love the freedom. I wouldn't want to burden them. I would tell them it wasn't all bad.

"I don't want my sons to think they owe me anything. But we are a family and I think you should help family. I don't think it's wrong to share your life with your children when they are grown."

Once again, we emphasize that while feelings are important, they are not always good predictors of behavior. Sons may love their mothers but act inappropriately. Mothers may sympathize with their sons' difficulties in growing up, but do things that compound, instead of ease those troubles. Obviously, most parents and children develop strong feelings for each other. Between single mothers and sons, those feelings are complicated by stress and unusual circumstances. But when the issue is what mothers and sons do—to, for, and with—each other, a behavioral plan is essential.

Finally, mother should think about what is really important in her personal list of objectives.

If her fairy godmother appeared to grant one or two wishes, about her son, what would they be? How many mothers would say such niggling things as: "I want my son to call me on the phone more," or, "I want my son to be nicer to me."

More likely, they would ask what they asked the day their sons were born; that as men they achieve success and contentment, and fulfill their destinies as husbands, fathers, lovers, and friends.

When mothers remember to set penultimate goals, they are at the same time reminding themselves to stop complaining about and concentrating too much on trivial things that interfere with good feelings and good behavior. (In this chapter and the next, incidentally, we suppose that sons have grown to be relatively successful and law-abiding members of society. In the distressing case of sons who are not, who are failing because of career, marriage, drug or alcohol problems, and so on, a much different approach is needed. Such mother-son relationships are the subject matter for other books.)

In summary, mothers should ask what it is they really want out of an adult son and mother relationship. Then, armed with these specifics, mothers can adapt ideas explained and promoted throughout the book. Here's how:
• Pay attention to behavior, instead of guessing at motives. If independence, self-confidence, and tolerance of others are what mothers of grown sons truly want for them, then it is more important to react to what sons at this stage actually do than to worry whether they do it out of "love for mom" or any other desirable emotion.

It is better to listen and watch, to understand what is important to older sons than to engineer showy displays of gush or make demands that they prove their love and respect for mothers. Mothers who believe that their sons want to, or ought to, keep a parent at the center of their adult lives are probably doomed to disappointment. And mothers who anticipate adult mother-son relationships built on the if-he-loved-me school of behavior are booking themselves on a fast jet out of their sons' lives . . . "If he loved me he wouldn't act this way," is a familiar lament. But such statements are illogical in view of what behavioral parenting tells us about why and how people learn and what controls behavior. They are also irrelevant.
• Catch 'em being good.

When a son reaches late adolescence, mom will begin to look for signs of maturity and independence that she can be proud of and reward.

These signs, by the way, appear in unexpected places at unexpected times. Because they tend to be overshadowed by activities that drive mothers up walls, mothers need to be alert.

When Adam and his first truly serious "steady" were in the process of breaking off, the alternating days of tirades and blues were painful to Adam, and seemed endless to Joann. She decided to treat them sympathetically as just another adolescent misery for him to get through, although attempts to soothe him with "I know how you feel" sentiments were met with hostility and denial at that point.

Then one night he told her, through tears, that it was definitely over. The pain of losing someone you cared about was "overwhelming," he said, and he "would never feel the same way about anyone."

The words "I know how you feel" slipped out before Joann

could bite her tongue. She expected an angry, "No, you don't." Instead, she saw Adam's eyes widen with a sudden flash of insight. Mom's divorce was certainly similar in some ways with the breakup of a high school romance. They hugged each other and mingled a few tears, and Adam spent the next few minutes telling Joann that for the "first time" he understood "what it must have been like for you and Dad." He was proud of his behavior, of sharing a moment of mature intimacy and mutual respect with his mother. So was Joann, and she let him know it.

• Track your own behavior as well as your son's.

It may seem an obvious point to some, but many mothers who say they are genuinely delighted to see their sons emerge as independent adults don't fully appreciate the consequences of losing contact with them. They may see that things cannot stay the same, but they resist reacting positively to the change.

It helps if mothers will watch their own reactions more closely, and practice being positive.

Think about it this way: An older son's primary reinforcements no longer emerge primarily from his home base or even his extended family of relatives and neighbors. Between late adolescence and the early thirties, most reinforcements are outside the family. Would mom have it any other way? Really?

For single mothers, moreover, that shift is both intensified, and, somehow, easier.

It is intensified because mothers must bear the brunt of their newfound aloneness often without another adult to help them over the rough edges. Easier for some at least because they may have already learned to be more independent and less demanding of traditional "pay attention" relationships with men.

• Consider realistically what the world will be like for each— mother and son on his own—and what recent major social changes will continue to influence the behavior of men and their relationships with women, including their mothers.

Those changes that deal with feminism, parenting, male-female equality, the demise of the two-parent family, and personal goals have been dealt with in other chapters. But there is one other change worth special mention in regard to older sons and mothers who will share their lives. This change involves the narrowing of the social and intellectual gap between the generations. For many, if not most mother-and-son pairs, it is likely that both the parent and child generations will have reached the same educational level. Mother is not the gray-haired lady in sensible shoes concerned primarily with knitting, Sunday dinners, and grandchildren, but a woman who has probably managed a career, a family, and a personal life that has thrown her numerous curves. She may have personal ambitions that rival or exceed her son's, and experiences in school, job, and the dating game that match his as well.

At the same time, there is some evidence that the current generation of young adult men and women will be the first in America's history who cannot automatically expect to do better—financially and educationally—than their parents. For that we can thank inflation and the realistic limits of economic and intellectual growth over the generations. In many single-parent homes, tight money meant truncated budgets and revised college plans for children. Dreams that mothers may have nourished when their boys were born had to be abandoned in the face of economic pressures.

It takes little imagination to realize that the world grown sons and mothers face today will place demands on them that were unknown to previous generations.

The current crop of middle-aged mothers is more likely, for example, to have made friendships across generational barriers than did their mothers. They may date men young enough to be their sons or have business friends who are much older.

Mothers may, in one way or another, compete on grounds that once were considered the rather exclusive territory of their sons.

One sixty-year-old mother we know is angry when her son, who lives in the same city as she, gives a party and does not invite her. Another we know, a little younger, is puzzled when her son does invite her.

These trends might at first seem legitimate cause for distress. But the real message in all this, from the standpoint of behavioral parenting, is that the trend toward social and intellectual parity between mothers and older sons is not nearly so important as the substance of the activities they choose to share in their relationship.

The goal of adult relationships is to find common ground

and share activities that are mutually enjoyable, rather than focusing on those that cannot be.

Notes Michael: "My job as an adult son is to find things I can and want to talk about with adult parents who stopped their formal education earlier than I did, rather than wonder about all the things we can't talk about. The task, whether mom has a PhD or not, or son has one or not, is to look for a common ground and build on the older generation's history and wisdom."

Ideally, the grown son we are speaking of has emerged from his mother's adventure in single parenting as a better man because of it. At the least, he is certainly not doomed by the experience. Rhona Rosen's 1979 study of ninety-two children of divorce, ages nine to twenty-eight, found that a bad marriage is in many cases more likely to create emotional problems in children than a divorce. Her findings further revealed "no difference in the ultimate adjustment of children reared by mothers and those reared by fathers." Her study included sex-role function, school achievement, self-confidence, independence, and social behavior of each of the subjects.

• Pay special attention to conditions that demand changes in mother, rather than son.

As a son enters full adulthood, and mother-son contact diminishes, some conditions will demand that mom phase out some of her own behavior patterns much the way she worked to phase out some of *his* when he was younger. Moreover, those that are to be discontinued won't be replaced with improved versions of similar behavior, but probably need to be replaced or dropped altogether. Son doesn't want or need classic mothering. He doesn't have time to devote to it, even if he does want or need it—not in the real world, anyway. There are too many competing distractions and demands for his time and energy.

So here is mother in a Catch-22 situation. She is not able to use the repertoire of actions that stood her in good stead for eighteen or twenty years (directing, guiding, reinforcing, punishing, instructing, stimulating), nor can she build up substitutes for the role she has enjoyed and found rewarding all those years. On top of all that, she is advised to be sensitive to and, in fact, celebrate the very behavior in her son that is creating all this havoc!

Joann recalls Adam's senior year in high school when he was applying to colleges. Weeks of his time went into writing the all-important application essay, that controlled and tortuous exercise in autobiography. His final version was, in her opinion, a mini-masterpiece. It mentioned all the events and ideas that he saw as the highlights of his life up to that point. The only mention it made of Joann, however, was a reference to her occupation as a writer. It wasn't easy ("After all I've done for him!"), but she celebrated.

- Give plenty of time to consideration of her own future goals.

This is a real departure from the emphasis in the rest of the book. Where once the focus was on having a son change his behavior to meet mother's plans, now mother needs to change her behavior, both to meet her future needs for her own self-development and to meet her son's changing needs.

The single mother, particularly if she has been working and independent, has a head start over other homemaker mothers, because she has had some experience building new roles and creating new patterns of behavior to fit them.

Mother's goal-setting should now focus on herself as much as on her son so that her son's separation from her will not set the stage for disaster.

It's best if she doesn't wait for her mothering repertoire to be wiped out by default (son's leave-taking), but to have some plans in the works, and to have new outlets for her intellectual and emotional energies.

She might take for herself the plan she earlier designed for a successful son: to test and challenge the outside world with new kinds of behavior.

An outstanding characteristic—and problem—among single mothers who continue to peddle old mothering wares (advice giving, instructions, problem-solving scenarios, etc.) is that they work too hard to find problems they hope will capture their sons' attention. Nine times out of ten, those problems don't require sons' intervention. Situations and difficulties mothers would not have asked sons to solve when they were fourteen or sixteen, are now presented as full-dress crises that demand her twenty-, thirty-, or forty-year-old: finding a plumber to fix the leaky faucets; doing her income taxes; cleaning the attic; getting dad to pay alimony on time; keeping her entertained; shopping for a new car, and so on.

A mother may attract her son's attention with these requests. Occasionally, son may even feel gratified that she is "treating me like an adult." More likely, however, she will earn his irritation, his resentment, and his patronization. After all, what can he really do about most of these things that a healthy woman cannot? Even if he can do something definitive about the plumbing or the taxes, doing it requires a great deal of time and energy, which he may (rightly) prefer to spend on the rapidly-growing demands of his own life. Is this mother-son trip worth it? We don't think so. Mom should save the attention-getting devices for those times she really needs attention, and not use them to test her son's filial devotion. If a son complies with nonessential demands, mother may have the instant "relief" of knowing her lessons were well learned. But the price for such moments of satisfaction is not usually fair to sons. Mothers win something they don't need; sons are less likely to give attention the next time mother asks for it; sons may feel guilty or angry about that. Everybody loses.

Mother is far better off if she prepares herself to recognize and avoid the danger signs and shift to appropriate time-sharing activities. A frantic increase in attention-getting activity with her son signals that she must find new situations in which to be with and work with her son. By developing reinforcing activities to replace the constant contact of earlier years, she will avoid much of the risk of "behavioral depression."

If a single mother becomes depressed over the "empty-nest" syndrome, her son cannot "fill her up" now any more than he could when he was a child. The chore is hers, as it always was, or should have been, to set her own goals and meet them. More than ever, a single woman's life must not be defined solely by what she does for others. That will lead to misery when the definition outlasts the job.

• Keep a firm grip on realistic expectations.

Under the best of circumstances, and with the best of efforts, sons on their own cannot deliver all that mothers want or need. No one could. Sons may resemble other grown men who did meet her requests in the past (husband, lover, dad), but they are still sons and have a distinctly unique relationship with mothers. They are grown, but they are no more able to replace husbands or lovers than they were as children.

This is especially true in those years when sons are building their own families and careers.

- Mother shouldn't be surprised if there are long periods of time when she doesn't see a lot of behavior she would count as "good" in her son.

Her son hasn't lost the know-how to behave well. If it was there, it isn't gone. What's happening is that the signals which prompt the actions she is looking for are less frequent.

The principles of behavioral parenting reveal that the most influential factor in the loss or retention of a certain behavior is not time, but the events that signal and reinforce the behavior. Therefore, although the behavior might not occur if the triggers are missing, it hasn't been dropped out of the behavior inventory. If you don't have access to a bicycle or a typewriter, you may not ride or type for years. But that doesn't mean you will forget how to do either.

Mothers can and should expect that sons in their twenties, thirties, and older will behave the way they were taught more often than not. She can take comfort from it and be ready to recognize it at times when it seems sons have forgotten their mothers and everything they learned from them.

She shouldn't worry that "new ideas" and "new friends" will wipe out her efforts. Such things won't influence behavvior nearly so much as eighteen or twenty years of behavioral parenting. But mothers may have to wait years to see it proven.

There is a parallel to be found in what happened with mother-son behaviors during son's adolescence. This was a time when it was often best to tide over the relationship with what was already in the behavioral bank, and not get too far afield with new and important instructions, directions, and behaviors.

The rationale was that adolescence is a time when biological and environmental events are making chaos out of previously stable patterns of behavior and thinking. During the teen years, sons needed time to sort things out, and mothers were most effective when they helped sons discriminate and make their own choices, rather than suggesting or reinforcing mother's choices.

Similarly, as sons grow into full manhood and begin to accept the full responsibility for their own lives and behavior that their mothers always hoped they would, the mothers can expect *sturm und drang*. It will resemble adolescence in style if not in substance. Sons need time and energy to sort things out, test the various waters, discriminate among the reinforcements and punishments operating in the outside world, and a good deal of tolerance.

Fortunately for single mothers, especially, this approach is likely to dovetail with her need for and enjoyment of private time and self-renewal.

Most of the single mothers of older sons whom we interviewed had already begun to taste the fruits of their own liberation from "minute-to-minute" mothering and to reap the benefits of sons on their own.

"At first I thought I would be a wreck when my son got his driver's license," the New Jersey mother of a seventeen-year-old remarked. "But suddenly here was this competent person, able and willing to do things for himself and for me and his younger brother. For the first time in seventeen years, I had some real time to myself."

Among the older sons we spoke to, two points of special interest emerged.

First, as one, a Broadway producer phrased it, "There comes a point in every man's life when he realizes that his mother may not read the *New York Times.*" What he meant was that grown sons must not only have their own dreams and ideas, but also begin to savor many things that their mothers (and fathers and other close relatives and friends) do not and cannot share with them. Although parents should and do care about their kids' marriages, jobs, goals, or lifestyle, they do not always approve, respect, or accept them. In the case of the producer, his mother now delights in his creative and financial success. But she once fought hard to lure him into a medical career and no doubt still has trouble understanding or appreciating the profession he chose.

For mature sons, acceptance and acknowledgment of this separation of interests is seen as a natural progression. For too many mothers, however, it is seen as "proof" of a sudden and rapidly growing "generation gap" that could not be bridged without demands, intrusions, and criticism.

"Why all of a sudden is he not interested in what I think," grumbled one mother of a medical student. "Just because I don't know much about medicine doesn't mean I'm stupid. He just doesn't want to be bothered." One can almost hear the "After all I've done for him . . ." line rising in her throat.

Since this man had spent the past several years immersed in medical studies, such a situation should hardly surprise his mother. For most of his waking hours, he has been reinforced for little else but learning anatomy and diagnosis. Little wonder he finds it tough to respond to much else, even at home. From this mother's point of view, the son who was once "perfect," and interested in family, friends, sports, and school, has turned into a stranger. She didn't stop to consider his new interests and influences.

- By the time sons are in their late thirties and forties, mothers can expect that their behavior will have begun to settle into predictable patterns once again. They are likely to be married and to have children of their own. They are now parenting and displaying behavior that was the mainstay of their relationships with their own mother.

During these times, a mother may see more of her influence than at any time since her son left boyhood. Although he may avoid or openly disdain her advice about his activities and his relationships with other adults or his children, a close look will often reveal behavior that indicates otherwise. The way he treats his wife, decorates his home, shares household chores, and spends time with his children belies his declarations of independence. Sometimes, the influence is absurdly sublime. Joann knows one mother who, on a visit to see her grandchildren, saw that both of them had been taught to fold their clothes and put them away in the same drawers (socks on top, underwear in the middle, shirts below) as her son was taught three decades earlier.

By middle age, sons have had relationships with many individuals: teachers and bosses, lovers and enemies, co-workers and underlings, police and lawyers, doctors and salespersons. These relationships have been wonderful, painful, helpful, and destructive. Sons will have learned a good deal. They will at the very least have learned what adults call street wisdom and learned to judge parents with honesty and tolerance.

At this stage sons may come to view their relationships with their mothers as increasingly valuable. And mothers can expect more "respect."

However, mothers are unlikely to be successful at programming major behavior changes in sons at this stage of their lives, or of having any of their advice followed, even if sons request changes or advice. There are just too many pressing day-to-day needs. Single mothers ought to recall the difficult days when their status as a married woman changed; how much energy it took to set priorities, find all the reins and pick them up. Sons on their own are going through a similar major life change.

• Mothers shouldn't target in on details of behavior in an attempt to support or extinguish them. Overlook what you might consider minor acts of social deviance and add your two cents only for those acts that count.

We know a man who, when he began graduate school, bought a motorcycle, a vehicle his mother forbid him to have when he was a teenager, and one she continued to criticize openly and frequently. With much justification, she considered motorcycles extremely dangerous.

He lived away from home, however, and she could no longer apply consequences that would force him to give up the motorcycle, short of refusing to help with his tuition or to welcome him home—Draconian measures likely to cause more problems than they solve.

For her to expect him to follow her demands is expecting too much. On the other hand, she might find ways to encourage him to become a more safety-conscious cyclist. She might buy him a safety helmet, and discuss her concern for the fact that some motorists disdain motorcyclists and consider them "punks" who deserve little consideration.

Instead of condemning his behavior outright or attempting to force him to choose between "mom" and "motorcycle," she could find occasions to demonstrate her concern for the problems *he* may have and suggest ways around them.

Jared's long flowing locks are a thorn in the side of many "establishment" adults in school and the business world. Some adults fairly bristle when they see long hair on a teenager, immediately labeling the boy as unreliable and filing them in whatever negative niches their own behavioral histories suggest.

As he gets older, his mother knows that such negativism may increase as the indulgences displayed toward young adolescents break down. ("Sure, it's understandable when he's fifteen, but at twenty?")

Joann might use any number of tough consequences that will produce a son with shorter hair. But that kind of moth-

ering behavior, even if it works, is based on unrealistic expectations about the outcome and is therefore fraught with
problems. He might be forced to comply, but the goal will
be to reduce her anxiety, not his potential problems with a
short-haired world.

In this case, her position is also hypocritical. She happens
to like his long hair. It is also not a priority problem at his
age.

Realistically, the best she can hope to do without outright
criticism (which usually gets mom nowhere) is to help Jared
finesse the unpleasantness his flowing tresses creates in some
circles, and to smooth reactions that may interfere with his
own desired goals for success.

Joann searched for opportunities to point out and reinforce
other behaviors that seem to mitigate the negative effects of
long hair among older adults. Two received special emphasis
and had usefulness in other situations: politeness and metic-
ulous grooming. The result: Joann has often seen Jared dis-
arm and win over the sternest crew-cut "square" with nothing
more than a firm handshake, warm smile, shined shoes, and
a friendly greeting.

The emphasis for mothers of sons on their own, as we said
before, should be on finding new ways to be essential in their
sons' lives.

An overall strategy is for mothers to forge the new relationships not on the basis of their role as mothers, but on
what psychotherapist and author Dr. Elissa Melamed refers
to as their "authenticity" as independent women.

By 1990, Melamed points out, thirty-six million American
women will be forty-five years old or older. They will be a
big-time political force and a big chunk of them will be single
mothers. For the first time, such women will have lots of
company and lots of clout which they can put to use for
themselves and their sons.

Instead of making vain efforts to recapture youthful mothering (and other) roles, the task is to evolve.

"Choosing a bathtub mat can only take us so far," she
writes. "Older women can no longer afford to remain the
world's most underutilized resource. And as we begin to use
the second half of our lives authentically, our youth hangup
will lose its deathly grip on us."

Melamed also notes that although they are motivated to make this shift to authenticity for their own sakes, women can and should hold onto their "helping, nurturing behavior." The survival of human life, she argues, may depend on women who can combine their new power with what have long been deemed "feminine" concerns.

We couldn't agree more—or miss the chance to add that working mothers, a large number of whom are single, have a considerable head start on the road to authenticity. With this perspective, mothering is no longer something to miss and mourn, but something from which to build and grow. Letting go of older sons can serve, therefore, as a potent behavioral signal for mothers to develop new interests. And the payoff is that these new interests are more likely to get mothers the attention they want than old ones, and will do so without devouring sons' time or engendering guilt.

Another grand strategy is to retain those "mothering" habits that reinforce what mother sees as positive and valuable in her relationship with her son.

Important among these is availability. As a maternal behavior, *being there* is a long-term winner. Let her son know she will be available to him if he wants to talk. "I'm going back to school three nights a week, but here's where you can reach me anytime."

Older sons are not likely to abuse this offer, if for no other reason than the fact that mother-son times together are far less frequent than they once were. Personal contact is often limited to holidays, vacations, summer visits, or phone calls on weekends.

Moreover, availability of parents tends to draw reciprocal treatment. Michael lives in a city several hundred miles from his parents and has now arranged for his parents to call or to call them regularly on Sunday mornings. It is a satisfying contact because it supports availability (both ways) and because it is predictable, brief, and unlikely to interfere with plans and obligations that require more of his time and energy.

The appropriate use of money also remains an important reinforcer for mother-son relationships. But a word of caution: Once sons are living away from home, mothers should be especially careful how they use it.

Mothers must distinguish between the money power they

have or have had for sons' essentials (tuition, for example) and gifts. The former was or may still be a matter of survival for sons; the latter is not. In cases where sons really need the funds, and mothers are able to provide them, linking money to demands to "do as I say" distracts a son from pursuing precisely those goals that are most important to his success in order to pay attention to mom. It may also introduce a lot of guilt if he gets the money without giving in to the behavior (which is often the case), or resentment if he does give in. Nobody wins.

Sometimes it is not necessary for a mother to find new ways to be essential in her son's life, but simply to find new ways of taking advantage of those times when he finds them for himself.

In this regard, a final major strategy for helping mothers and older sons get along is the *Contrast Effect*. Watch for it. Then play it for all it's worth.

The contrast effect occurs when a set of circumstances takes on special value because it is set off by another set of circumstances.

For example, Tom grows up at home with his divorced mother, and has come to rely on certain reinforcements in his life and activities at home. He reaps benefits that are tailored to home base. These include everything from meals he likes, to entertainment, money, and attention from mother. Then he goes off to college.

For a few weeks or a month, he is totally distracted by the unique environment and what is offered there: junk food for breakfast, no one nagging him to pick up his clothes, new friends, and freedom to cut class.

But the beer-for-breakfast trip soon wears off and Tom begins to think about the conveniences and benefits of home. He grows homesick. Pot roast and green vegetables take on a whole new meaning even if they emerged only rarely from the kitchen of a full-time working mother.

What Tom had at home assumes more value not only because it is absent at school, but also because of what transpired in the interval since he was home. It was not just the absence of pot roast and mom, but the presence of other events and conditions—junk food and hangovers, for example—that created the contrast effect.

Such experiences tend to heighten the quality of the relationship with the person who still operates home base: mother.

By the time Tom is thirty or forty, he has had lots of different away-from-home experiences. His time away from his mother, combined with the nature of those other relationships, cannot fail (unless things have always been rotten between them) to place more value on the relationship he has with the person who once was a major if not *the* major mediator of his behavior and influence in his life.

He will also have had hundreds of adult relationships. But he never will have another similar to that with his mother. If she is single and a behavioral parent, that relationship has been all the more unique. At this stage, the mother-son relationship may become as valued for son as his birth was for mother and for the same reason: By contrast, there is nothing that can match it.

As one thirty-seven-year-old son put it, "As men seek relationships with other adults, they realize there are no other people who hold them in as much esteem as their mothers. No one else shares so much history, that many memories, with them as mothers. Even a man's wife cannot compete with that until the couple is in the senior citizen range, and a wife still cannot equal the experience shared by a single mother and her son."

A word of caution: If there is anything that can foul up the contrast effect, it's too much contact, because intense contact destroys the uniqueness that makes the contrast effect work in the first place.

For example, when grown children plan a return to the family home for Christmas or other special holidays, the mood is upbeat. The first hours or day or two at home are marvelous: everyone exchanging the latest news and ideas and putting his best foot forward. But by the end of a week, there may be a full blown case of holiday blues. Intense close contact within the old parent-child framework too often means a return to parent-child behavior patterns ("Are you really serious about this girl you brought home?" "You might offer to take out the garbage!") that trigger old tensions.

In sum, to help the contrast effect work, intense contacts should be kept short and upbeat. Both should resist with all their might getting hung up on old parent-child confrontations. Mothers should support and reinforce social occasions as happy times that have nothing to do with mother-child relationships and everything to do with adult-to-adult relationships.

Keeping social occasions free as much as possible of "help me" sessions or discussions of essential needs is desirable. On social occasions, mothers shouldn't lecture, instruct, advise, or bring mothering behaviors into the picture, and should avoid "If you do this, I'll do that . . ." discussions.

Many single mothers have a more active social life than their sons. If they are active politically or a member of a profession or firm that holds interest for their adult sons, an invitation to one of mom's parties or Sunday brunches may be highly valued by adult sons and their wives or friends.

Single mothers may also provide continuity for family functions. Joann, for example, takes turns with her first cousins in hosting the entire family for certain holidays. Her sons look forward to these occasions and she plans to continue them when they are on their own.

There are times when mothers need their grown sons to pay attention to them—really need them. These are usually times of sickness, loss of their own parents, or money problems.

The good news for mothers is that these needs are likely to be met.

When we spoke to sons growing up and growing older, it was rare to find one who did not find the prospect of giving help satisfying. In part, they may be motivated by guilt and social propriety. "What kind of a son doesn't help his mother?" Being genuinely helpful and dependable and relied upon, is, from a behavioral point of view, a very positive reinforcement to most adults.

All those skills his mother encouraged him to learn must have meant a lot to her or she wouldn't have bothered teaching them. When he has finally mastered them, that's satisfying. But if he has the chance to show his stuff to his teacher, Nirvana!

If mastery and competency as a "parent" to his mother is reinforcing to a son, and if his activities with his mother are reinforcing because of the contrast effect, then the combination of the two is likely to be even more rewarding to him, as well as helpful to her.

More hosannas are likely to come from friends, relatives, and colleagues, further reinforcing a son who comes through for his mother.

If sons have learned in childhood and adolescence to value such rewards, they will continue to value them as adults. A final bonus: Helping mother often means keeping her healthy and happy and therefore enabling her to continue giving all kinds of positive encouragement to her son. A happy cycle. Everybody wins.

It bears pointing out, however, that situations in which mothers need help from sons may also be threatening to sons. Sons may worry about failing their mothers, or if the time they must spend with them will jeopardize their own families and careers.

Such tensions can result in serious efforts to avoid contact or to listen to the real needs, especially with mothers who have set the stage by making myriad nuisance demands or who, because they seek "proof" of their sons' continued devotion, ask sons to meet needs that aren't genuinely important.

We have talked to several grown sons who moved as far away from their mothers as possible. They find they are more willing to deal with the guilt than with the demands. "If it's something really serious, I'll know it and I'll come," one told us. "But out here, I don't have to say no to a lot of things I can't find time for."

Putting it all together, from a behavioral parenting point of view, mothers of older sons can assure a maximum of good contacts with their son and minimum of unpleasant ones if they look for or arrange situations that help sons provide painless, relatively brief, and successful meetings with mothers. Just as mothers find benefit in "liberation" from the daily tasks of motherhood, sons find liberation from daily filial obligations necessary and pleasant. And that is as it should be.

CHAPTER ELEVEN

Destinies: Toward New Paths for Mothers and Sons

Philip Wylie's "*momism*" and the anti-mother fanaticism it bred and reflected in the 1950s had as its base the observation that mom dominated dad in the young boy's household. How ironic that the 1950s was in fact a time when men were still considered the supreme and proper rulers of the roost. Few scholars seriously suggested at the time that if boys grew up badly, entropy created by fathers might have had as much to do with that as any alleged excess by a generation of female vipers.

But a further irony worked to mothers' advantage. The dethroned and disillusioned moms of the 1950s finally had motive and impetus to reevaluate their roles realistically. If they were no longer on the historic Earth Mother pedestal, they were also no longer content with the illusion of power in the home and outside of it. If motherhood was a form of parental malpractice, then rehabilitating it was to be forever part of the penalty.

How well have mothers done with their sons? And where are the twin paths of motherhood and feminism leading? Will it ever be true that, as W. R. Wallace observed in 1865, the "hand that rocks the cradle is the hand that rules the world"? Is that what mothers want? Is it something sons will accept?

In fact, single mothers we interviewed and those from Michael's clinical experience want two things. They want to know how to enjoy, to the fullest, the experience of raising their sons; to minimize the hassles, rebellions, and everyday trivia that compete with the intensely positive aspects of having and rearing their children. At the same time, they want to prepare their sons for a future they cannot fully predict, or live in.

200

Single mothers (as with mothers who are married, fathers, and grandparents) may have vastly differing fears about the future and how it may affect their sons. Each of them carves her own *bête noire* out of her son's traits, achievements, and shortcomings. Is Johnny shy and withdrawn? That produces one set of fears. Is he Don Quixote or Don Juan? Still another. Is he a perfect student or a poor one? A third.

Whatever the worry, however, all that a mother has at her disposal with which to fulfill her parenting goals are all she ever had in any period of history: how well she operates day to day and how well she can anticipate the future.

In the 1980s, of course, there is yet one more irony that complicates the mission. As the grand commercial success of *Kramer versus Kramer* and several TV shows points up, mothering, like every other job, has real status only when men do it. Mothers must still pay dues in a man's world.

In fact, much of what passes for mass entertainment in our society still depends on separating "real" men from "real" women on the basis of muscle-bulge, aggression, and blind ambition. Society—male and female—is still titillated by tough guys who shoot first and ask questions later.

Still, there is reason to hope that future generations of boys and girls will grow into men and women who will think of negotiation instead of resorting to or giving in to muscle power. If that happens, then behavioral parents will have played their roles well.

The behavioral approach to human relationships focuses on what works, but of course what works in any given time may range from rough-talking macho and insensitivity to flexibility, willingness to bend and compromise, to persuade and shape, to foster empathy and sensitivity. In behavioral terms, the outcome of human relationships is best measured not in wins and losses, but in how the game is played.

There is ample evidence that playing it behaviorally will become increasingly valuable in the twenty-first century, as today's young sons fulfill their social destinies.

The evidence comes from several sources. First, those whose job it is to analyze future trends point to rapid change as the only constant over the next thirty or forty years. The popularity of such books as John Naisbitt's *Megatrends* is a testimonial to the public's acceptance of the promise of continuous change as both a worry and a complicated challenge.

Second, technological and biomedical advances will make physical characteristics and limitations less important in human relationships. As we conquer more of nature, such things as the ability to select the sex of our offspring, artificial conception and gestation, and treatment for genetic disorders will shake the foundations of traditional family life even further than they have been already. The family will not die, but its form and function will be dramatically altered. Thus, although personal skills will remain the currency of social and occupational success, the skills with the highest demand will be dramatically altered as well. Where once swordsmanship, chivalry, and formal rules of behavior separated the "men from the boys" in the reach for success, tomorrow it will be computer literacy, sensitivity to others, and rapid adaptability.

Third, rising economic expectations and the political vigor of women and minorities are likely to produce large numbers of cooperative ventures, particularly in child rearing and education. In the past, the physical necessities of life—food, shelter, clothing, health—were the primary forces that shaped family life and social structure. Today, the struggle to meet basic physical needs has been eased by modern conveniences. What concerns us at least as much today are getting ahead, spending our time happily and constructively, mobility, and personal power. As a consequence, there will be far greater demand than ever for those with "people" skills.

Diagnosing and treating illness will be easier and more comprehensive thanks to computerized X-rays, better drugs, and efficiently-run hospitals. But finding compassionate physicians who can reassure us and treat our anxieties will be harder. It takes very little imagination right now to figure out that as our population ages, the highest rewards will go not to the high-flying neurosurgical whiz, but to the gentle and patient family practitioner who will care for the chronic ills of the elderly.

Many of the biggest challenges to our human-to-human skills will occur in male-female (including mother-son) relationships. Some will be continuations of trends begun with the women's liberation movement. Others will move women into new realms of openness. One mother we interviewed spoke easily of a trip to Paris with her oldest son, part of a promise to take each of her children abroad individually as they graduated from high school. From Paris, they brought back only one souvenir, she said: a promise to hug, kiss, touch, and display their feelings for each other in appropriate physical as well as verbal ways.

Other challenges will be less intimate: legal guarantees of equal rights, for example, and more attention to fathering as well as mothering. Still others may signal changes as radical as any that have come before, including large numbers of women choosing single motherhood, some through artificial insemination.

Less and less social stigma will be attached to a woman who is, or chooses to be, a single parent. More middle-class white women now openly elect motherhood outside of marriage. Among some black women, according to one source, "It is more acceptable to have a baby (out of wedlock) than to have an abortion."

What this means in terms of future trends is hardly subtle. A study released by the Rand Corporation, a California think-tank, cited research estimating that 46 percent of children born in the late 1970s will spend some part of their youth in single-parent families.

Finally, the future will see women become more demanding. Unless there is a total loss of ground won in the past twenty years, an unlikely situation, they will certainly gain substantial political power and, like men before them, abuse it.

"Dominance" will be defined not by physical prowess but by social and occupational success. And it will be achieved not by physically overpowering others, but by a combination of cooperation and superior negotiating performance.

Perhaps the most stunning mark of the change in the "battle of the sexes" over the past twenty-five years is not so much that it occurred as that many of us never imagined it happening so fast. It's a good bet most never watched for it, and that one reason for the hardships the change created for both sexes rests right there.

Now we know better. Change, rapid change, is occurring and women are far more alert to it than in the past. In such a world, the skills that will be most highly valued will be those that involve adaptation and flexibility. And if this vision of the future is accurate, behavioral parenting and the ideas it introduces can, with certain adaptations, serve sons as they fulfill their own destinies as husbands, fathers, lovers, and friends.

The reinforcements may change of course. What society will reward will shift as life-styles and social demands change. But the principles will remain valid.

When we spoke to single mothers about their sons' sons, the women all wished to make an impact on the destinies of their grandchildren.

Clearly, they wanted these boys to continue their own commitments to cooperation, equality, and fairness between the sexes. They also hoped to inspire a commitment to families as the best environment in which to rear children.

Those families may be defined and formed differently in the future. They may consist of mothers and fathers; of single mothers or single fathers; of combinations of parents and child-care workers, and even of groups of unrelated individuals. But all will involve at least one responsible, loving person willing to devote a major part of her or his energies to child rearing for fifteen or twenty years.

Not one of the mothers we interviewed said they did not want their sons to marry and have children. Their young sons, moreover, shared that vision of successful family life, and few found anything terrifying in the prospect of divorce or rearing their children alone.

In the not-so-distant future, sons of single mothers will be part of a cohort of millions. They will have learned skills unique in the history of the family. If they have learned those skills well and if they have the courage to use them as their mothers did, they will be a force unmatched for helping future generations meet destinies we can only imagine.

Appendix: How Do I Answer That?

Questions asked single mothers often fit the "Have you stopped beating your wife?" category: "You know, I think your son's poor grades could be related to your divorce, don't you?" (from a school guidance counselor). "Couldn't you ask Uncle Harry to teach him how to throw a ball the right way?" (from grandmother). "You're *not* going to go to bed with that guy, are you?" (from son). "Why does he (the son) always seem upset around you?" (from ex-husband). "How do you manage to have a private life with your teenage sons around?" (from a woman friend). "You and Dad messed up. What do you expect from me?" (from son). "What's wrong with him? (the son). Ever since your separation, he's so quiet" (from grandfather).

Other questions arise in the mind of the single mother herself: "Is he confused about his masculinity?" "Does he resent my feminist views?" "Why doesn't he take more responsibility?" "Why does he act as if he's running things?" "What is his father telling him about how to act around girls?" "Am I being fair?" "Why does he copy the behavior of men I don't like?"

As any good defense lawyer will tell you, such questions are inflammatory because they couch an issue in the language of a problem. In that way, they beg for trouble.

The way we choose to think and speak about something often determines the way we deal with it. In the case of questions such as those above, the questioner is not seeking information so much as affirmation of his or her anxieties and perhaps faulty assumptions. Such questions are toxic.

Sometimes, the questions are triggered by pity and fear; in other cases by the need to patronize and put down. Whatever the situation, there is this: they put a mother on the defensive. They cut.

205

If, however, a mother practices behavioral parenting, they also present opportunities: to identify issues and solve problems; to instruct the questioner; and to reduce some of the negative situations and expectations we have been talking about here.

Mom need not let anyone, son, family, or friend, get away with questions that reinforce the Myth Of The Woebegone Mother.

Joann recalls the first such question directed at her. Jared was eight. A few days after his father moved to an apartment, Jared had a nightmare about falling. Joann comforted him and he went back to sleep quickly. In a conversation with her own mother the next day, she mentioned it. The question came fast: "Don't you think the dream is a warning that he's upset about the separation and feels cut loose, without security?"

In the calm restrospect of six years, Joann agrees that Jared's dream probably did reflect the changes taking place in his life. To her mother that day, however, she retorted, "Don't be ridiculous, he just had a normal nightmare!" and angrily ended the conversation.

What Joann really needed was a way to deal with the substance of a question (her mother's valid concern over Jared's reaction to the separation) without letting the question's toxic message (if your marriage hadn't failed, wouldn't Jared feel secure?) distract her.

Jared's dream also illustrates how easily single mothers interpret a situation or event common to most boys (dreams of falling) as unique to their mother-son family, and how easily they attribute every problem to single motherhood.

We can't emphasize enough the folly of linking things that have nothing to do with single parenting of sons to the absence of husband and father. This in itself creates imaginary problems and a vicious cycle becomes established.

In raising sons, a major task for mothers is to distinguish between real and unreal problems and help sons build repertoires for doing likewise.

We're certain you know some people who just naturally seem very good at finessing such questions and avoiding defensive cycles.

These individuals also make the person asking the question feel satisfied. Jared had a teacher like this. On his first day of school after Joann's separation, he had an encounter with her that illustrates this quality. Both Jared and the teacher remembered the conversation this way.

Jared: Did you know my parents are getting a divorce?

Teacher: No, I didn't, Jared.

Jared (After a long pause. He seemed to be waiting for some further response from the teacher to his question.): Well what do you think about that? Do you think that's bad?

Teacher (warmly, but in a matter-of-fact tone): Right now, it must seem that way to you, I know. I'm sorry to hear about it and I know you must feel sad. That's all right, though. You have a right to feel sad. I feel very good that you told me about this. Anytime you want to talk about it, I want very much to listen.

In this exchange, Jared showed that he felt much the way single mothers do when they are asked painful questions: freakish, different, uncertain about how the world will see them. He didn't want to be pitied or patronized or ridiculed. Sometimes children (and, according to many observations from parents, teachers, and social scientists, boys especially) are more direct about letting others know what their worries are. So Jared asked the tough question first.

The answer he got from this wise and sensitive teacher was critical. It guided Jared's view of himself and his parents in a positive way. The teacher did not display pity or anger. In both words and manner, she recognized his fear and uncertainty and gave them validity without unduly attending to them, positively or negatively. She did not patronize him with an "everything will be for the best" line of blather. She acknowledged the event, offered her guidance, and very definitely let him know that his family's change of status in no way altered her good feelings toward him as a person. If she did consider what happened "bad," she kept her judgments on hold. She did not try to read his mind or predict his feelings. She did not assume anything was "bad" or that his world was crashing in.

She took her cues from his behavior, which was appropriately curious, worried, and embarrassed. She did not call up simplistic generalizations about divorced families or Psychology 101 courses.

Somewhere in her training, Jared's teacher learned the art of answering toxic questions. She learned to listen to the nature of the question, to consider the motive, relationship and history of the questioner, to observe the behavior of the questioner, to consider the consequences of any answer she might give, and to answer in language that is not defensive or aggressive.

Whether designed to stab or not, tough questions arise for everyone, but single mothers of sons tend to become unnecessarily intimidated by them.

As we have said often in these pages, the key elements in successful behavioral approaches to mother-son relationships are preparation and rehearsal. Therefore, in this appendix, we offer questions frequently asked of—and by—single mothers of sons.

They cover subjects from discipline to hotel sleeping arrangements, and all were suggested by the women and boys we interviewed.

We have tried to construct the question in such a way that both mothers and sons can quickly identify the issues (and the traps) it embraces.

Thus, a question may not be asked in words you or those around you use. Instead, it is posed in a way that demonstrates the technique we think works best to turn a potentially toxic question into one that provides the best opportunity for analysis, thoughtful response, and desirable behavioral change.

Question One: How can I make sure there are enough men around to provide masculine role models for my son?

Answer: Even if you need and want more men in your son's life, it is not usually necessary to recruit them. Here is why:

A model does not necessarily have to be available and accessible. In a forced masculine setting such as a military school or boy's camp, the models may be so numerous and varied that the messages for your son are confusing or inappropriate.

Numerous studies confirm that all-male institutions, for example, have no inside track on encouraging behaviors that lead to traditional male sexual choices. Indeed, in some cases, they may serve as fertile ground for just the opposite. (See Question Two.)

Before considering any move to bring more men into her son's life, mothers ought to first identify what it is her son perceives as a desirable model for himself.

Johnny may admire prizefighters, but may be personally

turned off at the thought of beating another human being to a pulp. He may admire military heroes, but disdain military values. He may think well of scientists, but worry about being an "egghead."

More than just making sure there are "men" around their sons, mothers need to decide what kinds of men they want for models and what kinds they do not.

They also need to consider human qualities that are modeled by both sexes, such as competence in dealing with others, courage, and compassion.

Only then can mothers find and exploit (in the good sense of that world) male role models from among friends, relatives, teachers, and even public figures, celebrities, and fictional characters.

With the preteen boy, a mother can get a lot of mileage from simply labeling male behaviors, according to her preferences, as good, bad, desirable, or undesirable. The point here is that a mother may just as easily achieve a behavior-modeling goal with a poor role model as with a good one. The young boy who wants to please his mother, and who is rewarded for doing so in some way, will be likely to copy the behavior of the models she praises.

Teenagers, who are more under control of peers, will tend to imitate individuals who are being rewarded in ways they want to be rewarded.

If the high school newspaper editor gets VIP treatment from campus jocks who want their name in print, and if your son wants in on that treatment, you may well find him suddenly interested in the morning paper and journalism courses.

Question Two: Is it a good idea to send my son to an all-male school or camp?

Answer: This "good idea" is often recommended by owners and operators of camps, military academies, and one-sex private schools. And it may be fine for your son, as it is for many boys, to enjoy the camaraderie, discipline, skill-training, and experiences of an all-male world for periods of time.

After Joann's divorce, a gentle, athletic Scotsman, a counselor at a New England boys' camp, became the first adult man besides his father with whom Jared, then age nine, was able to drop his cool, diffident, I-can-handle-anything pose and let his feelings out.

On the last day of camp, and in front of his mother, his

bunkmates, and his brother, he jumped into Rob's open arms for farewell hugs and the first open tears since the divorce. They continued their friendship by correspondence for some time, and Jared's behavior toward younger children and adult men reflects that warm relationship to this day.

That question behind the question, of course, is whether a boy reared by a woman needs all-male experiences in order to develop "masculine" traits and abilities.

Questions of biology and hormones aside, there are risks and benefits to the "all-male-environment" strategy. The benefit, mothers will say, is to immerse a child in a male environment. But packing her son off to an all-boy prep school is no guarantee he will learn only what she wants him to learn.

There is no doubt that sons in these situations are in a great position to learn and to imitate male behaviors, but they could include some she would rather have him ignore, including undesirable language, dress, and career goals. Boys in all-male schools and camps are also exposed to boys of many ages, whose behaviors may be copied inappropriately.

Even if mother's time with her son is limited, she has a good chance to influence the selection of appropriate role models if she keeps close watch on her son's behavior, and if she understands how her son learns any given behavior.

And, she is much more likely to be able to do this if he is with her part of each day or week, rather than apart from her most of the time.

As we have explained, what sons do will depend on the environment his mother structures and the skills she gives him with which to discriminate.

Make no mistake. A son will learn from his mother and anyone else who gets his attention. The job for mother is to make the information he gets positive, important, and relevant, and to teach "sifting" strategies a son can use later on his own.

Sons will learn their mothers are not always right and they will reject some of her lessons. But if properly taught, they will always keep with them the skill of analyzing models (and other demands for attention and events) and making thoughtful choices.

Question Three: A lot of people say my son and I should get psychiatric or psychological counseling because of my situation. How do I know if we need it?

Answer: Once again, stick to what you know and observe. If you use behavior and functional success as your yardsticks, it is not that difficult to measure the need.

If your son does well in school, has friends, enjoys eating, playing, and other activities appropriate for his age group; if there are no sudden and radical shifts in his behavior and focus; if you are functioning well, if not perfectly in your job, and at home; if there are no signs of serious depression, withdrawal or drug use, you probably need not worry.

Experienced psychologists and counselors have learned that even if one or more of these crises occurs, the critical consideration for seeking professional help is whether and how long a problem persists over time.

After breaking up with his first serious girl friend, Joann's son, Adam, was blue for days. Taken out of context, his behavior was clearly one of serious depression. But he continued to study for exams, go to track practice, and juggle apples at the dinner table. There was nothing depressed about these activities. His crisis eventually dissolved when a new girl friend appeared.

On the other hand, the principles of preparation and rehearsal apply to possible behaviors as well as to actual behaviors. So plan ahead. If you have read through the previous chapters, you know how important it is not to wait for problems to arise. We don't mean to suggest that you take action before there is evidence that action is needed (no mind reading, please!). But common sense tells you that there will be times when you will need guidance.

From a behavioral standpoint, successful people, as we have said repeatedly, prepare and rehearse. They don't rush around in the middle of a crisis trying to make decisions. They try to develop and have in place a number of helpful individuals who will be available if needed.

A good illustration of what we mean can be found in a subject most of us are familiar with: health care.

One way to approach health is to wait until you are sick, then find a doctor or hospital or dentist or surgeon to help. That has obvious built-in weaknesses.

A second approach is to view the world as a sea of health threats and surround yourself with a host of specialists who will be glad to check you out at the first sneeze.

A third is to find experts who can help you learn to stay healthy, thereby preventing health problems.

To us, the sensible approach to health or successful parenting is to evaluate and select someone who can advise in a time of relative calm and noncrisis. Stay in touch from time to time with a note, a call, or a visit. When you feel the need for professional guidance, preventive or otherwise, call on it.

Much of behavioral parenting is not only knowing how to handle a problem when it arises, but how to minimize the likelihood that problems will occur in the first place.

Many of the women we interviewed reported seeking professional counseling for brief periods. And several sought guidance from women's groups, religious leaders, family physicians, and friends.

A few of the sons took unilateral action as well, including Joann's son Jared, when he was ten. "I need a shrink," he announced one day after school.

"Okay," Joann said. "Anything I can offer right away?"

"Nope," came the response. "You're a mother, not an expert."

After a brief consultation with Joann for background, the psychologist set up the appointment. Joann delivered Jared and after an hour, Jared emerged into the waiting room with a smile wrapped twice around his face. "The doctor wants to see you and he said to tell you that he won't discuss anything I said with you unless I say it's okay and it's not. Okay?"

The psychologist kept his word, but reassured Joann that Jared's request for counseling was sensible and helpful. "He just had some questions and I answered them the best I could. He seemed very satisfied," the psychologist said. "I also gave him a card with my phone numbers on it and told him to call anytime."

(Jared never did. "The problem," he told me sometime later, "was solved.")

Question Four: "After almost a year, my teenaged son still won't talk to his friends or family members about his father's remarriage or my dating. He becomes angry if anyone mentions such subjects. How can I get him to be more open and honest about all this?"

Answer: The chances are good that this kind of behavior has emerged because there were some painful consequences for him when the subjects were discussed. Teenagers are notoriously embarrassed by any parental behavior that is unusual.

First determine what kind of peer group your son has. Are they mostly children for whom single parenthood is an unknown? It's possible that it is not the subjects per se that distress your son, but that he simply does not know *how* to talk about them.

Try providing some sample dialogues he might use that rely on neutral, not judgmental language. Demonstrate ways in which he can provide information without having to explain personal family affairs. For example, if one of his friend's asks "Why can't your Dad drive us to the movies tonight?" he need not go into a long explanation about separate houses and separate family obligations. "I just tell people his wife needs the car," one fifteen-year-old said.

Suggest ways in which your son can speak of your family life matter-of-factly. "My mother's busy tonight," rather than "My mother has a date." One mother recalls that when a neighbor expressed an uninvited negative opinion about her current lover ("A lot of people find him hard to talk to"), she made a point of telling her son what her response was. "I asked her with a smile whether she thought Gallup would do a scientific survey for me so I could have a really sound basis for my selection." She heard her son use a version of that in response to an insensitive question from one of his friends sometime later.

Teenagers, like everyone else, need a behavioral repertoire, a storehouse of skills, verbal and otherwise, to apply to uneasy situations.

We aren't born with the ability to ask gracefully for a date or finesse a verbal thrust.

Moreover, not only do they need a repertoire, but some guidance in how and when to use it and when to say nothing at all. Not every statement or question needs or deserves a response.

Tell your son to be alert to what kinds of responses work and what kinds do not. Tell him about some of your awkward encounters and how you handled them (well or badly). Reassure him that saying the wrong thing is not only okay but guaranteed to happen. The message is to pay attention to the responses your comments get and adapt them.

Help your son to think about who is asking the question,

and what happens after he answers. And advise him to offer no more than what he feels comfortable giving. A good way to give people information is to do so a little at a time. Set up foundations and build on them.

Question Five: What do I do when my son asks why he can't live with his father?
Answer: Most sons will say something like this from time to time. In some cases, they mean it. In most, however, they have found that it is an effective way to get a rise out of mother, sympathy out of dad, and score a manipulative triumph with both. This is particularly likely to be the case if the question has arisen before and not dealt with in a reasonable manner.

As always, consider the context of the question. If it is asked in a moment of calm reasonableness, your son may be seeking reassurance that you don't want to get rid of him or reassurance that his father does still love him. If it has been asked during an argument, however, it is likely the son is using it as an effective weapon, particularly if he has been successful using it that way before.

One good approach is to avoid the temptation many mothers have to launch into a global analysis and defense of current living arrangements. Speak only to the question at hand and ignore the rest for the moment.

Your son should already have basic background on the subject. He should already know that he is living with his mother for legal, economic, or other reasons that have been decided by the adults who are responsible for him.

There is no need to explain that all again. If the question is the verbal equivalent of a tantrum, as an attention-getting device, it may not be what he wants from you anyway. There is no point in trying to read his mind; construct your answer from the context of his question and his behavior.

"You can't live with Dad because it has already been decided that you will live with me," or some version of that response may be best, at least initially.

If you keep getting the question ("But *why* can't I live with Dad?") again and again, remember that you have already given him the information he wants and that what is maintaining the question's vitality is your reaction and attention to it.

If mothers are really uncertain about why the question is being asked, the best approach in some cases is to delay your response so that you don't risk reinforcing the "tantrum" value if that is what is in play.

For example, if you are in a pitched battle and the question comes out, don't instantly respond as if your son needs reassurance or feels insecure. Let the air clear and promise to give him an answer a short time later. (Be sure to let "later" come. Don't just forget about it, even if he does.)

One of the best ways to neutralize a painful question is to say, "I'd like to talk about this a little later when we both have time and more patience."

Question Six: I drink occasionally, but I don't want my teenage son to. He says all his friends drink beer and if he doesn't he will not be considered manly, and be ostracized. What do I say to him?

Answer: Questions like these seek to produce guilt and challenge mothers about their own behavior. The goal, for the son, is to receive permission to engage in a behavior that bends or breaks family rules.

The very fact that the questions are asked suggests that most of the time, sons know that these rules are fair and operative. If they considered them otherwise, they would not seek permission, but would simply defy the rules without asking.

From a behavioral parenting standpoint, therefore, the question should first be neutralized, then used as the basis for a positive lesson. The drinking question is representative of a whole category of questions that deal with behaviors perceived as "macho": driving, taking drugs, staying out late, and others that are very much influenced by a son's social group.

The son is using the mother's anxiety about "masculinity" to test her convictions, his values, and the fabric of the family's rules. But most of all, he is using her anxiety to get permission to do something he thinks will impress his valued peer group.

So begin your answer by reminding yourself and then making clear to your son that drinking (or driving a car, or whatever) is no more tied to masculinity than your highball before dinner is tied to your role as a woman; that girls his age are just as likely to want to drink, drive, and raise hell as he, and you doubt they want to in order to feel "macho."

On the more positive note, remind him of some of the times he has felt masculine and good about himself when not drinking. Reinforce his apparent acceptance of your rules by telling him how good it makes you feel that he has asked the question.

"I know you feel it is unfair that I can have a drink before dinner and you are not allowed to. I'm glad you brought it up so we can discuss this. Your concern about this shows me you are approaching the rules in your life as an adult would and not just childishly going off to break them."

Without becoming defensive, it also helps to remind your son that adults have established operational patterns for their lives that are firm enough at this point to withstand occasional chemical escape. Sons have not, but are still forming those patterns.

Because, as we have said, preparation is essential to behavioral parenting, mothers must assume that at some time, her son will explore "forbidden behavior" and test the rules. Their job is to make certain sons understand, by the nature of their rules and their willingness to back them up, that there are social and personal consequences to all behavior.

Moreover, because the reinforcement for drinking among men is often social and heavy, it may be a wise course to teach controlled drinking by negotiating a contract for drinking behavior in the home that reinforces the goal of responsible adult behavior. That may mean mother permitting one glass of beer at a family barbecue or wine with a special dinner.

What is more important, mother should point out the acceptable ways her son can impress and influence his age- and classmates. He may be good at a sport or have some special creative talent. That is his strength, his unique strength. Anyone can drink, but not everyone can do what he is good at doing. He can use his special talents or interests to gain approval just as he should develop and use his skills throughout life.

Question Seven: My high-school-aged son recently asked me what I thought of his plans to "go all the way" with his girl friend. We've talked about sex of course, but why is he asking me this now and how do I respond?

Answer: We can't emphasize often enough that behavior does not occur in a vacuum. Think about the context in which he is asking the question and considering the activity. Are you involved in an affair that he has expressed an opinion about? Does he want permission? Does he want to see your reaction? Next, consider the consequences of what you say and do. What do you want to demonstrate to him by your reaction? What's important about this to you?

If you disapprove, make up your mind that it will happen anyway, if not this week, then another time soon. And construct your answer in that context. Sons who ask this question are not seeking permission so much as approval or disapproval; they are looking for traffic lights to get them through the intersection.

As always, look for the opportunity to achieve your parenting goals and for ways to reinforce your values about the subject at hand, and to use any occasion like this to help your son prepare for the short- and long-term future.

The following conversation took place between a forty-two-year-old divorced mother and her fifteen-year-old son. We think it demonstrates the need for preparation and rehearsal (she had thought about the subject a good deal as her son began to date regularly) and the object of behavioral parenting.

Son: What would you say if I told you that Jane and I are ready to have intercourse?

Mother: I wouldn't be surprised. You both spend time here and feel comfortable around me, so I've been aware that your feelings were not Platonic! As a matter of fact, I am happy that you are entering a stage of life that is very wonderful and fulfilling.

Son: Do you think I'm ready?

Mother: I can't really put myself in your position. As a woman, though, I have been thinking about whether Jane is ready. I know you care about her very much, and we've talked a lot about not exploiting or hurting people who are especially vulnerable because they are in love. (Mother may not particularly care about Jane and it is likely she cares a lot more about her son. But with this approach, she can introduce some clear signals about what she wants her son to consider in deciding on a course of action. Here she is saying "I don't want your behavior to be exploitive. I do want your behavior to be fulfilling for you and it can't be if your partner is not considered." And she can introduce these ideas without criticizing or preaching to her son.)

Son: Are you saying that I shouldn't?

Mother: I'm really thinking out loud about how your plans for sex will influence Jane and her goals. Women think about a sexual relationship from a physical standpoint, of course, but Jane is also very romantic about you. It's possible that Jane wants to expand your sexual experiences out of a concern that she not disappoint you romantically. Perhaps you should discuss that possibility with her.

Son: You're implying she only wants to have sex because she's afraid I'll be angry if she won't?

Mother: It's not possible for either of us to know that without talking to her about it. She may not realize her own fears. I'm only saying it's a possibility because people who love each other sometimes think that way. Men as well as women.

Son: I love her. I wouldn't do anything to exploit her.

Mother: I believe you. And I think just talking about this lowers the chances even further that that could happen inadvertently. Just being aware of the possibility is a big step.

Son: Well of course Jane and I will talk about this a lot before we decide. It has to be a decision both of us make, don't you think?

Mother: Absolutely. I wish my boyfriends in high school had been as loving and sensitive as you are with Jane. She is a very lucky girl.

For this mother, what was important was not when her son had sexual intercourse with his girl friend, but whether the decision to have sex was mutual and nonexploitive.

She saw in the question the chance for her son to learn that sexual relationships are fragile and wonderful. And she wanted to reinforce her belief that in order for sex to be satisfying for a man or a woman, a man must want to please a woman and respond to her needs as fully as he wants her to respond to his.

Her conversation with her son expresses that, while it also lets him know that she feels good about his emerging manhood and desires.

One mother, a widow with sons fifteen and thirteen, told us: "Thank God I have sons, not daughters. My brother's daughters are so socially advanced and sexually aggressive I keep thinking about the poor boys who will be asked to perform beyond the call of duty."

The mother who brings up these subjects has given her son the emotional room to explore the possibility that *he* may be unsure about his plans. He learns that sex is a positive element of life, but one that calls for responsibilities.

Question Eight: My son has asked if he can dress up in my clothes or put on my lipstick and other makeup. Is this a sign that he is developing male identity or sexual problems?

Answer: That women worry this is the case probably reflects the fact that this is how male society reacts to the issue.

Cross-dressing and playing opposite sex role models is a standard part of childhood and growing up. It's just that society tends to see it as abnormal for boys, although perfectly acceptable for girls. It is, in fact, considered quite fashionable these days for girls to wear boys' clothes and many of the most exclusive teenage clothiers offer boys and mens' sweaters, slacks, shirts, shoes, and jackets in "feminine" colors.

Among the latest couture fashions are women's suits and dresses modeled after male military uniforms, work clothes (such as jumpsuits and overalls), and man-tailored business suits.

Several sons we interviewed described the importance of having their girl friends wear their jogging shorts, sweatshirts, and letter jackets. And many mothers reported wearing hand-me-downs from their growing sons. Joann has a wardrobe of blazers, sweatshirts, and button-downs her sons have outgrown over the years.

The obverse, of course, is a social taboo.

From a behavior standpoint, several opportunities emerge out of this question to reinforce important goals in the relationship between mothers and sons. Among them: tolerance for sexual differences; the superficiality of many sex role "markers"; the intellectual poverty of sex role stereotypes.

First, pay attention to the context of the question. If your grade-school son is watching you dress for a special occasion and you are applying a rainbow of colors to your face, a mother might consider this a natural part of childhood curiosity. Just as her son might want to apply his dad's shaving cream and cologne, it is perfectly normal for him to want to try her perfume and powder. (This occurs, of course, in two-parent as well in single-parent families.)

On the other hand, if her preadolescent son is dipping into the rouge pot on the sly, he may be signaling some concern for his masculinity.

In either case, mothers can point out that in history many men have dressed in frills, powder, and paint; that she feels no less a woman if she wears overalls or slacks; and that it is not abnormal to want to "try on" other identities. Actors spend their lives doing just that, and to the extent that maturity is an outgrowth of empathy, trying to "walk in another's moccasins" is a sign of growth, not sexual perversion.

In most cases, this phase of boyhood passes quickly, provided mothers don't actively encourage or reinforce the practice. Peers take care of the rest.

Adam: I wouldn't be caught dead in a pink shirt.

Joann: Many successful men wear them.

Adam: Well, maybe when I'm the president of General Motors I will, too.

Again, we emphasize that the difference between a distressing or puzzling situation which is likely to dissolve of its own inherent lack of force, and one which needs more attention (mom's or a professional's) is one of persistence.

If her son's interest in cross-dressing, for example, lingers for weeks or months; or if it consumes large amounts of his time or curiosity, it may be time for guidance for both of them.

Question Nine: Is my son having problems because he lacks full-time male influence in his life?

Answer: By now readers will recognize that this question arises because the "problem" is often implied in comments from teachers, coaches, ex-husbands, relatives, and authorities, despite a consistent lack of evidence for its validity.

What is important in your response is not so much what you say, but what you don't; that is, the answer must not assume the worst.

Try this: "People seem to think that if my son had a man around, he would behave differently. Because it is not possible for a man to live here with us, I need to have some alternatives."

This approach will gently but firmly state your point of view without directly contradicting the assumptions. It may be all the invitation he or she needs to get a discussion off the defensive track and onto the subject at hand.

You might also point out that boys generally grow up, whether their mother is single or not, under predominantly female influence in their early years, both at home and in school. (The vast majority of teachers are still women in the lower grades.)

Closely coupled with this question is whether there is any evidence that boys need a father figure when they are growing up in order to assure a strong male identity.

The social research in the past, that is called upon to substantiate the need for a father figure is based primarily on two kinds of studies. First, on *abnormal* rather than normal boys and their behavior; and second, on boys who did not have a father present. But this kind of research begs the real question: Why is it desirable for boys to have good relationships with fathers or other grown men?

Put another way, is male sex role identity the most important consequence of those relationships?

In an important review of the professional literature, Joseph H. Pleck, the author of *The Myth of Masculinity*, says most studies are inconclusive, contradictory, or present data that has been "cooked" to fit a foregone hypothesis on the part of the researcher.

At best, research on this topic is circumstantial anyway. One can hardly conduct an experiment, randomly assigning groups of boys to be reared in various ways in order to prove or disprove an hypothesis!

"Proponents of boys-need-male-model hypothesis explain . . . inconsistencies by claiming that father absence can make boys either more or less masculine depending on their personalities and circumstances," he notes. Just so. As noted earlier, role modeling is not a question of gender (who), but a question of behavior (what).

Question Ten: But surely a divorce can be expected to affect a son's development, right?

Answer: Absolutely. *Everything* that happens to boys growing up and to their parents will influence their behavior and attitudes. The point of behavioral parenting is to spend less energy guessing at what may happen or what others warn you may happen, and more energy on structuring your home environment so you determine what in fact happens.

Question Eleven: Biology may not be destiny, but aren't there some ways that boys are inherently different than girls, and don't I need to pay attention to those things?
Answer: Yes and yes. But the real question here, once again, is what *kind* of attention to pay. There is accumulating evidence that from the time he is a fetus, a male's thought patterns and learning abilities develop differently than those of a female.

There are studies which demonstrate that under the influence of male sex hormones, boys are by nature somewhat more aggressive, and that these same hormones have differentially influenced brain development so that boys tend to excel in left-brain activities such as mathematics and spatial relations.

The thing to keep in mind, however, is the overwhelming amount of research which also demonstrates that genetic and biologic influences produce a wide spectrum of results, and they are basically unpredictable in any given individual. In addition, many studies of normally intelligent and retarded individuals have shown that what we learn in our environment may not only overcome but overrun biological influences.

Educators have repeatedly demonstrated that, overall, girls can learn math as well as boys, and if they haven't in the past, it is probably due to lower expectations and subtle discouragement rather than to biology.

For mothers, it is less important to single out differences or similarities among males and females than to help sculpt competent people, males or females, by having clearly defined goals and a knowledge of what they approve and disapprove in their sons' behavior.

Question Twelve: How can I get it across to my son that physical fighting is something I can't condone under any circumstances and something I don't want him to do? He and his father say all boys have to learn when not to back down from a fight or they'll never survive.
Answer: As with any other kind of behavior, mothers can encourage or discourage physical fighting as a response to certain conditions or provocations. Most of the mothers we spoke to found that the most sensible approach (i.e., the one

that worked best and gave up the least) was a seriously negotiated menu of options.

When your son insists that there are times when he cannot avoid a fight with the schoolyard bully, for example, it's a good time to list those incidents and situations that make him feel that way.

Then it is possible to discuss the consequences (for him and his would-be victim) of fighting, including reactions from school officials, teachers, and friends. It is also possible to discuss alternatives and options, ways of avoiding or interrupting the steps that lead up to confrontations.

It is also necessary for mother, in this situation, to compromise her "absolute pacifist" stand. For credibility's sake, she must acknowledge those instances (and she can make them few indeed) when it may be necessary to fight back.

The behavior she wants in her son—to value the life and health of all human beings and find nonviolent ways of solving problems—will not be guaranteed or foreclosed by such negotiation. It will, however, raise the issue in a way boys can understand. As a bonus, her willingness to negotiate the point is an object lesson as well in finding ways to resolve conflict without bullying or passivity.

Question Thirteen: If I ask my son to clean floors, cook, iron, sew, and help with baby care, will he become too feminine?

Answer: Boys who learn to nurture will often be regarded by others as having "feminine" qualities. In fact, they will have learned human qualities that are no more likely to diminish male behavior than learning to pump gas will make a woman less of a nurturing mother.

Problems are not rooted in what boys may learn about nurturing from their mothers, but what they don't learn.

Don't be afraid to praise the nurturing side of your son. Just don't leave out praise for the other traits he exhibits, such as independence, initiative, ambition, competitiveness. Because you as a woman have those traits, too, point them out to him (and your daughters) as well. Acknowledge them. Call attention to the fact that they are positive for you and in you.

Question Fourteen: Now that my son is growing up, don't I need to be more careful about nudity around the house?

Answer: Most mothers we talked to found that their sons began to develop their own sense and rules of modesty by about age nine or ten. From the standpoint of behavioral parenting, learning is a two-way street. Take your behavioral cues from your son. If he begins to close the bathroom and bedroom doors, to wear a robe or towel after his bath, you can bet he'll appreciate your knocking before entering, and covering up as well.

Above all, don't force your own behavior into niches that aren't comfortable, and don't be upset if there are occasional lapses in your intentions. Joann, for example, will sometimes dash for a telephone or a boiled-over pot in bra and underpants, and a few times her sons have unintentionally seen her bare to the world. (These confrontations invariably produce hilarity and awkward retreats. Theirs, not hers.)

From time to time, she also asks Adam and Jared if her leisure wear around the house (sweatshirts or T-shirts without bra, robes, and such) concerns them. (It doesn't.)

Some mothers told us that they have forced themselves to be less inhibited around their sons in the belief that this would teach them to be relaxed about women and sex. That's fine, as long as the mother is truly comfortable with that role. Otherwise, her behavior may backfire, inviting the notion in her son that women can and should submit to sexual behaviors they do not prefer.

Many single mothers told us that when they travel with their sons, they share a room to save money. This may require some negotiated traffic patterns if nudity is a concern.

At times of illness (mothers' or sons'), exposure of the body may be necessary, and in keeping with principles of behavioral parenting, a sensible, negotiated set of guidelines is a good idea.

There is no question that mothers and sons can be sexually aroused by the sight of the others' bodies. That does not mean either acts upon it. The important lesson is to teach respect for others' preferences and for the human body as a functional (and to many beautiful) apparatus whether it is on your lover, your parent, or your child. It is also important to help your son discriminate between what is acceptable behavior at home, among close family members, and what is acceptable in others' homes or in public.

As a corollary, it's important for single mothers to be aware that nudity among males—in gym locker rooms, public rest rooms and the like—is commonplace, but may also cause some boys woe. Several sons we interviewed confessed to years of constipation because school bathrooms provided no privacy. Modesty is not, as many mothers believe, a predominantly "feminine" concern.

Question Fifteen: My high-school and college-age sons bring a lot of their friends home and some of them openly flirt with me. My sons blame me and are sometimes upset about it. Sometimes I just hide out when they come. How can I handle these situations without hurting their feelings, or my sons'?

Answer: Don't hide out. Do speak privately to your sons about the problem and examine your behavior to see if there is something you are doing, wearing, saying, that particularly provokes the flirting. Then try modifying that behavior. Remember, nothing happens in a vacuum.

Mothers are entitled to certain freedoms in their own homes and it may be that the sons' friends need some guidance. One mother we know has a swimming pool and frequently wears scanty bikinis around the house in the summer. She quickly put an end to a predictable round of provocative remarks by reacting without laughter or encouragement.

Question Sixteen: How can I deal with my son's accusation that I was to blame for our family's breakup? Whenever I say or do something he doesn't like, the usual comment is "No wonder Dad left." Whenever something goes wrong, he says, "This wouldn't happen if Dad were around."

Answer: Behavior can occur for many reasons. Such statements as these may grow out of true resentment or simple dissatisfaction over a restriction.

What mothers must remember at these times is that the topography of behavior—what shows—does not necessarily explain or imply what lies beneath.

When mothers are unsure what's behind a statement like that, a good approach is to try and figure out the direct root of the behavior. If, for example, the divorce is very recent, the son is more likely to be expressing resentment. If it happens years later, it may be a "getcha" game.

If mother decides the resentment is honest, her answer must clearly point out that there is nothing to be done about it and they must both make the best of the situation. If it's a tactical move in mother-son pull for power, a good response is that dad's absence or presence would not be likely to change the issue at hand.

Question Seventeen: How can I get my son to stop acting as if he were in charge—of me, his younger siblings, and the house? He seems to have picked up where his father left off.

Answer: Sex role stereotypes do not stop at the front door of the house. The stereotypes are many-sided, but from a behavioral standpoint they involve dominance in males and passivity in females.

The answer to this question is for mother to be firm in her parenting goals and not let sex role anxieties get her off track. Within reason, you can get your way by negotiating a compromise with behaviors that are not acceptable. Forging good mother-son relationships is not a task for the timid.

By word and deed, let your son know that women, too, can be skillful at running things; that management of a home or family is a process in need of continuous refinement, not boy dictators; and that he has a way to go to match your management skills. In short, don't abdicate and don't fight. Just structure the rules so sons know who is chairman of the board.

Question Eighteen: When I have to punish my son, I worry that he won't take me seriously. His father used to enforce discipline, whereas I would just get upset or yell. What is the best way to discipline boys, especially when they get beyond grade school? What if they absolutely refuse to obey and they are too big for me to restrain?

Answer: Many mothers feel they cannot be forceful in discipline, that it is unfeminine or unnatural for them to undertake this role. But those feelings emerge from a confusion of discipline with intimidation and physical force.

With the proper use of behavioral principles, a five foot handicapped mother can have as much control as a six foot marine.

If you want to be taken seriously as a parent, you must be serious, consistent, and firm. The rules you establish and the penalties for breaking them must be applied not for your convenience, but for the sake of family unity.

Mothers sometimes worry that their older sons will hit them.

And some will. But research suggests that in extreme forms, male temper aimed at mothers (though not necessarily women in general) results at worst in verbal abuse or pushing, not hitting.

If you are struck, the consequences for your son should be the same as for any serious rule violation. If he strikes out of anger and is clearly out of control, the immediate consequences must focus on the behavior, not the trigger of the behavior.

Behavioral goals must be clearly established. The parent is responsible for ensuring that there are rules and that the consequences for rule keeping or rule breaking are properly managed. If this is done, size is not usually an issue because your son's action will be automatically governed by its consequences. By the time a boy is in his teens, without a proper "rule and consequence" system in place, there are going to be problems, regardless of his size.

Remember, teenage boys are not only physical but increasingly independent. The small teenage boy with a big father at home may not strike out so easily, but he will still express his frustrations in other ways.

Question Twenty: What chores are appropriate for my son to do around the house and what chores are not?

Answer: Modern sons often complain about the lack of "manly" chores to perform around a house or apartment. There are few calls for hauling wood, felling trees, shoeing horses, or hunting for dinner.

Mothers we spoke to try hard to find substitutes in activities such as cleaning the cellar, clearing drain spouts, changing bulbs, taking out garbage, mowing the lawn, and so on.

The problem with this approach is two-fold. One, such tasks are periodic or seasonal. They rarely require daily attendance or attention to personal family needs. In the single-mother household, it is the latter kind of chores that need doing. Second, the "men's work" approach reinforces sex role stereotypes that will hardly prepare sons to cope realistically with future divisions of labor.

What jobs are appropriate for boys? Just about every one that is appropriate for girls. The few exceptions are those that require brute strength or height, but even with these, there are girls and women who can outperform some males.

Chores, including obligations and aid to other family members, should be divided up fairly according to time available and the nature of the job. The goal is not to teach sex roles, but to get the daily needs of the household filled without nagging and reminders.

Make a list of daily, weekly, and monthly household duties. Negotiate and then produce an assignment roster. Teach whatever skills are necessary. And stick to it.

More than half the mothers we interviewed had taught their sons to cook, iron, sew on buttons, use the laundry equipment, and food shop. Others made use of the family car contingent on driving younger brothers and sisters to Sunday school, orthodontists, and leisure activities.

Question Twenty-one: I don't like the idea of hunting or rough sports such as football or boxing. I don't even approve of movies or TV shows that depict violence. But my son says I'm trying to make a girl out of him. What do I do when he wants to get involved in these activities?

Answer: The answer depends in part on your son's age. It makes good sense, from a health standpoint, to forbid certain contact sports in children whose height, weight, and muscle development aren't sufficient to withstand the training or physical punishment involved.

With older boys, there are other options. It's important to assess the quality and quantity of supervision and coaching. If these are inferior, they may be used as the basis for a negative decision. Encouraging substitutes such as soccer, tennis, and track for football, lacrosse, or hockey can be effective.

As for violent films and TV shows, mothers can control viewing to a point. Beyond that, your behavior and the selection of role models are the best countervailing power. Joann and her sons enjoy going to films, but Joann will not take them to, or pay for, films with gratuitous violence. On the other hand, she has no problem with language or sex and has taken her sons to numerous R-rated films.

Question Twenty-two: How do I get my son to dress more neatly? He looks like a rag picker even though he has a closet full of nice clothes.

Answer: Most of the mothers we talked to encountered this problem as their sons advanced into adolescence, as do most families with both parents living in the household. The answer is a question for mothers: Just how important is what your son wears to you and when is it important? Enough to make it a major issue of confrontation or just an annoyance when he is sloppy?

In general, dress and hairstyles are benign expressions of a boy's emerging independence and highly sensitive to peer pressure. If ever a situation called for negotiation, this one does.

We suggest the following: cleanliness and good hygiene are a must: clean nails, hair, teeth, and so on. At school and with his peers, dress is his option. With mother, family, or outside social activities, her opinions count.

Question Twenty-three: What if my son's father gives him different messages about behavior, responsibilities, privileges, school than I do?

Answer: Count on it to happen, and not just from fathers, but from peers, relatives, and other adults, both male and female. As the parent in charge, however, we remind you that you have governing advantages they don't. Your goal is not to counter what others say, but to reinforce what you want done. This will not work all of the time, but it will work much of the time.

Question Twenty-four: What if my son objects to the men I date? Should I seek his okay to have a man sleep over?

Answer: Good mother-son relationships demand privacy, respect, tolerance, honesty, and regard for others' needs by both mothers and sons. If your son objects, you may listen to his reasons and show respect for his opinion, without accepting his advice to reject the man.

Be prepared for sons to act out their displeasure when your date or boyfriend is around. It's a good idea to let the men in your life know how your son feels and to reassure the men that it may have nothing to do with them personally.

There should be rules of behavior that spell out what is and what is not tolerable when company comes.

The decision to have a man stay over is one that so troubled most of the mothers we spoke to that, by and large, they decided against it when sons were at home.

These women explained that they felt uncomfortable themselves about the arrangement and desired more privacy than they would have with their sons around.

Among those mothers who did have sleep-in boyfriends, the vast majority said they were involved in long-term relationships that included their children.

Keep in mind that your sexual behavior will be closely watched by your son, as will the behavior of the men with whom you are involved. It will be necessary to talk about the relationship, to reassure the son about his role in your life and yours in his, and to define clearly where the privileges and responsibilities of the lover begin and end in your household.

There is a corollary to this question a number of mothers raised: "What if I don't have or want romantic or sexual involvements, permanent or otherwise in my life?"

On several occasions, both of Joann's sons have asked or demanded angrily to know why she wasn't remarried, or why she did not seek a more permanent relationship with such and such a person.

"How come you're not involved or married again?" is a question faced by many mothers who choose to remain single and uninvolved.

Whatever you as a mother, and woman, do or do not do should be openly acknowledged as your choice and your right. For some women, the issue of a lover sleeping over will never be raised in the home because they would not themselves consider it a possibility. An issue is only an issue if it arises in your home. Be comfortable with your choices, consciously made.

Although a majority of newly single women do resume active social and sex lives, not all do. Single mothers' lifestyles reflect many ethical, moral, and social codes, all of which are to be respected.

Bibliography

Adolescence and Stress. Report of a National Institute of Mental Health Conference. Washington, D.C.: U.S. Department of Health and Human Services, 1981.

Baker, B. L., Brightman, A. J., and Heifitz, L. J., Murphy, D. M. *Steps to Independence: Behavioral Problems.* Champaign, Illinois: Research Press, 1976.

Bandura, Albert. *Social Learning Theory.* Englewood Cliffs, NJ: Prentice-Hall, 1977.

Becker, W. C. *Parents are Teachers: A Child Management Program.* Champaign, Illinois: Research Press, 1971.

Biller, H. and Meredith, D. *Father Power.* New York: Anchor Press, 1975.

Callahan, Sidney C. *Parenting: Principles and Politics of Parenthood.* Garden City, NY: Doubleday, 1973.

Canter, Lee. *Assertive Discipline for Parents.* New York: Harper & Row, 1982.

Christopherson, E. R. *Little People.* Lawrence, Kansas: H&H Enterprise, 1977.

Eichenbaum, Luise (CX) and Orbach, Susie. *What Do Women Want?* New York: Coward-McCann, 1983.

Flaste, Richard. "The Invulnerable Children Who Thrive Against All Odds," *The New York Times*, July 22, 1977.

Flax, Carol C. and Ubell, Earl. *Mother, Father, You.* New York: Wyden Books, 1980.

Francke, Linda Bird. *Growing Up Divorced.* New York: Linden Press, 1983.

Friedan, Betty. *The Second Stage.* New York: Summit, 1981.

Gambrill, Eileen D. *Behavior Modification. Handbook of Assessment, Intervention and Evaluation.* San Francisco: Jossey-Bass, 1977.

Ginott, Haim. *Between Parent and Child.* New York: Macmillan, 1965.

Gilbert, Sara. *What's a Father For?* New York: Warner Books, 1975.

Hammer, Signe. *Passionate Attachments.* New York: Rawson Associates, 1982.

Hetherington, E. Mavis. "Children and Divorce," in *Parent-Child Interaction: Theory, Research and Prospects.* New York: Academic Press, 1981.

Hirsch, G. T. "Nonsexist Childrearing: Demythifying Normative Data," *Family Coordinator*, April 1974, p. 168.

Hunt, Morton and Hunt, Bernice. *The Divorce Experience.* New York: McGraw-Hill, 1977.

Janeway, Elizabeth. *Man's World, Woman's Place: A Study in Social Mythology.* New York: Dell, 1971.

Kagan, Jerome et al. "The Child's Differential Perception of Parental Attributes," *Journal of Abnormal and Social Psychology*, 1960.

Keniston, Kenneth and the Carnegie Council on Children. *All Our Children: The American Family Under Pressure.* New York: Harcourt Brace Jovanovich, 1977.

Kliman, Gilbert W. and Katz, Judith. *Maternal Depression as an Antecedent to Early Childhood Psychosis.* Center for Psychiatry Reprint, 1973.

Lamb, Michael E., ed. *The Role of the Father in Child Development.* New York: John Wiley and Sons, 1976.

Levine, James A. *Who Will Raise the Children?* Philadelphia: Lippincott, 1976.

Liley, H.M.I. with Beth Day. *Modern Motherhood.* New York: Random House, 1966.

Lips, Hilary M. *Women, Men and the Psychology of Power.* Englewood Cliffs, NJ: Prentice Hall, 1981.

Maynard, Joyce. "Rearing Children of 1970's Worries Children of 1950's." *The New York Times*, Dec. 24, 1976.

Melamed, Elissa. *Mirror Mirror. The Terror of Not Being Young.* New York: Linden Press, 1983.

Miller, W. H. *Systematic Parent Training.* Champaign, Illinois: Research Press, 1975.

Millett, Kate. *Sexual Politics.* Garden City, NY: Doubleday, 1970.

Money, John and Ehrhandt, Anke. *Man and Woman, Boy and Girl.* Baltimore: Johns Hopkins University Press, 1972.

Money, John and Tucker, Patricia. *Sexual Signatures: On Being a Man or a Woman.* Boston: Little, Brown, 1975.

National Academy of Sciences. *Toward a National Policy for Children and Families.* Washington, D.C., 1976.

Ogg, Elizabeth. *One Parent Families*. Public Affairs Pamphlet 533. Public Affairs Committee, 1976.

Olshaker, Bennett. *What Shall We Tell the Kids?* New York: Arbor House, 1971.

Patterson, G. R. *Families*. Champaign, Illinois: Research Press, 1971.

Patterson, G. R. *Living with Children*. Champaign, Illinois: Research Press, 1976.

Pear, Joseph and Martin, Gerry. *Behavior Modification*. Englewood Cliffs, NJ: Prentice Hall, 1978.

Peck, Ellen and Senderowtiz, Judith, eds. *Pronatalism: The Myth of Mom and Apple Pie*. New York: Crowell, 1974.

Pietropinto, Anthony and Simenauer, Jacqueline. *Beyond the Male Myth*. New York: Times Books, 1977.

Pogrebin, Letty Cottin. *Growing Up Free*. New York: McGraw-Hill, 1980.

Ramey, James. "Multi-adult Household: Living Group of the Future?" *The Futurist*, 1976.

Rappoport, Rhona and Robert, and Strelitz, Ziona. *Fathers, Mothers and Society*. New York: Basic Books, 1977.

Rice, B. "The Power of a Frilly Apron: Coming of Age in Sodom and New Milford," *Psychology Today*, Sept. 1975, p. 64.

Rivers, Caryl, Barnett, Rosalind, and Baruch, Grace. *Beyond Sugar and Spice; How Women Grow, Learn and Thrive*. New York: Putnam, 1979.

Rivers, Caryl, Barnett, Rosalind, and Baruch, Grace. *Lifeprints: New Patterns of Love and Work for Today's Women*. New York: McGraw-Hill, 1983.

Rosenfeld, Albert. "Who Says We're a Child Centered Society?" *Saturday Review*, Aug. 7, 1976.

Rubin, Nancy. *The New Suburban Woman*. New York: Coward-McCann, 1982.

Rubinstein, Eli and Coelho, George, eds. *Behavioral Science and Mental Health*. Washington, D.C.: National Institute of Mental Health, Department of Health, Education and Welfare, 1970.

Rutter, Michael. "Maternal Deprivation, 1972–77. New Findings, New Concepts, New Approaches." Paper presented to the Society for Research in Child Development, New Orleans, 1977.

Salk, Lee. *What Every Child Would Like Parents to Know About Divorce*. New York: Harper & Row, 1978.

Salk, Lee and Kramer, Rita. *How to Raise a Human Being.* New York: Random House, 1969.

Scarf, Maggie. "Which Child Gets Scarred?" *The New York Times*, Dec. 3, 1972.

Schaffer, H. Rudolph. *Mothers.* The Developing Child Series, Jerome Bruner, Michael Cole and Barbara Lloyd, eds. Cambridge, Mass.: Harvard University Press, 1977.

Segal, Julius and Yahraes, Herbert. *A Child's Journey: Forces that Shape the Lives of Our Young.* New York: McGraw-Hill, 1978.

Skolnick, Arlene. "The Myth of the Vulnerable Child," *Psychology Today*, Feb. 1978.

Smith, J.M. and Smither, D.E.P. Child Management. Champaign, Illinois. Research Press, 1976.

Steinem, Gloria. "Women's Liberation Aims to Free Men, Too." *The Washington Post*, June 7, 1970.

Stuart, Irving R and Abt, Lawrence. *Children of Separation and Divorce.* New York: Grossman, 1972.

Talbot, Nathan B. *Raising Children in Modern America.* Boston: Little, Brown, 1976.

Terman, Louis and Miles, C. *Sex and Personality.* New York: McGraw-Hill, 1936.

Thomas, Gordon. *Parent Effectiveness Training.* New York: David McKay, 1970.

Weiss, Robert S. *The Family Life and Social Situation of the Single Parent.* New York: Basic Books, 1979.

Yablonsky, Lewis. *Fathers and Sons.* New York: Simon & Schuster, 1982.

Yaeger, Deborah Sue. "Out of Wedlock; Women Who Choose Unwed Motherhood Face Unusual Problems." *Wall Street Journal*, Sept. 12, 1977.

Wallerstein, Judith S. and Kelly, Joan B. *Surviving the Breakup: How Parents and Children Cope with Divorce.* New York: Basic Books, 1980.

Index